IMAGES
of Rail

RAILROADS OF HILLSBORO

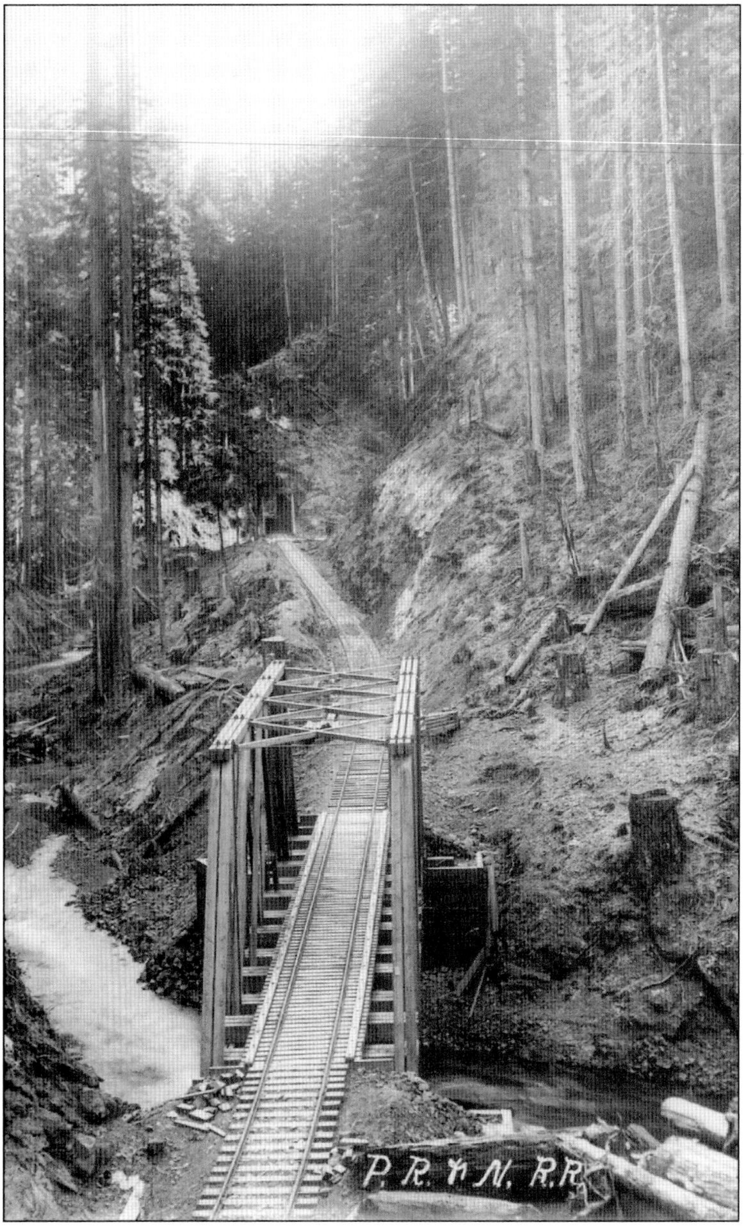

Bridges and Tunnels. In 1911, the Pacific Railway & Navigation Company (PR&N) became the last of three railroad companies to build a rail line into Hillsboro, following the Oregon Electric Railway in 1908 and the Oregon & California Railroad in 1871. Construction started on the PR&N's 90-mile-long route between Hillsboro and the coastal town of Tillamook in 1906, but due to challenging terrain, the line took five years to complete. (Collection of Curtis Culp.)

On the Cover: The Oregon Electric Railway (OE) opened an electrified branchline to Hillsboro on September 30, 1908, and many of Hillsboro's citizens dressed in their finest clothing to attend a welcoming ceremony for the new rail service. By the end of 1908, the OE had extended the line westward by another six miles to reach the nearby town of Forest Grove. (Collection of Curtis Culp.)

IMAGES
of Rail

RAILROADS OF HILLSBORO

D.C. Jesse Burkhardt

ARCADIA
PUBLISHING

ISBN 978-1-4671-3236-7

Published by Arcadia Publishing
Charleston, South Carolina

Printed in the United States of America

Library of Congress Control Number: 2014935401

For all general information, please contact Arcadia Publishing:
Telephone 843-853-2070
Fax 843-853-0044
E-mail sales@arcadiapublishing.com
For customer service and orders:
Toll-Free 1-888-313-2665

Visit us on the Internet at www.arcadiapublishing.com

To my daughter, Clare, who hiked around many obscure trackside locations with me when she was a youngster

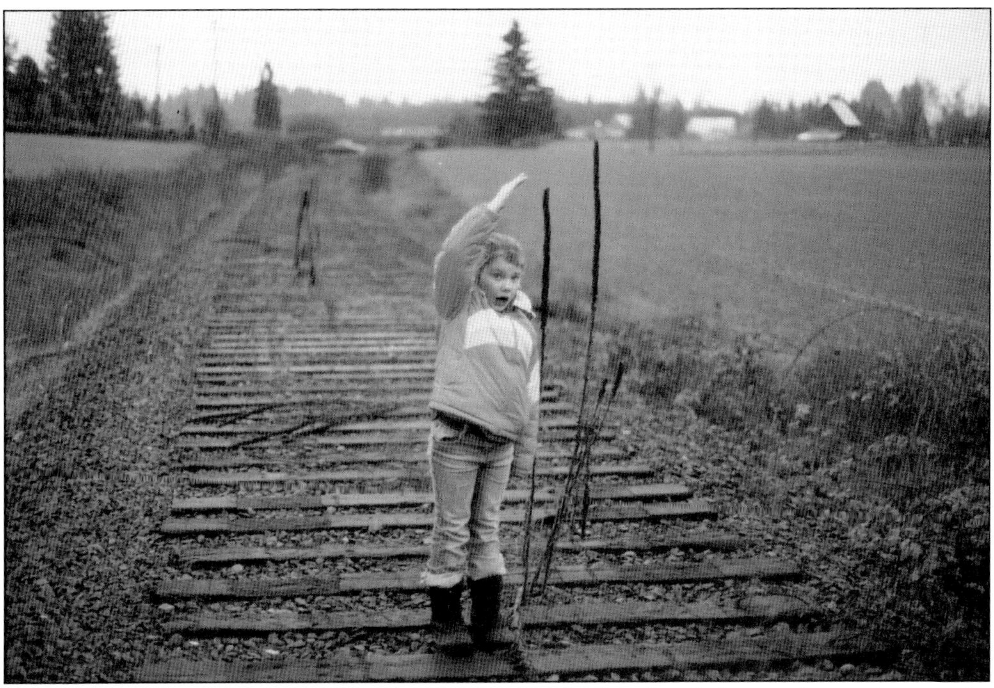

Weeds Take Over. Clare Burkhardt is amazed at the height of the weeds growing on the abandoned roadbed at Bendemeer, Oregon, on Christmas Eve 2006. (Photograph by D.C. Jesse Burkhardt.)

Contents

ACKNOWLEDGMENTS

The following individuals and organizations contributed to this project: Karen Lange and Beth Dehn, Washington County Museum, Hillsboro, Oregon; Curtis Culp, Salem, Oregon; Randy Nelson, North Richland Hills, Texas; Judy Donovan, Beaverton History Center, Beaverton, Oregon; Jan Zweerts, locomotive engineer, Portland & Western Railroad; Kathy Fuller, Hillsboro, Oregon; Chase Allgood, Portland, Oregon; Don Skinner, Friends of Historic Forest Grove, Forest Grove, Oregon; Ray Deeth, Banks Historical Society, Banks, Oregon; Colleen Clark Cornish, Forest Grove, Oregon; David Anzur, Portland & Western Railroad; Rob Drake, city manager, Cornelius, Oregon; Debbie Raber, Hillsboro Planning Department; Bob Melbo, Oregon Department of Transportation; Michael Smith, director, Hillsboro Public Library; Scott Sparling, Lake Oswego, Oregon; Tom Lacinski, Maple City, Michigan; Larry "Moon" Yaek, St. Clair, Michigan; Tina Jacobsen, owner of Jacobsen's Books in Hillsboro; Tonya Macalino, president of Hillsboro-based Northwest Independent Publishers Association; John Schrag, publisher, *News-Times* and *Hillsboro Tribune*, Forest Grove, Oregon; and the volunteers and staff at the Pacific Northwest Chapter of the National Railway Historical Society in Portland, Oregon.

Special thanks to Rebecca Coffey, editor at Arcadia Publishing in Mount Pleasant, South Carolina; Robert and Lois Burkhardt, for constant support; and to Marie Burkhardt, for keeping the "home fires" organized and on track while I took time out to produce this book.

I sincerely appreciate the support from all of you.

—D.C. Jesse Burkhardt
Aloha, Oregon
March 11, 2014

Introduction

Even before the community was incorporated in 1876, Hillsboro, Oregon, seemed destined to become an important railroad town. Located in the northwest corner of the state just 20 miles west of Portland—a booming regional center of manufacturing and trade—Hillsboro became a key junction for trains moving to and from the Oregon coast to the west and the rich agricultural lands of the Willamette Valley to the south.

The first trains began rolling toward Hillsboro in 1871. In that year, the Oregon & California Railroad (O&C) carved a right of way into the area, but Hillsboro came close to being bypassed because the town's leaders refused to give the railroad company land to entice it to build into the heart of Hillsboro. Because of that refusal, the O&C skirted the city, laying its tracks about a mile south of the growing Hillsboro community.

In an era of extensive railroad construction across the nation, it was surprising that after the O&C put down tracks, it was to be nearly four decades before another company brought steel rails to Hillsboro.

As it turned out, there were three main phases of railroad construction in and around Hillsboro. Following the O&C's entry into the area in 1871, it was not until 1908 that another railroad came to town.

In early 1908, newspapers in Washington County were reporting that Hillsboro, Forest Grove, and the western part of the county would soon be linked to Portland, as the Oregon Electric Railway (OE) was building a new electrified passenger train route from Portland that would connect the towns. By late summer of that year, construction of the line reached the outskirts of Hillsboro, and the excitement of the townspeople was so great that dozens of newspaper articles were devoted to tracking the new railroad line's progress, as well as its setbacks. In September 1908, one local newspaper dramatically reported that an Oregon Electric construction train had reached Hillsboro "amid the ringing of bells, explosion of bombs, and the cheers of the populace. The whole town, attracted by the engine's repeated whistling, lined the track," the article read. "Citizens and boys galore came up Washington Street to Second, where hundreds of citizens . . . gave three cheers for the Oregon Electric."

It was a grand occasion, and on September 30, 1908, when the first interurban passenger train from Portland reached Hillsboro, hundreds of people gathered near the new OE railroad depot to celebrate the achievement. In the months after that celebration, the OE extended service westward to Cornelius and Forest Grove.

The arrival of the Oregon Electric's interurban trains meant Hillsboro residents could get to Portland essentially within an hour's time. There were numerous trains coming and going each day, as well as an overnight train operating to and from Eugene.

After the OE's dramatic and long-awaited arrival, however, the townsfolk did not have long to wait before yet another railroad began laying track into Hillsboro. In fact, even before the OE came to town, the Pacific Railway & Navigation Company (PR&N) had been busy constructing a rail line from Tillamook, a small coastal logging town on the west side of the Coast Range.

Starting in 1905, PR&N track crews worked northeast from Tillamook, punching a route through the region's rough mountainous terrain. In part because of the treacherous landscape, the line between Hillsboro and Tillamook took several years to complete, finally opening in 1911.

The importance of Hillsboro as a transportation hub accelerated in the early 1900s. It hit high gear when the PR&N opened its line to Tillamook, thereby directly connecting Hillsboro with the Oregon coastal region.

When the era of railroad construction ended, several vital rail lines branched out of Hillsboro. The PR&N's line headed west to Tillamook, where the railroad tapped rich timber resources along the Oregon coast; the Oregon & California route cut south to McMinnville and Corvallis, accessing prime dairy and agricultural lands in the Willamette Valley; and the Oregon Electric line cut through Hillsboro, moving passengers and goods to and from Portland to the east and the growing communities of Forest Grove and Cornelius to the west.

Yet changes were brewing in the railroad industry. In 1910, the OE became a subsidiary of a much larger railroad, the Spokane, Portland & Seattle Railway (SP&S). Similarly, in 1915, railroad giant Southern Pacific (SP) took control of the PR&N and the O&C, operating the routes for roughly the next 80 years. Further, the popularity of interurban train service proved to be relatively short, because with the advent of automobiles and improved roads in the 1920s, the need for passenger rail operations began to wane.

As a result, by the early 1930s, electric trains were no longer running into Hillsboro or elsewhere in the Willamette Valley. The last of SP's "Red Electric" trains left Hillsboro in 1929, while the OE ended its electric interurban passenger service in 1933.

In the modern era, more changes have unfolded. After many decades of service and with dramatic regulatory changes and economic challenges in the railroad industry, many large railroad companies sought to eliminate lightly trafficked branchlines. In 1993, SP leased most of its Oregon branch routes to a startup shortline company, the Willamette & Pacific Railroad. In 1995, the Portland & Western Railroad—a new shortline under the same corporate ownership as the Willamette & Pacific—took over more SP branches, as well as much of the old Oregon Electric trackage.

The Willamette & Pacific was folded into the Portland & Western in December 2000, and the combined routes—totaling approximately 520 miles—officially became the Portland & Western Railroad (P&W). The P&W is now the sole freight railroad serving Hillsboro.

Somewhat surprisingly, there has even been a bit of new railroad construction just a few miles down the tracks from Hillsboro. In November 2013, the P&W began building a connecting track at Wilkesboro, a rural station between Banks and Hillsboro. The new trackage, two-thirds of a mile in length, was designed to more directly connect the former OE Vernonia Branch with the ex-SP Tillamook Branch, thereby removing a time-consuming backup move at Banks for freight trains moving between Portland and Albany. The $3.1-million project, dubbed the "Banks Rail Connection," slices at least an hour off the previous transit times on the route, which passes directly through Hillsboro and generally sees through movements on a daily basis.

The Banks Rail Connection project, which was given a big boost by way of a $2.4-million ConnectOregon transportation grant from the State of Oregon, opened for service in the summer of 2014.

Although there are fewer trains in Hillsboro in contemporary times, and some rail routes radiating out of the city have been truncated, freight trains still carry logs, lumber, and agricultural products through the city, and the railroad remains an important facet of the region's economic strength.

Tracks also continue to carry passengers into and out of Hillsboro, but they are light rail operations these days. It is striking that traditional passenger trains on the route have given way to electric-powered transit operations in a clear instance of 21st century technology going "back to the future." Similarly, in December 2013, the Forest Grove Planning Commission set having a light rail station in the community within 20 years as a specific goal in the city's comprehensive plan, so the development of new ways to move passengers around the Portland metropolitan area truly appears to be coming full circle.

For nearly 150 years, railroads have hauled goods and passengers to Hillsboro and surrounding communities. With infrastructure improvements such as the one in nearby Wilkesboro demonstrating an ongoing commitment to providing efficient rail transportation, it is apparent that steel wheels will continue to roll through Hillsboro for many years to come.

One

Tracks into Hillsboro

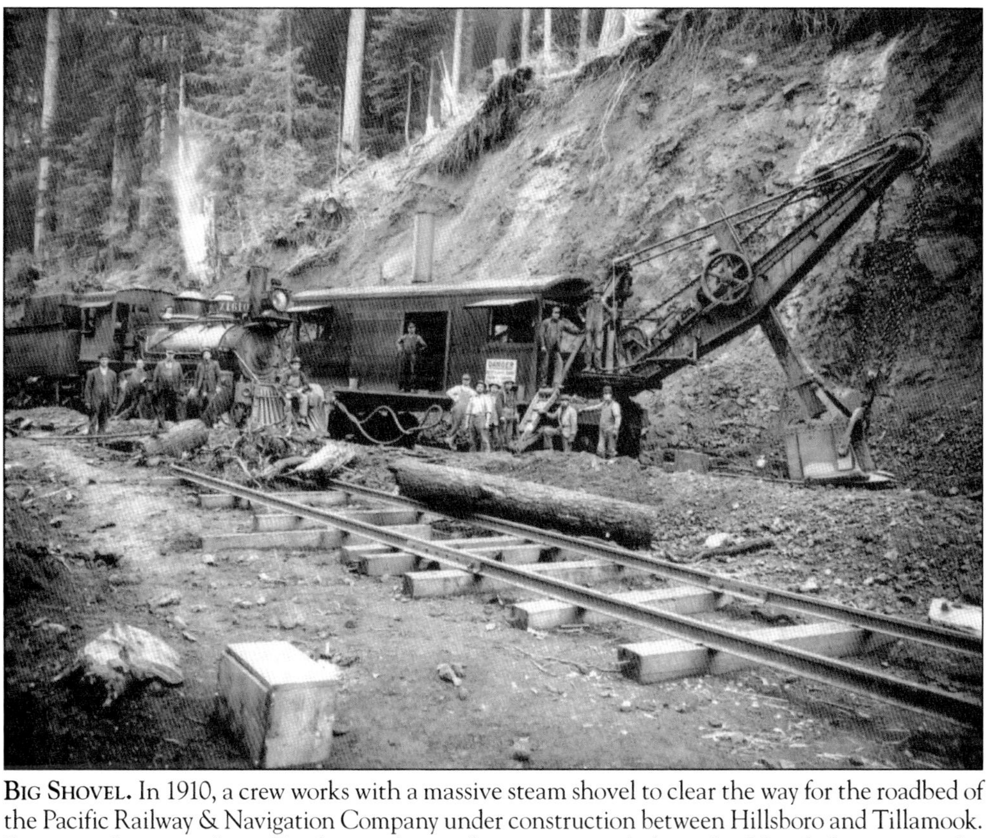

Big Shovel. In 1910, a crew works with a massive steam shovel to clear the way for the roadbed of the Pacific Railway & Navigation Company under construction between Hillsboro and Tillamook. Because a large number of bridges and tunnels were required along the 90-mile-long route, the new rail line took about five years to complete. Service started on the PR&N on November 10, 1911. (Collection of Curtis Culp.)

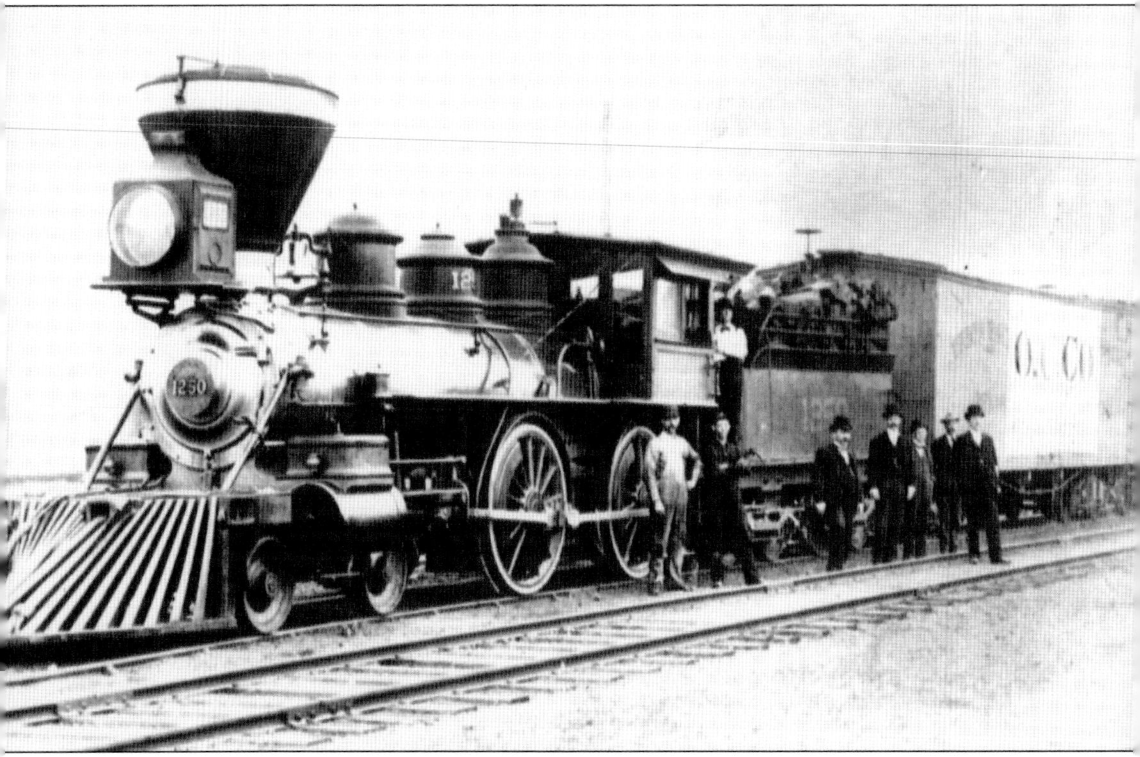

First to Arrive. Oregon & California Railroad locomotive No. 1250 poses with its crew and a handful of dignitaries. The O&C became the first railroad to build tracks into the Hillsboro area, completing a route from Portland to Hillsboro on December 23, 1871. Note the large "O.C. Co." banner on the boxcar directly behind the locomotive. A milestone—possibly the arrival of rail service to Washington County—was being celebrated. It would be nearly four decades before two other carriers—the Oregon Electric Railway in 1908 and the Pacific Railway & Navigation Company in 1911—brought railroad lines into Hillsboro. (Collection of Curtis Culp.)

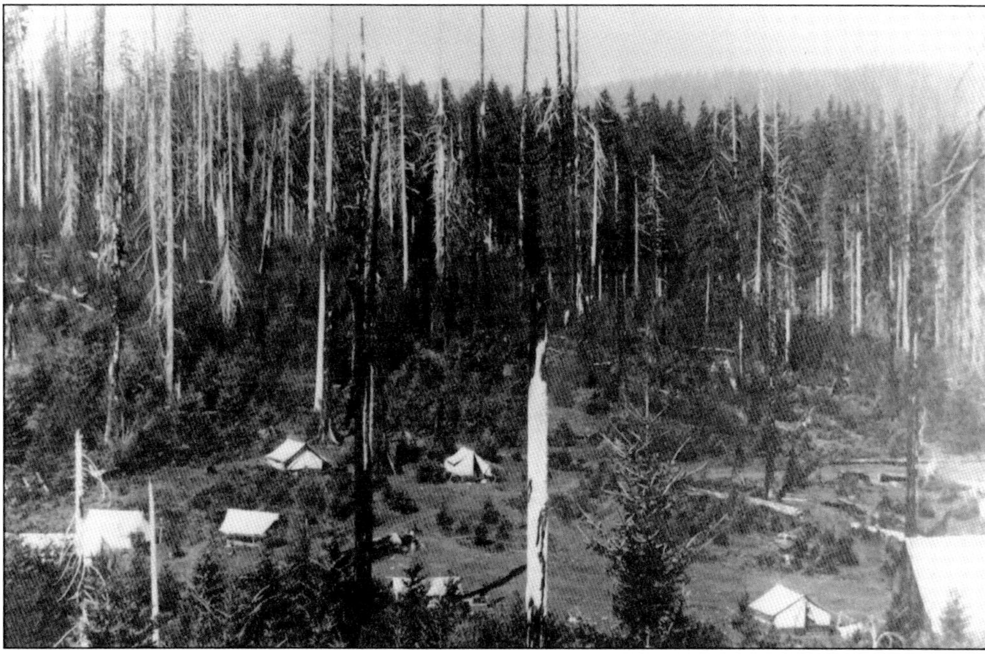

Camping Out. This 1905 photograph shows a group of tents set up by a team of engineers and surveyors trying to locate the best route for the Pacific Railway & Navigation Company line between Hillsboro and Tillamook. This campsite was in the Coast Range somewhere between the two end points; the camps were moved as surveyors hunted for the least challenging—and least expensive—places for the tracks to go. (Collection of Washington County Museum.)

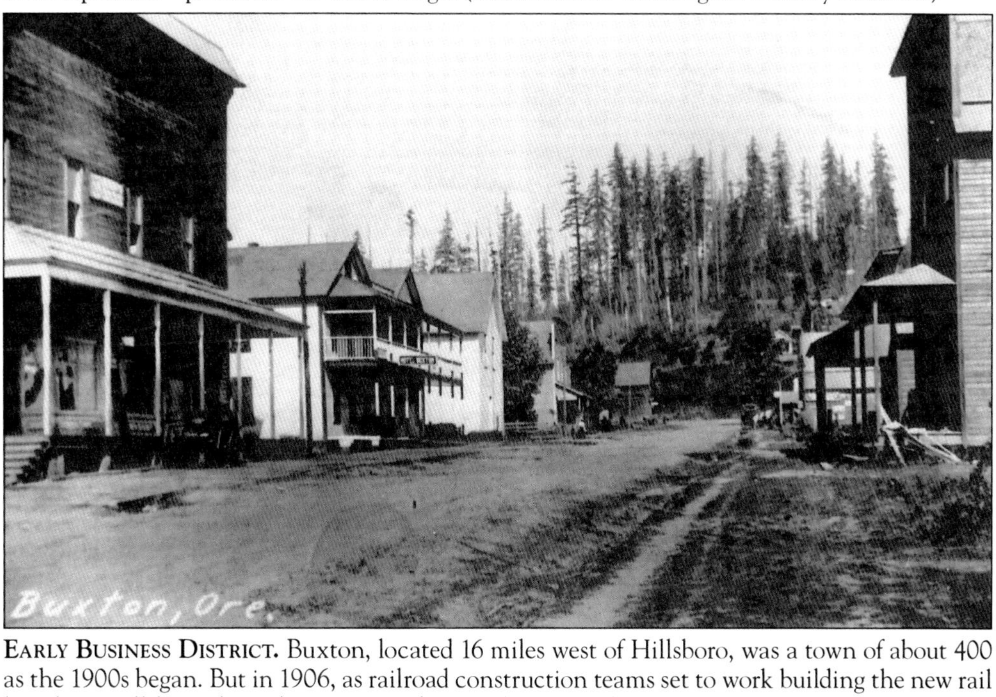

Early Business District. Buxton, located 16 miles west of Hillsboro, was a town of about 400 as the 1900s began. But in 1906, as railroad construction teams set to work building the new rail line from Hillsboro through Buxton and on to the coast, the town started to grow as it became a staging center for workers and supplies. (Collection of Banks Historical Society.)

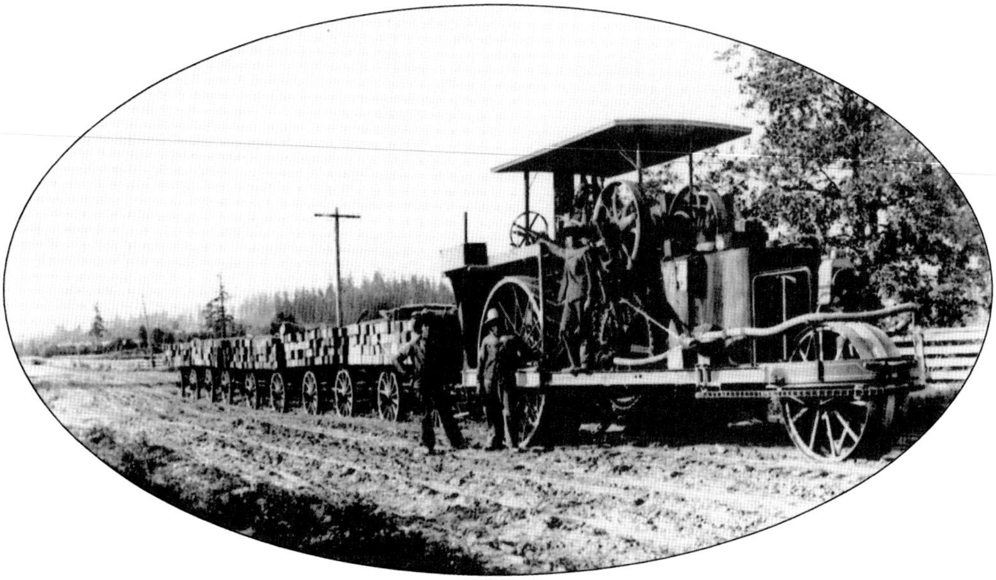

Roots of a Railroad. A team of employees from Potter's Mill, a sawmill in the Cedar Mill area northeast of Hillsboro, uses a 50-horsepower Russell steam tractor to pull several wagonloads of railroad ties through the mud to the construction site for the Oregon Electric Railway. In 1905, when this photograph was taken, the OE was building a 50-mile-long electrified mainline between Portland and Salem, as well as a 19-mile-long branchline from Garden Home to Hillsboro and Forest Grove. Both routes opened in 1908. (Collection of Washington County Museum.)

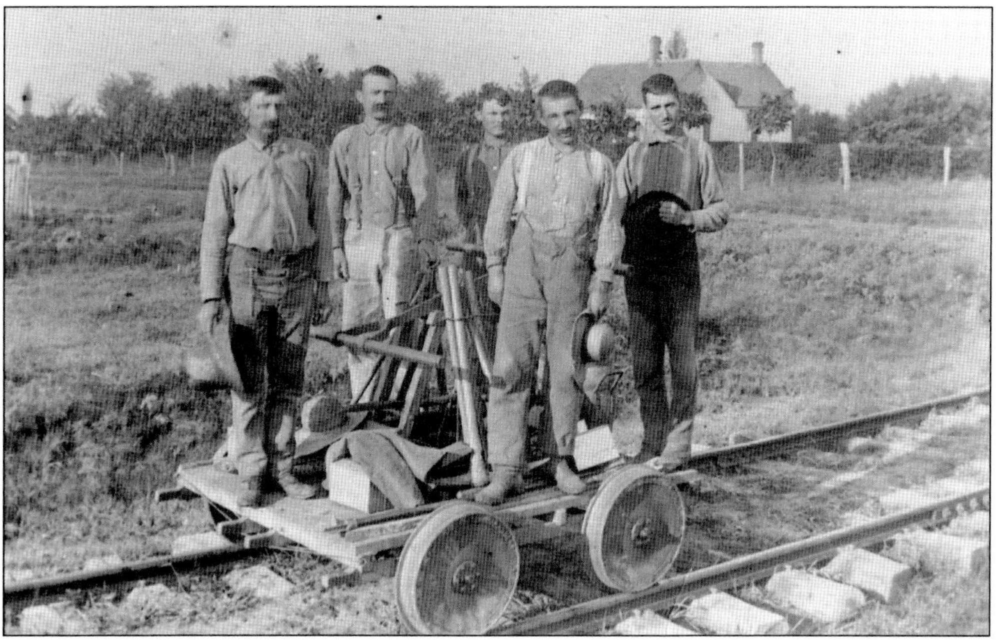

No Shortage of Tools. Railroad workers pause with their handcar on a section of the United Railways line between North Plains and Wilkesboro around 1910. These workers were likely part of the crew building the United Railways line between Wilkesboro, a rural station roughly nine miles northwest of Hillsboro, and United Junction, a few miles west of Portland. The new line opened in 1911. (Collection of Washington County Museum.)

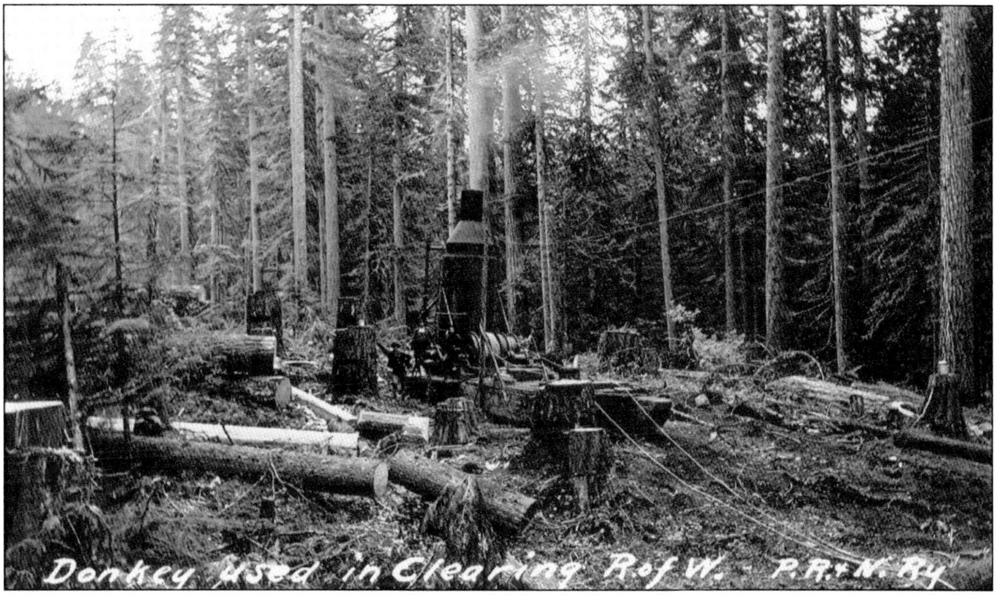

Donkey in the Woods. "Donkeys" were steam-powered winches that could be transported where needed for a variety of heavy-duty operations. This donkey is shown at work in the Coast Range, helping to clear the way for the Pacific Railway & Navigation rail line from Hillsboro to the coast. Note the heavy cables used to pull logs and other debris out of the way of the new roadbed. (Collection of Washington County Museum.)

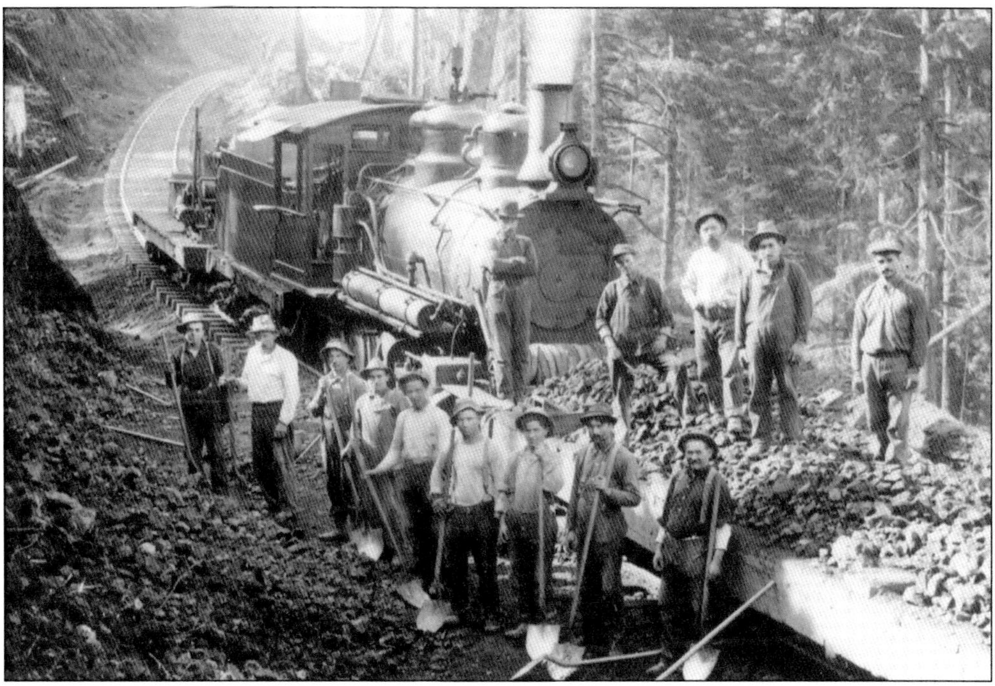

Put Your Backs into It. A group of men take a break from clearing a rock slide on the PR&N's line out of Hillsboro in this photograph from around 1909. With steep slopes and a lot of rain, slides were not uncommon, and men wielding shovels were the first line of defense in clearing blocked tracks. (Collection of Washington County Museum.)

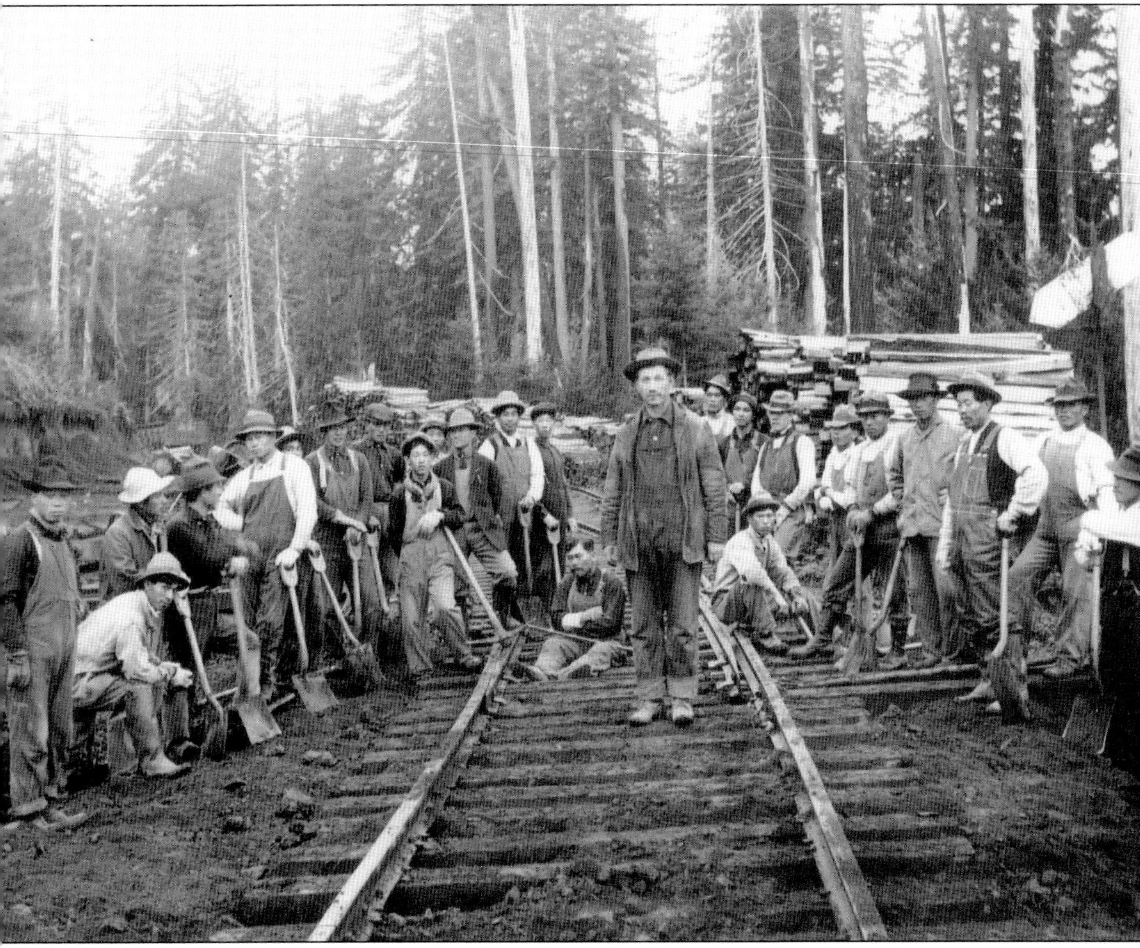

HARD WORK AND LOW PAY. Immigrants from all around the globe came to the United States in the early 1900s, and many were put to work building the grades for new railroads and laying track. In this photograph, taken near Buxton during construction of the PR&N route to Tillamook, a crew of Japanese workers poses during a break in the grind. The immigrants typically settled for low wages, so they were attractive employees for the railroads. (Collection of Curtis Culp.)

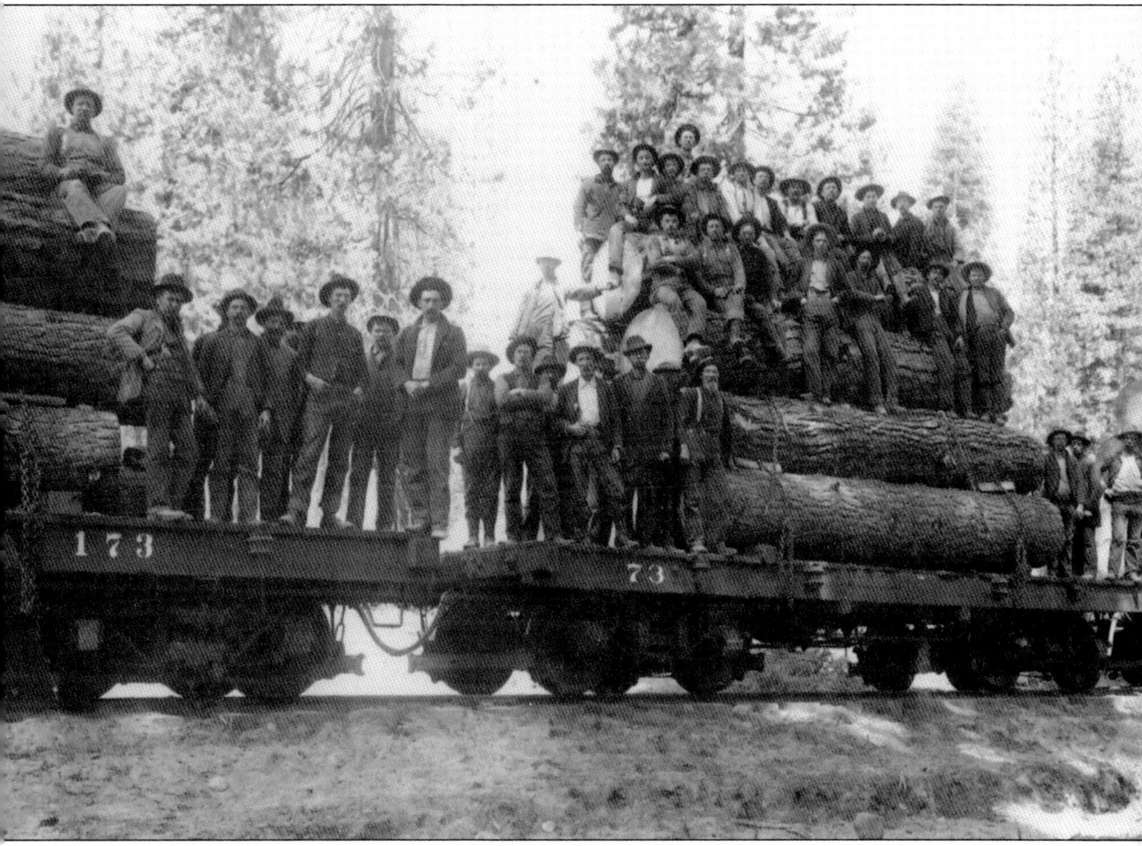

LOGGERS. With the PR&N tracks going in, trees needed to be cut down to clear the new railroad's right of way through the forests of the Coast Range. With a growing market for lumber, especially with the area beginning to be more heavily populated, crews loaded the felled logs onto flatcars for transport to local sawmills. In this scene from 1910, a group of sawyers near Cochran, a small railroad town about 35 miles west of Hillsboro on the mainline to the coast, poses on flatcars laden with massive logs. Although the loads do not look quite like this these days, the transportation of logs remains a significant slice of business for railroads in this part of Oregon. (Collection of Washington County Museum.)

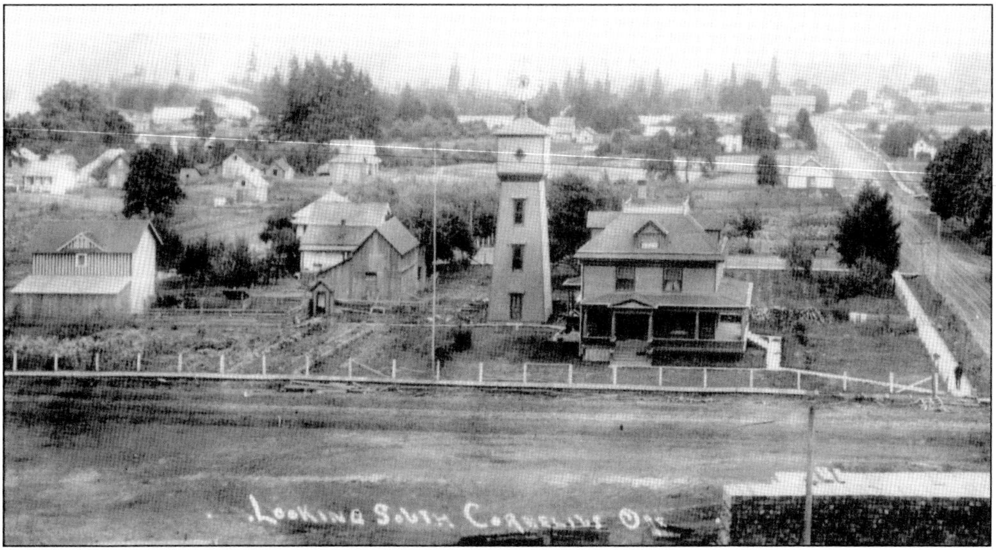

Cornelius on the Move. In 1908, the Oregon Electric Railway built a new passenger train branchline route between Hillsboro and Portland. On September 30 of that year, the OE's first interurban train reached Hillsboro, and three months after that, the railroad was extended westward to Cornelius and Forest Grove. In this photograph of Cornelius taken in early 1908, the small town appears quiet, but note the immense stack of railroad ties in the foreground. The railroad is about to come to Cornelius. (Collection of Curtis Culp.)

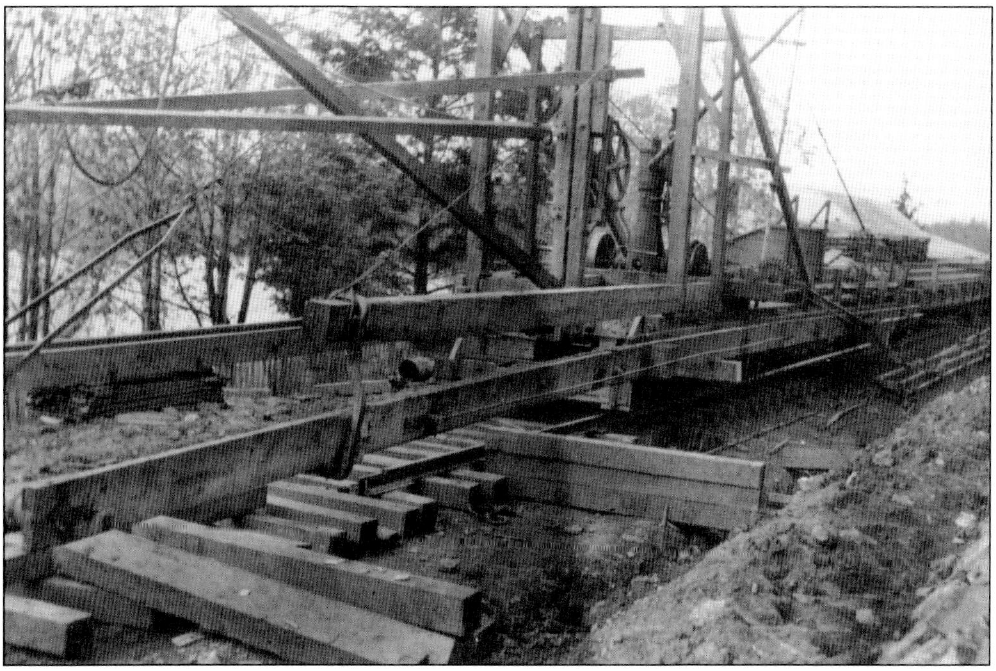

Labor-Saving Tool. This odd contraption is described as a "track-laying machine." It was used in the building of the Oregon Electric's interurban lines in the Willamette Valley in the early 1900s, including the line that reached Hillsboro and Forest Grove in 1908. When the OE trains first arrived in Hillsboro, the city had a population of approximately 2,000 residents. (Collection of Curtis Culp.)

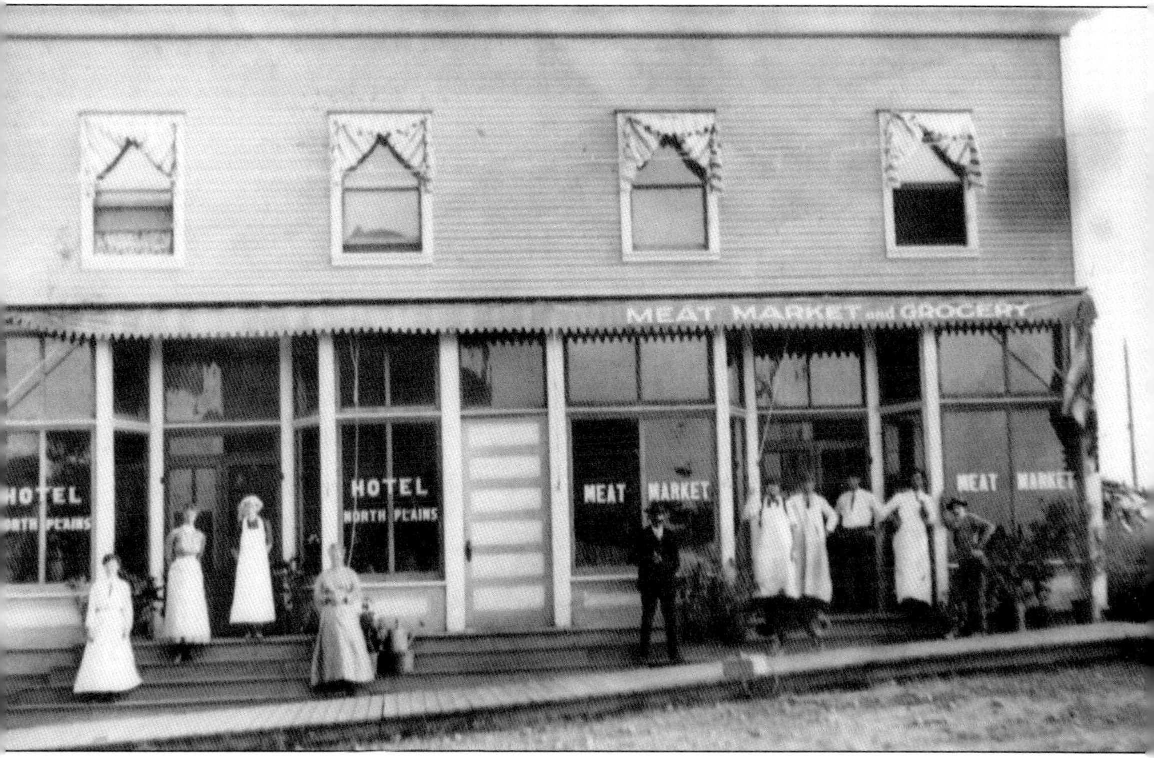

A Growing Community. With the opening of the United Railways line in 1911, North Plains began growing to meet the needs of more residents and more travelers. In this 1912 photograph, townspeople pose in front of their stores—a hotel and a meat market—along Main Street. The market seen here reportedly furnished all the meat for the railroad construction crews that brought the tracks to North Plains. The Spokane, Portland & Seattle Railway took control of United Railways in March 1911 and made the route through North Plains part of its Third Subdivision, which extended 38 miles from United Junction to the town of Vernonia. In 1912, North Plains had a population of approximately 400—twice what it had before the building of the railroad. Reflecting the optimism that greeted the arrival of the trains, an early advertising brochure for North Plains publicized the city as the "Metropolis of North Tualatin Valley." (Collection of Curtis Culp.)

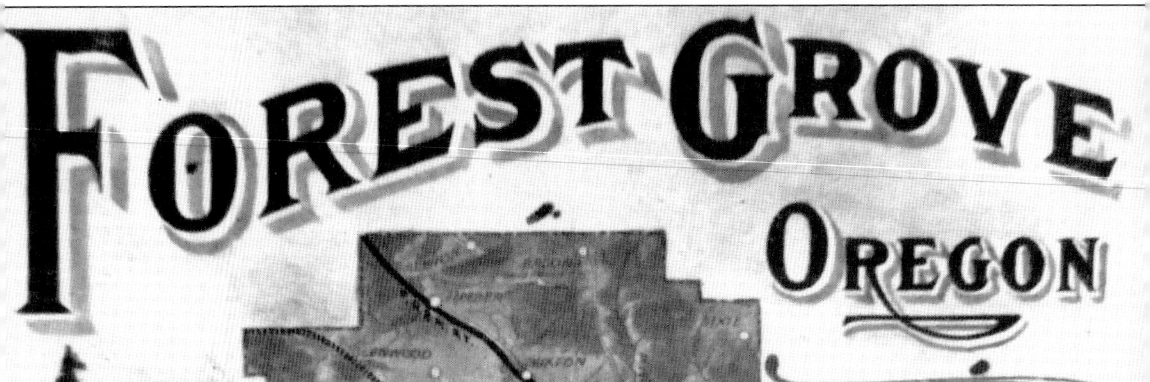

WELCOME TO WASHINGTON COUNTY. An early map shows rail lines in Washington County, with a clear tipoff as to which community the mapmakers believed was most important in the region. This map, designed to be on a postcard, was created in 1914 by the Forest Grove Commercial Club to promote the region. Note the dotted United Railways line leading west out of Banks. United Railways originally proposed to build a rail line to the coast along this routing, but economic realities led the company's owners to shelve the project, and the carrier never laid tracks west of Banks. The map's focus on farming, dairy cows, and timber accurately represented the key economic engines of the era. To this day, all three of these business sectors remain important to the county's economy, although high tech manufacturing has taken over the top spot. (Collection of Washington County Museum.)

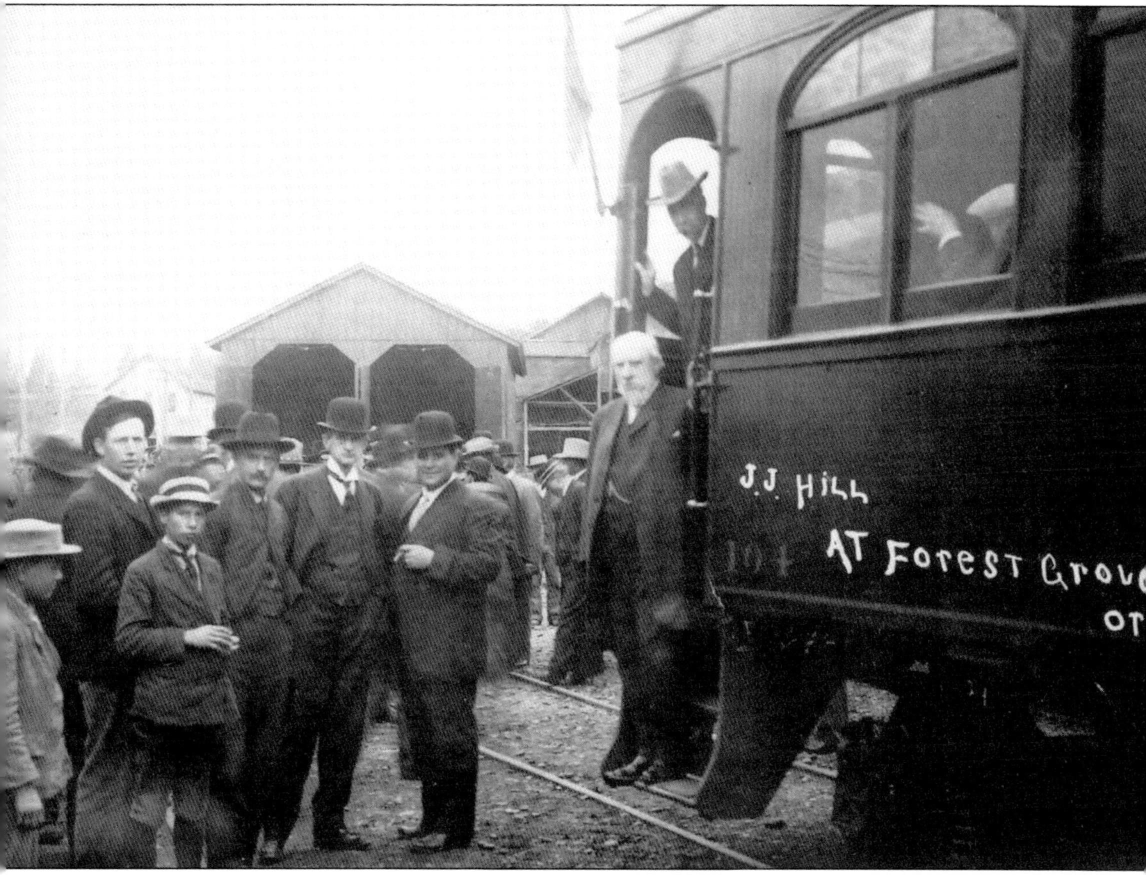

EMPIRE EXTENDS TO FOREST GROVE. In May 1910, James J. Hill—owner of the Great Northern Railway—visited Forest Grove as part of a "victory lap" celebrating his March 1910 purchase of the Oregon Electric Railway. In this photograph, he is seen standing on the steps of his private railroad car, surrounded by Oregon Electric employees and local townspeople. Hill was nicknamed "the Empire Builder" because of his extensive railroad holdings, which, in addition to the Great Northern, included the Northern Pacific; the Spokane, Portland & Seattle Railway; and the Chicago, Burlington & Quincy. After Hill bought the Oregon Electric, he extended the interurban line first to Albany—beginning service there on July 4, 1912—and later all the way to Eugene, where service began on October 15, 1912. (Collection of Friends of Historic Forest Grove.)

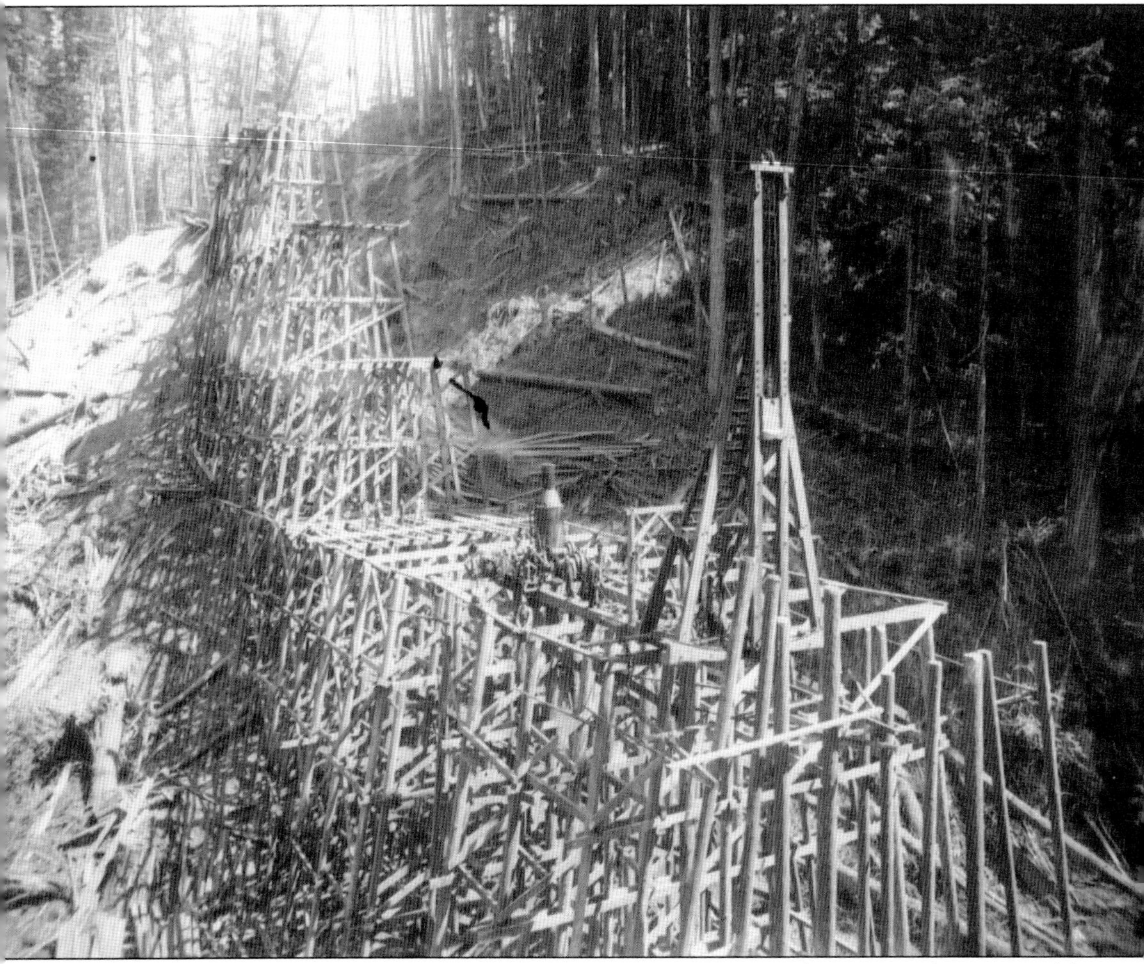

Rugged Terrain. In this scene from 1910, a construction crew works on a trestle over Heidel Creek just east of Cochran on the Pacific Railway & Navigation Company's line between Hillsboro and Tillamook. This four-story-tall bridge, which was about 590 feet long, is being built in an area representative of the unforgiving terrain the builders of the PR&N line had to conquer. Approximately 60 bridges were needed on the 90-mile line. The route, finally opened in November 1911 after more than five years of toil, linked Hillsboro with the timber-rich Oregon coast. (Collection of Curtis Culp.)

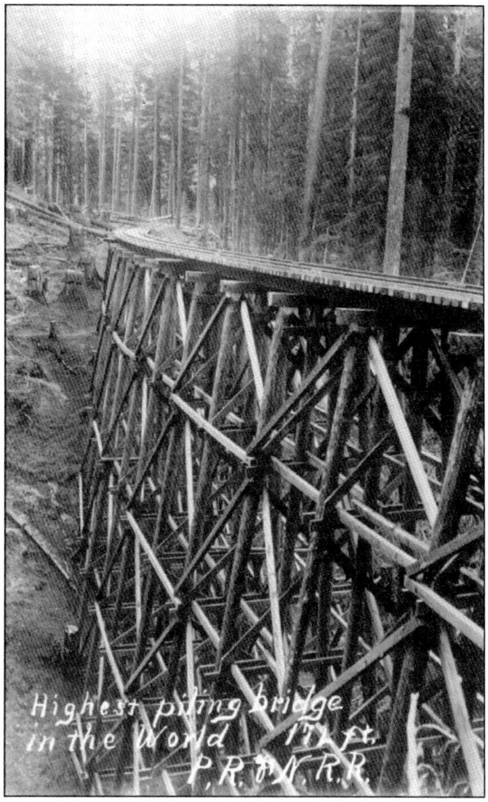

High Bridge. When completed in 1911, the Big Baldwin trestle on the PR&N rail line was 172 feet high and considered the "highest piling bridge in the world," as the inscription on the top photograph attests. The photograph below shows the view from the same vantage point but looks the other way from the scene at right. The newly constructed bridge swings over a wide canyon and immediately enters a tunnel, all of which probably caused some anxious moments for train crews who reportedly could not even see the bridge they were riding on as they swung around the tight curve. Note the big timbers and intricate lacing of the supports that went into this amazing project. (Both, collection of Washington County Museum.)

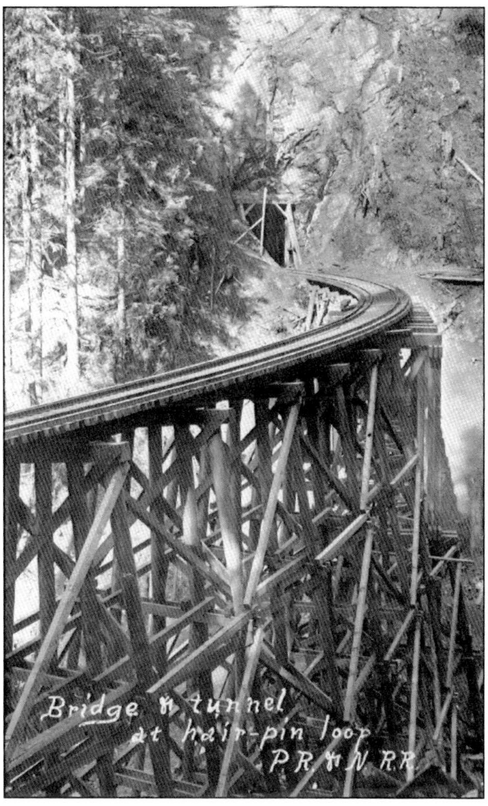

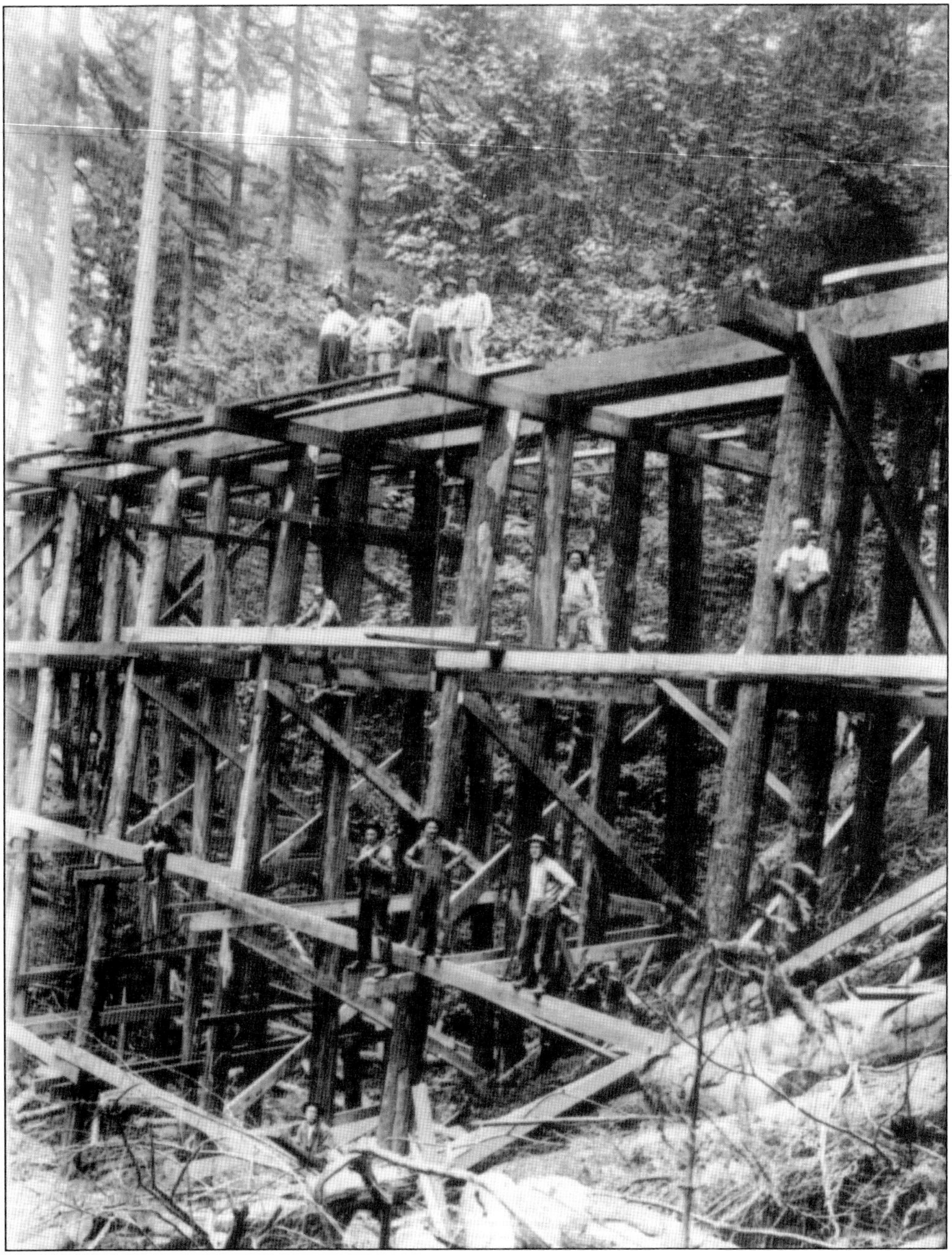

Bridging the Gap at Buxton. The PR&N's route between Hillsboro and Tillamook was an engineering marvel, given the rugged landscape and the many canyons that had to be bridged. In this photograph from 1910, a crew of builders hammers away to complete a trestle near Buxton. (Collection of Washington County Museum.)

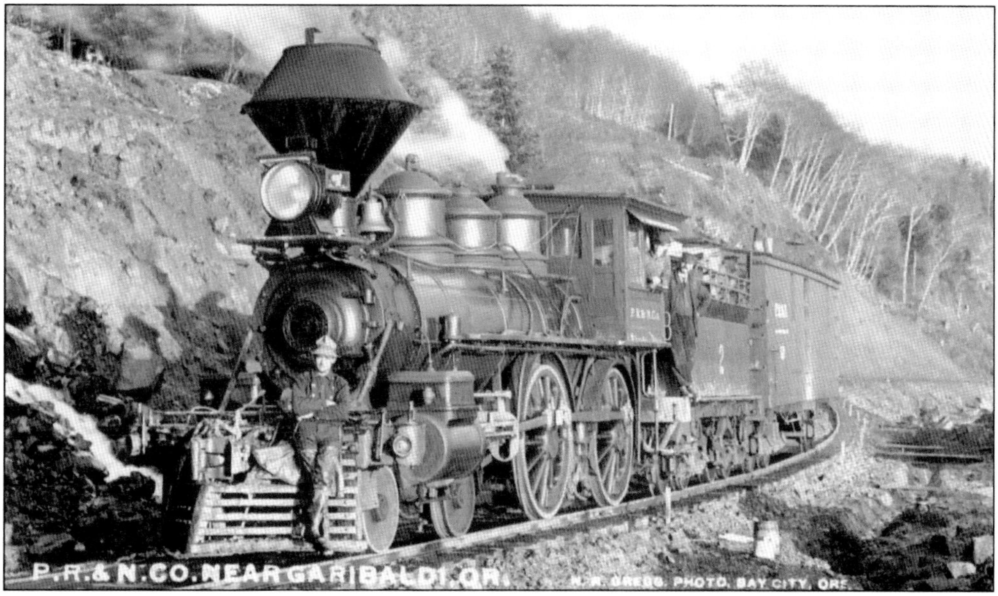

Under Construction. Pacific Railway & Navigation Company locomotive No. 2 steams away in work train service in this 1910 photograph taken at Garibaldi on the Oregon coast. The Baldwin locomotive, a 4-4-0, was built in 1872 for the Oregon & California Railroad, which in 1871 was the first railroad to arrive in Hillsboro. Note the wooden engineering stakes lining the tracks, an indication the railroad is still under construction. (Photograph by H.R. Gregg; collection of Curtis Culp.)

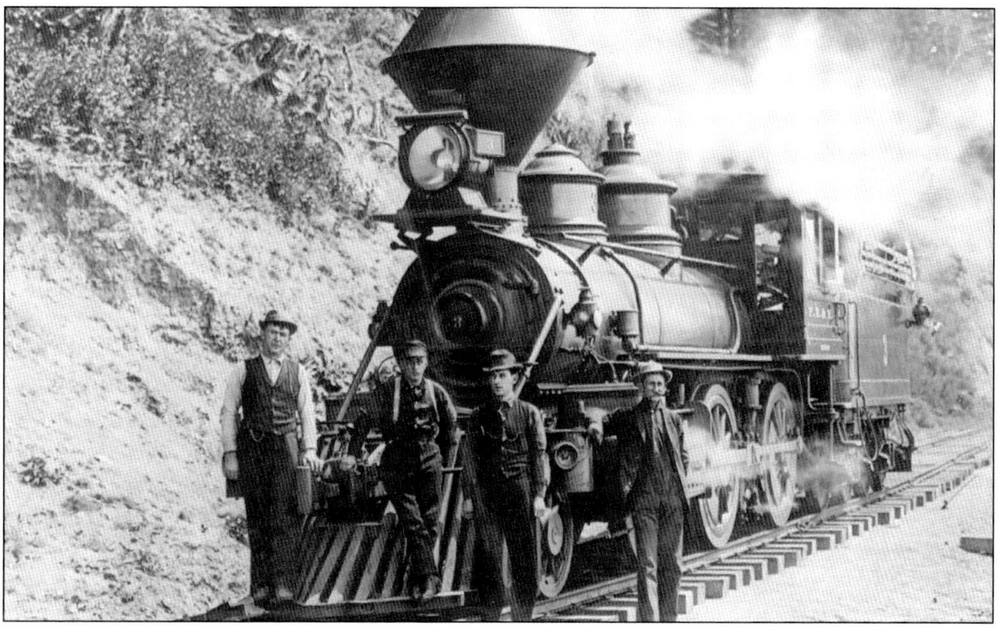

Added Muscle. With the tracks to Hillsboro nearing completion, the PR&N's managers decided it was time to bring in another locomotive to meet the needs of construction teams and shippers on the fledgling railroad linking Tillamook with Hillsboro. PR&N No. 3 was purchased from Southern Pacific in June 1910 and barged to Wheeler, a town on Nehalem Bay about 22 miles north of Tillamook. (Collection of Washington County Museum.)

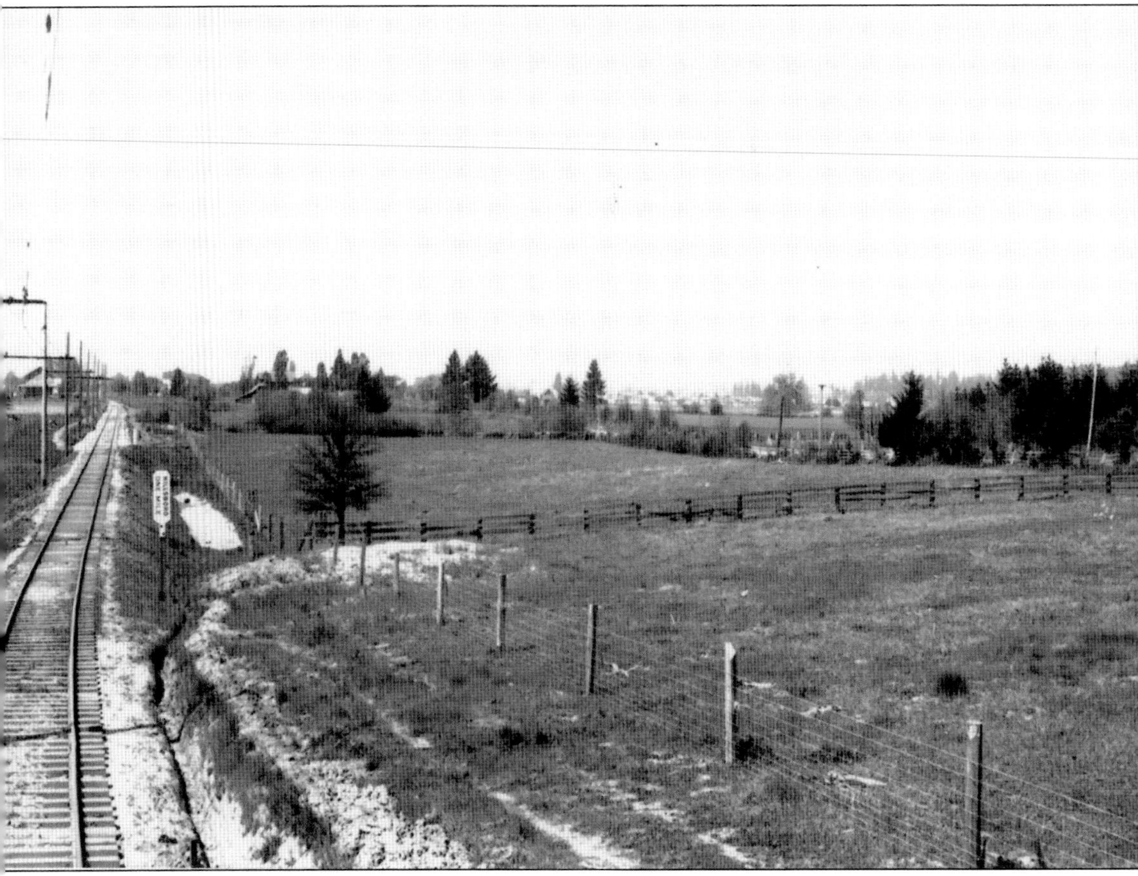

ONE MORE MILE. A sign alongside the Oregon Electric right of way just outside Hillsboro alerts the engineer there is just one mile to go before reaching the Hillsboro station. From the vantage point of this photograph, it appears the photographer has climbed one of the signal towers on the 19-mile line, which stretched from Garden Home—a station on the OE mainline a few miles south of Portland—through Hillsboro and on to the end of the OE's electrified interurban line at Forest Grove. (Collection of Washington County Museum.)

Two

Passengers on the Move

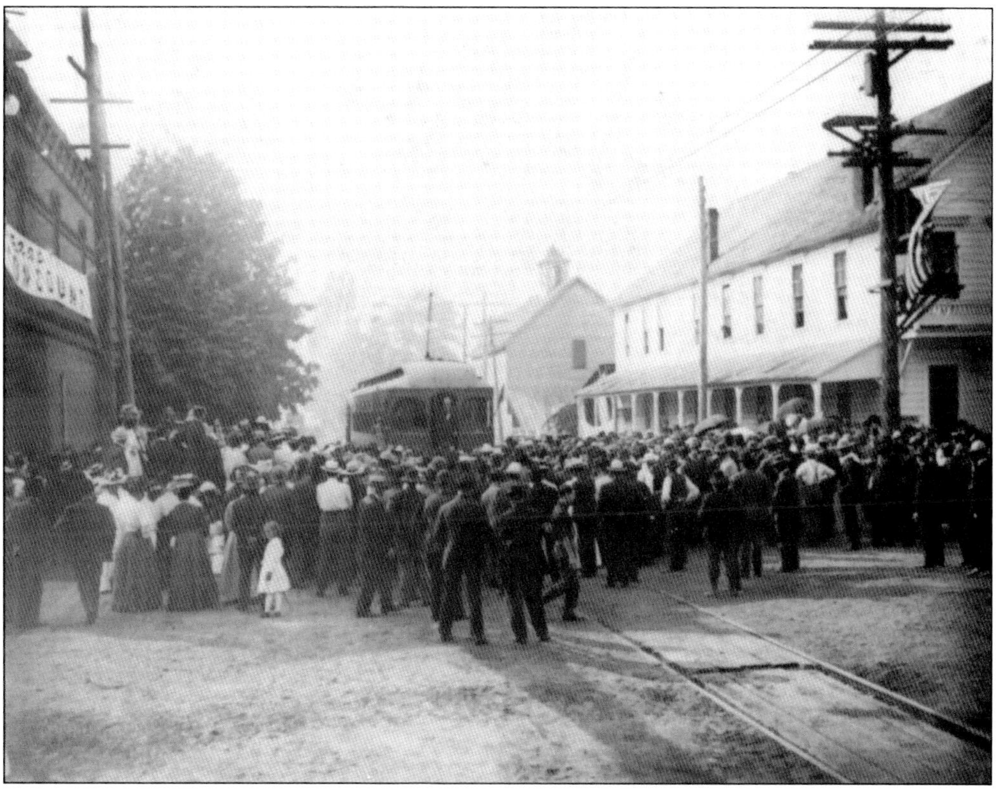

A Banner Day. The date is September 30, 1908, and the Oregon Electric Railway's first train into Hillsboro has arrived at the intersection of Washington Street and Second Avenue. Several hundred people turned out to welcome the new electric interurban train service, which would provide Hillsboro's residents with a direct rail link to Portland for the next 25 years. (Collection of Washington County Museum.)

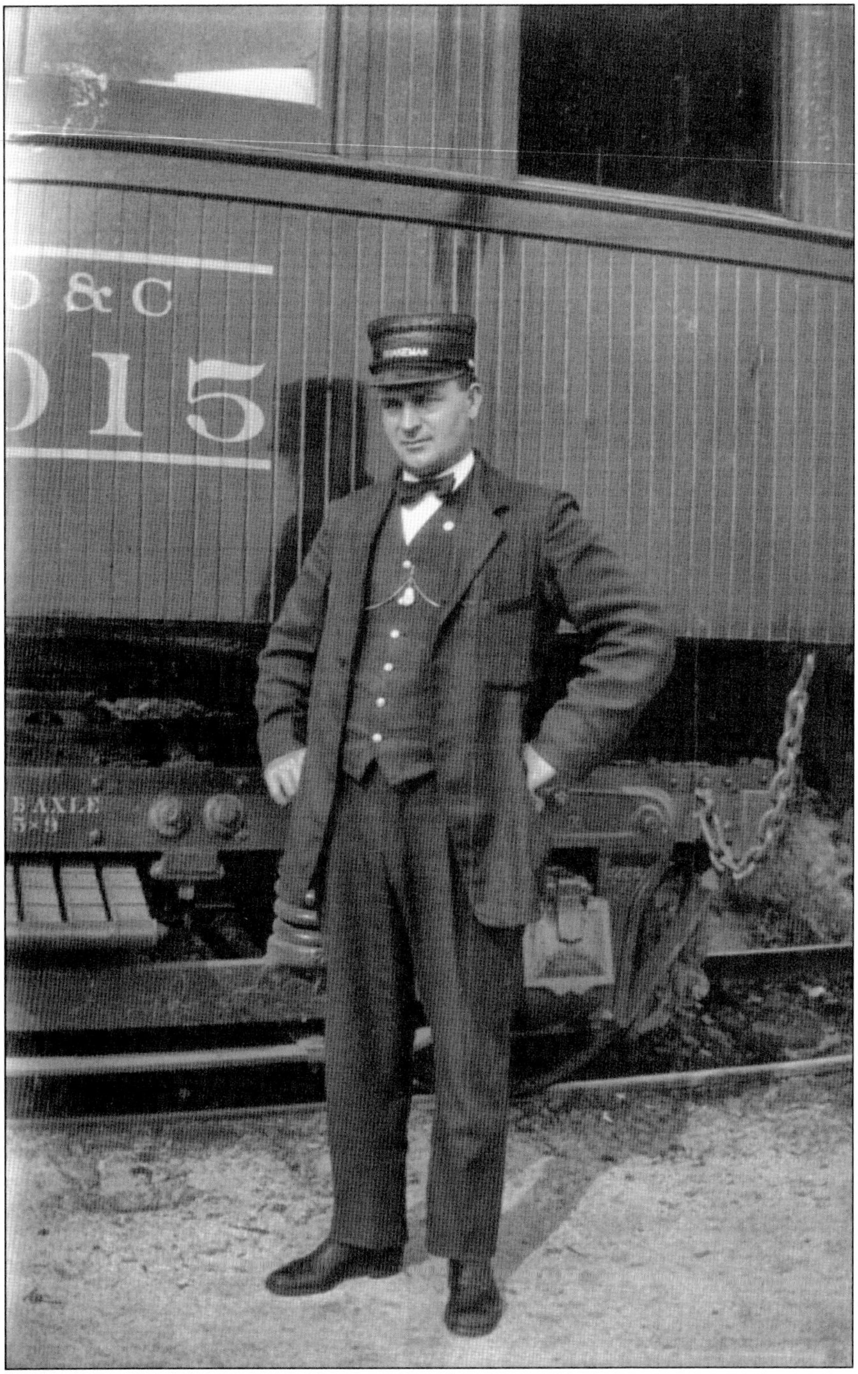

Brakeman. Railroad brakeman Carl F. Akin poses for a photograph alongside an Oregon & California passenger car during a station stop on the line between Hillsboro and Corvallis in 1918. Although the car is lettered for the O&C, Southern Pacific had taken over operations on the line three years earlier. Trains on this route operated between Portland and Corvallis via Hillsboro and McMinnville. The O&C was the first railroad to build tracks to Hillsboro, doing so in 1871. (Collection of Curtis Culp.)

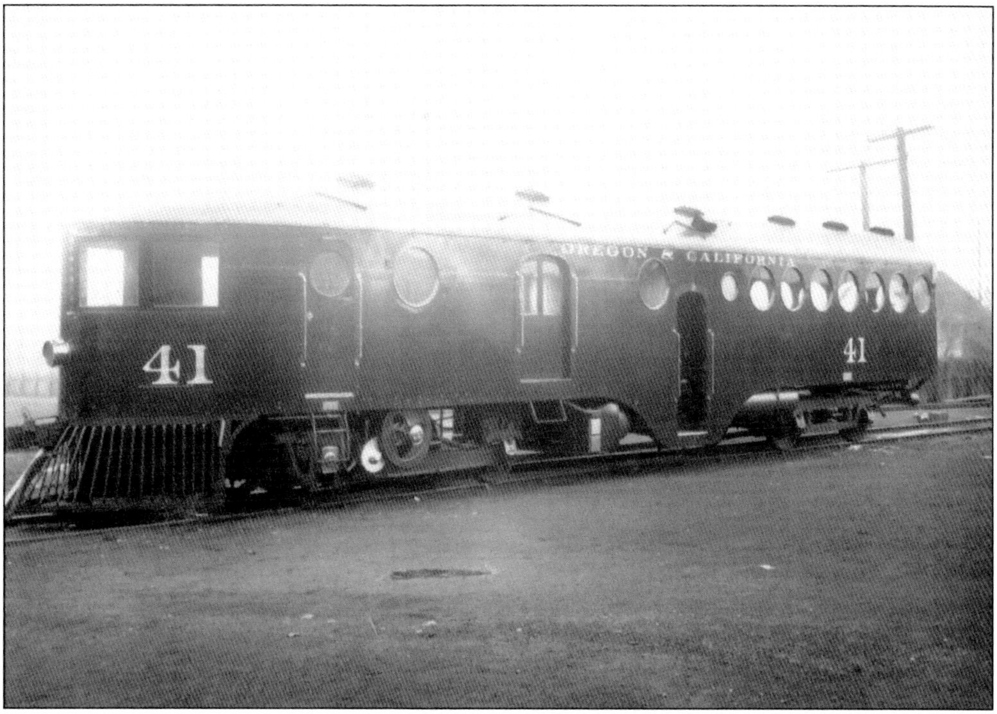

Internal Combustion. The McKeen Motor Car Company, based in Omaha, Nebraska, tried to find a more efficient way to move passengers in the early 1900s with these ungainly cars that ran on gasoline-fired engines. The Oregon & California Railroad purchased at least two McKeen cars for use on Oregon's Willamette Valley branchlines, including this one photographed in 1913. The cars were taken out of service in 1930. (Collection of Curtis Culp.)

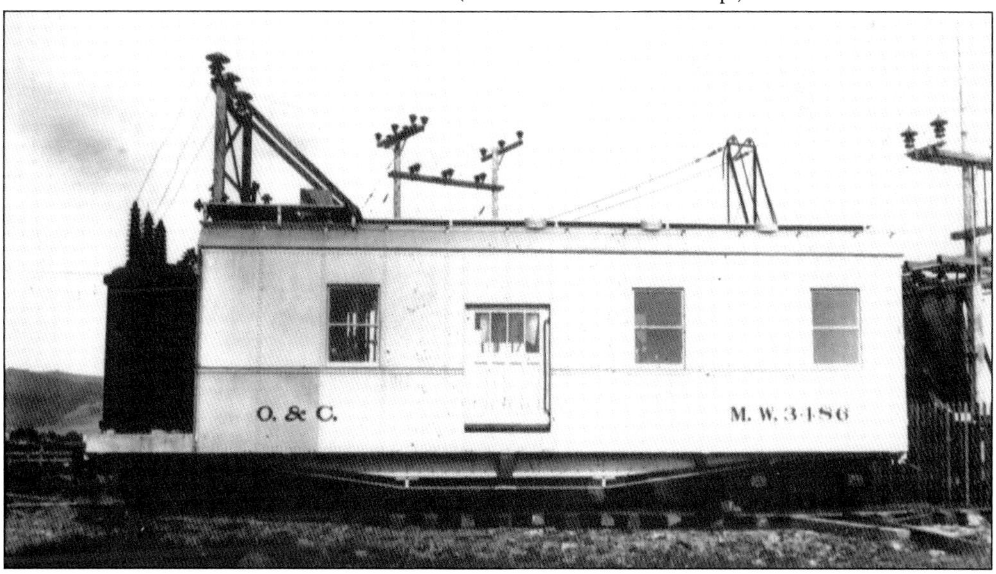

Portable Power. A mobile electrical power generator unit lettered for the Oregon & California Railroad rests on a spur track alongside the West Side Branch in the Willamette Valley in 1916. The units were used to generate electricity to power trains during times the substations along the route were out of service for repairs. (Collection of Curtis Culp.)

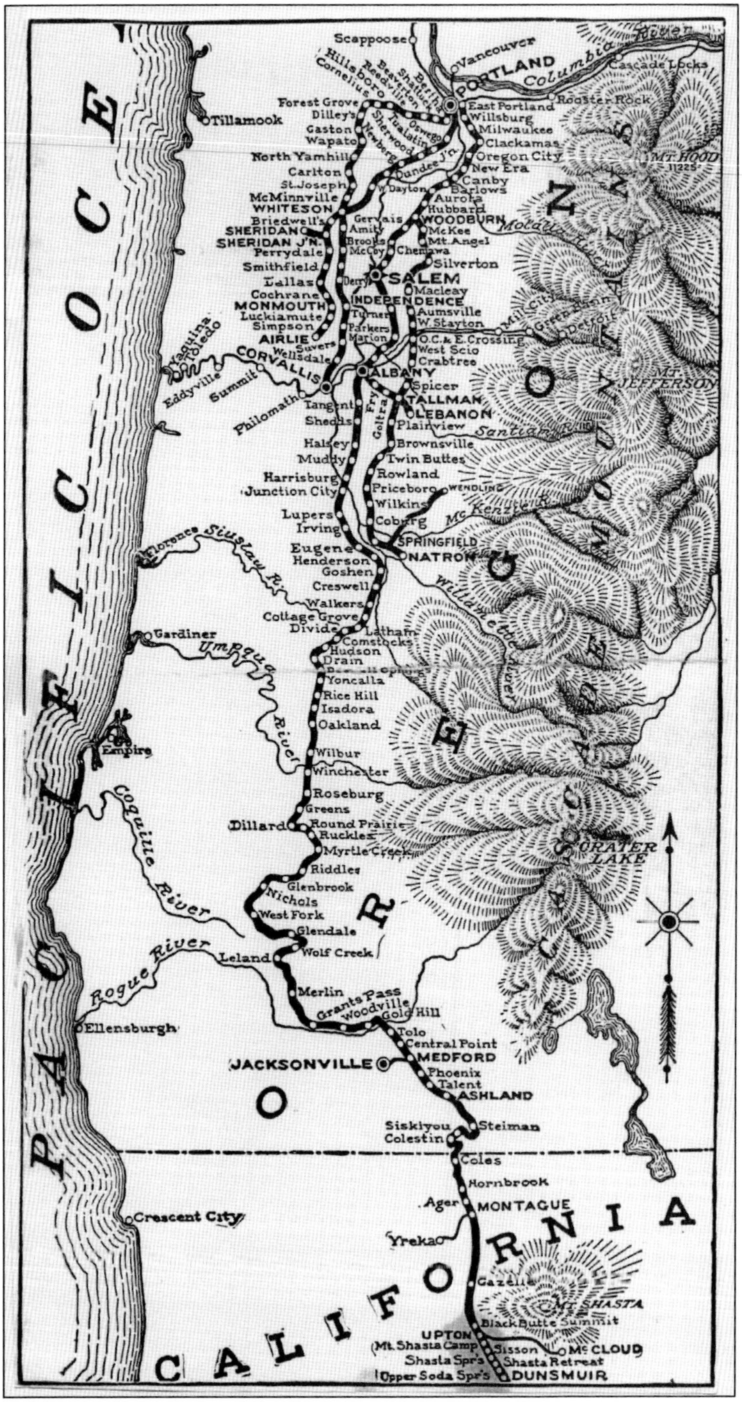

Oregon Lines. A map from Southern Pacific Railroad's Oregon Lines timetable of February 3, 1905, displays Southern Pacific's routes in Oregon at that time. In 1905, Hillsboro was not yet a junction point, as the Pacific Railway & Navigation line to Tillamook—which Southern Pacific absorbed into its network in 1915—would not be completed for another six years. (Collection of Colleen Clark Cornish.)

WEST SIDE TRAVEL. The stations of Southern Pacific Railroad's West Side Division are shown on the San Francisco–based carrier's timetable dated February 3, 1905. The timetable also provides the schedules of SP's daily passenger train operations on the railroad's route between Portland and Corvallis, which operated via Hillsboro and Forest Grove. Although the railroad south from Portland reached Hillsboro on December 23, 1871, the route to Corvallis would not be completed until 1879. (Collection of Colleen Clark Cornish.)

OREGON LINES

PORTLAND AND CORVALLIS

4 Ex. Sun.	2 Daily.	Miles.	STATIONS West Side Division.	1 Daily.	3 Ex. Sun.
4 50	7 30	0	Lv. ...... PORTLAND ...... Ar.	5 50	8 25
f 5 10	f 7 50	3	South Portland	f 5 28	f 8 08
5 20	8 00	6	Bertha	5 20	8 00
f 5 28	f 8 08	9	Shattuck	f 5 11	f 7 52
5 38	8 18	11	Beaverton	4 59	7 40
5 43	8 22	12	St. Mary's	4 54	7 35
5 52	8 31	16	Reedville	4 46	7 27
f 5 56	f 8 35	17	Witch Hazel	f 4 42	f 7 23
f 6 01	8 40	19	Newton	4 36	f 7 19
6 06	8 44	21	Hillsboro	4 31	7 14
6 15	8 54	24	Cornelius	4 21	7 05
6 21	9 00	26	Forest Grove	4 16	6 59
6 25	9 05	28	Dilley	4 10	6 53
6 36	9 16	32	Gaston	3 59	6 43
f 6 48	f 9 27	37	Cove Orchard	f 3 46	f 6 32
6 54	9 33	39	North Yamhill	3 39	6 26
7 03	9 41	43	Carlton	3 30	6 17
f 7 13	9 52	47	St. Joseph	3 18	f 6 06
7 21	10 00	50	McMinnville	3 10	5 58
7 30	10 10	54	Ar. ...... WHITESON Lv	3 00	5 50
7 40	......	0	Lv. ...... Whiteson ...... Ar.	......	5 40
8 01	......	7	Sheridan Junc	......	5 23
8 07	......	10	Ballston	......	5 15
8 20	......	14	Sheridan	......	5 05
......	10 16	57	Amity	2 54	......
......	10 27	62	McCoy	2 42	......
......	10 46	70	Derry	2 24	......
......	11 00	76	Independence	2 10	......
......	11 11	81	Parker	1 58	......
......	11 16	83	Suver	1 53	......
......	11 23	86	Wellsdale	1 46	......
......	11 45	97	Ar. ...... CORVALLIS ...... Lv.	1 20	......

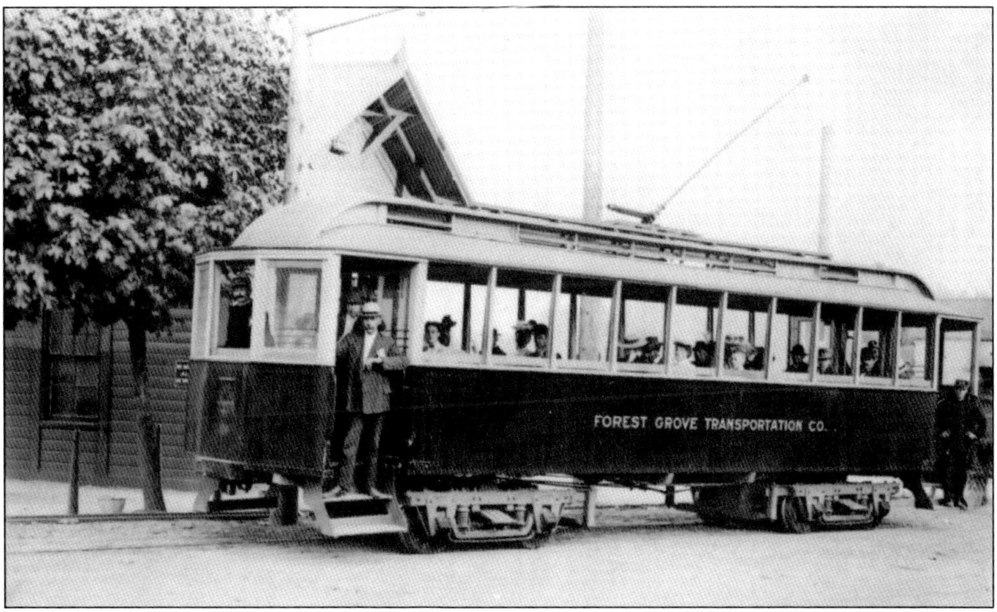

FALLS TO COMPETITION. With the Oregon & California Railroad station about a mile away from downtown Forest Grove, the Forest Grove Transportation Company was created in 1906 to move passengers to and from the O&C depot. However, with the 1908 arrival of the Oregon Electric's interurban passenger train service—which went directly from Portland to Forest Grove's downtown business district—the Forest Grove Transportation Company's streetcars saw a sharp drop in use and eventually went out of business. The trolley line ceased operating in 1911. (Collection of Friends of Historic Forest Grove.)

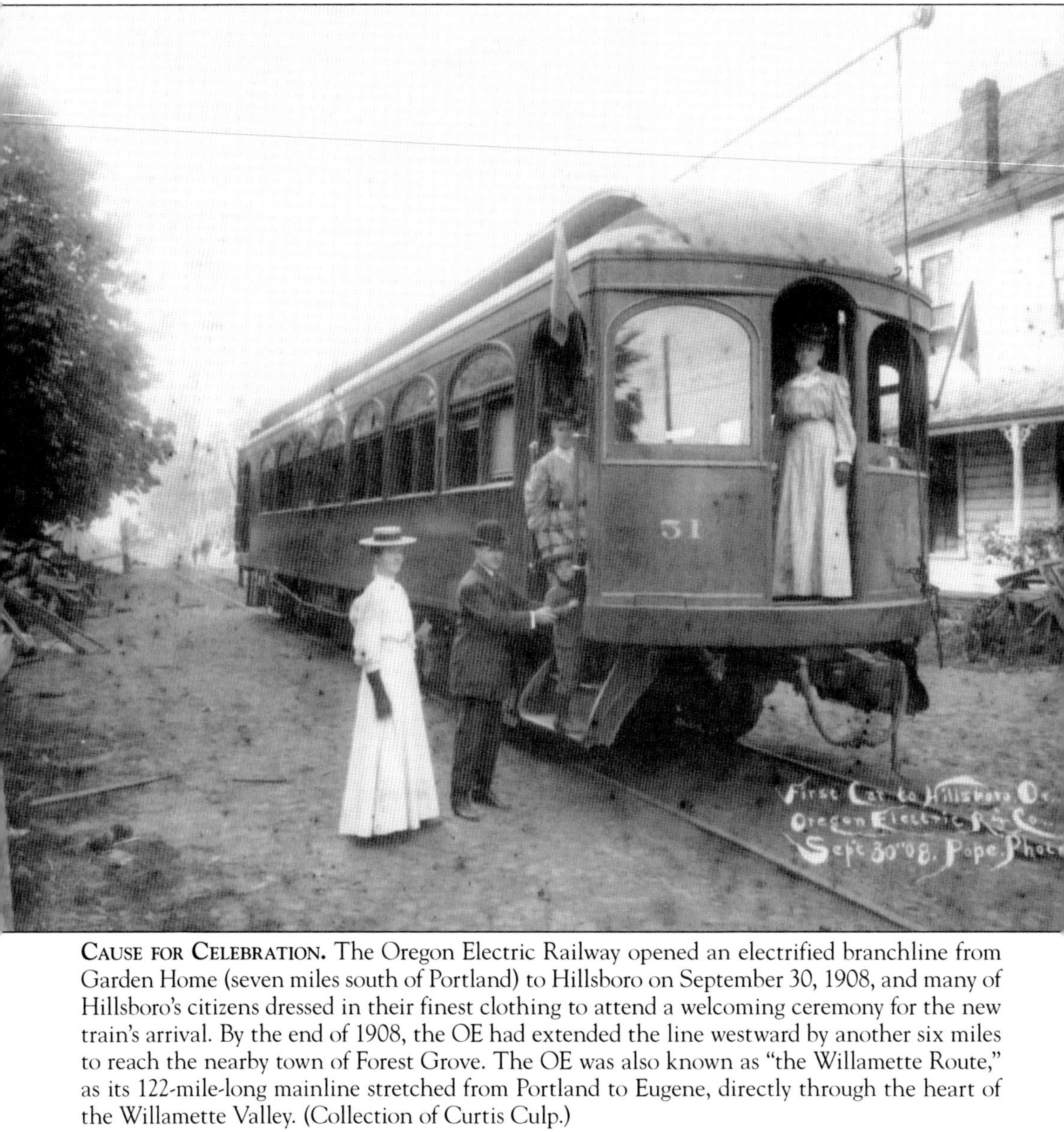

CAUSE FOR CELEBRATION. The Oregon Electric Railway opened an electrified branchline from Garden Home (seven miles south of Portland) to Hillsboro on September 30, 1908, and many of Hillsboro's citizens dressed in their finest clothing to attend a welcoming ceremony for the new train's arrival. By the end of 1908, the OE had extended the line westward by another six miles to reach the nearby town of Forest Grove. The OE was also known as "the Willamette Route," as its 122-mile-long mainline stretched from Portland to Eugene, directly through the heart of the Willamette Valley. (Collection of Curtis Culp.)

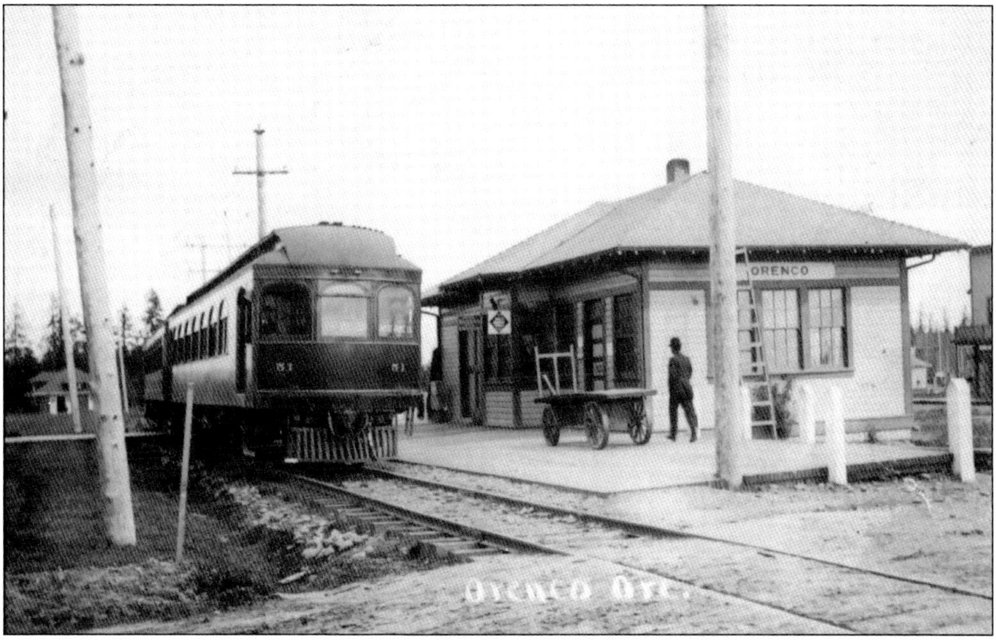

Orenco Station. In 1908, a new station on the Oregon Electric called "Orenco" was created after the Oregon Nursery Company located near Hillsboro. The company owned about 1,300 acres and shipped all types of trees and other nursery stock around the nation by rail. Because of the magnitude of the nursery's operation, the Oregon Electric agreed to build a passenger depot here and took the station's name by using letters from the company's name: OREgon Nursery COmpany. The massive building behind the OE interurban train in the bottom photograph—pictured here in 1910—is an Orenco packing shed. (Both, collection of Washington County Museum.)

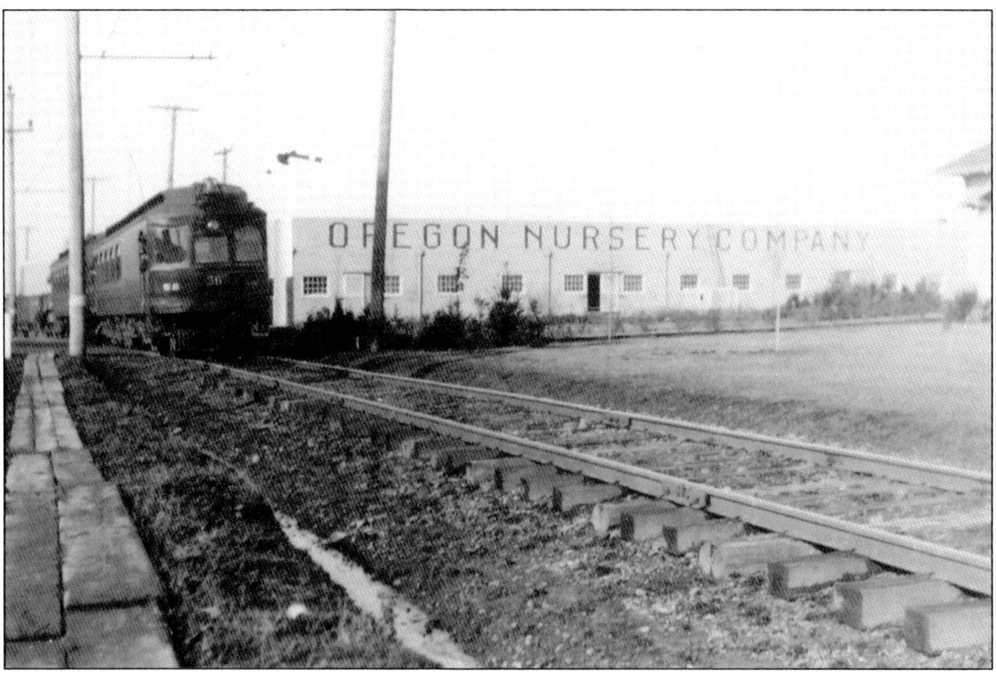

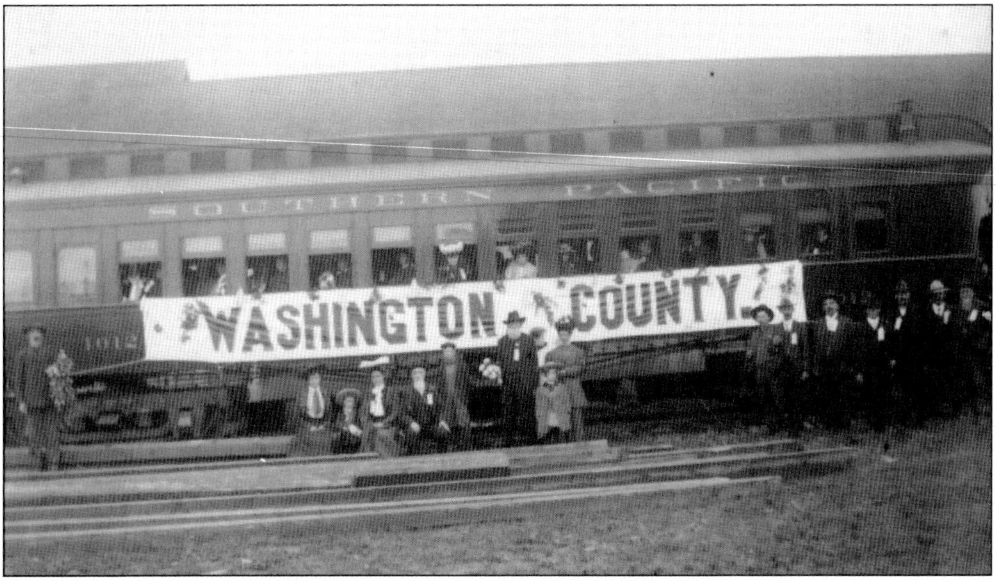

Opening Ceremony. When the Oregon Electric's new interurban trains started taking some of Southern Pacific Railroad's passenger business away, SP officials decided to electrify segments of their trackage to compete in that market. SP's "Red Electrics" began service to Hillsboro on January 17, 1914—more than five years after the Oregon Electric's arrival. (Collection of Washington County Museum.)

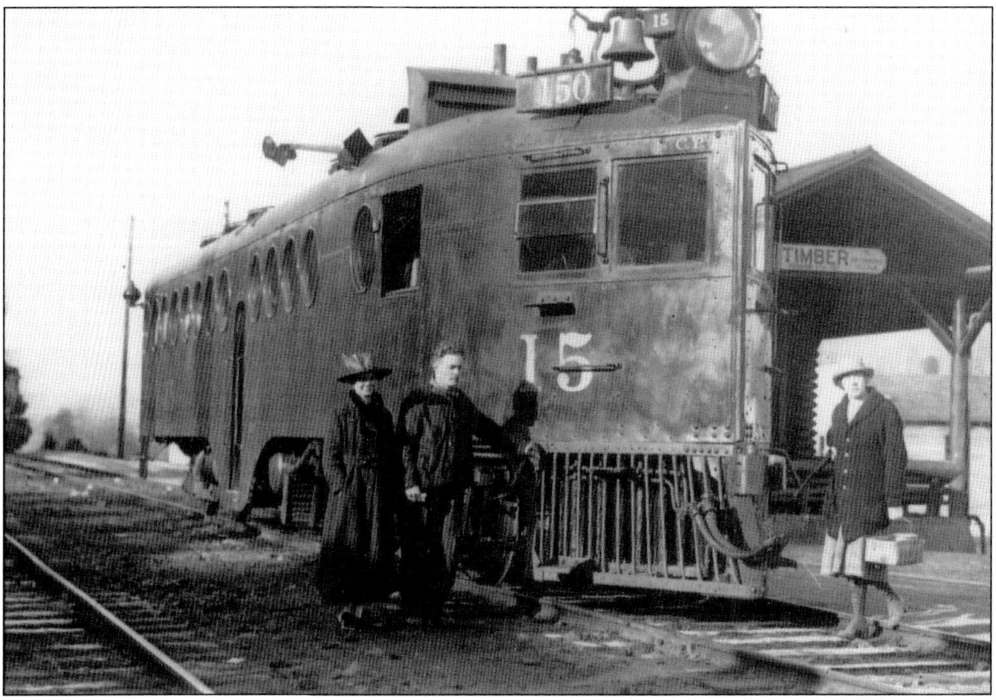

Train Time at Timber. Southern Pacific No. 15, a gasoline-powered McKeen passenger car, waits at the depot in Timber in the 1920s on SP's Tillamook Branch before heading on toward Hillsboro, 28 miles to the east. Note the woman on the right, casually carrying a rifle as she crosses the tracks in front of the car. (Collection of Washington County Museum.)

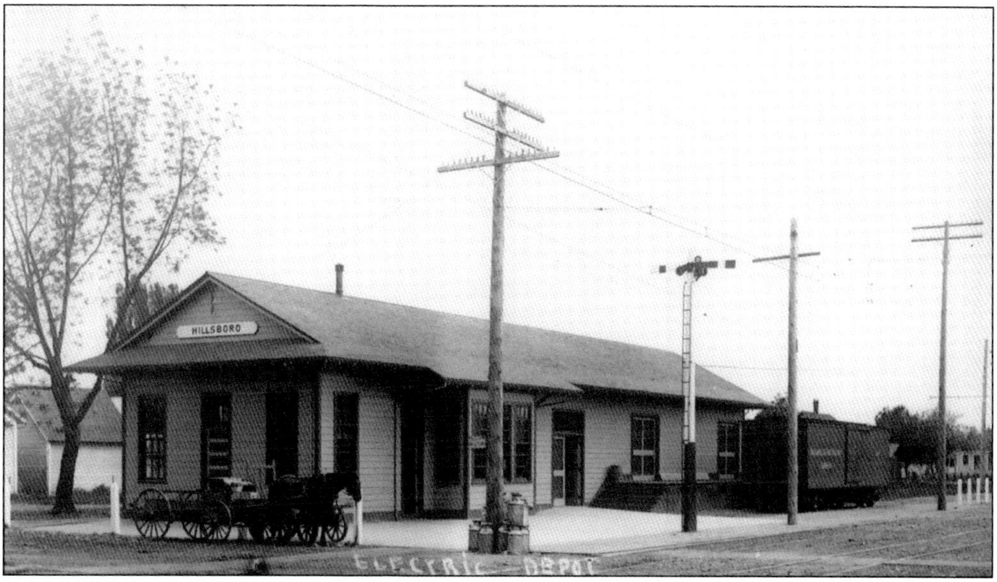

Don't Keep the Horses Waiting. In this photograph from 1910, the Oregon Electric Railway's passenger depot in Hillsboro appears quiet as the station awaits the next train. A horse-drawn wagon has arrived at the depot, perhaps to pick up incoming goods or to transport a passenger home. The depot area looks quiet, but that is no surprise: in 1910, the population of Hillsboro was only about 2,000. (Collection of the Washington County Museum.)

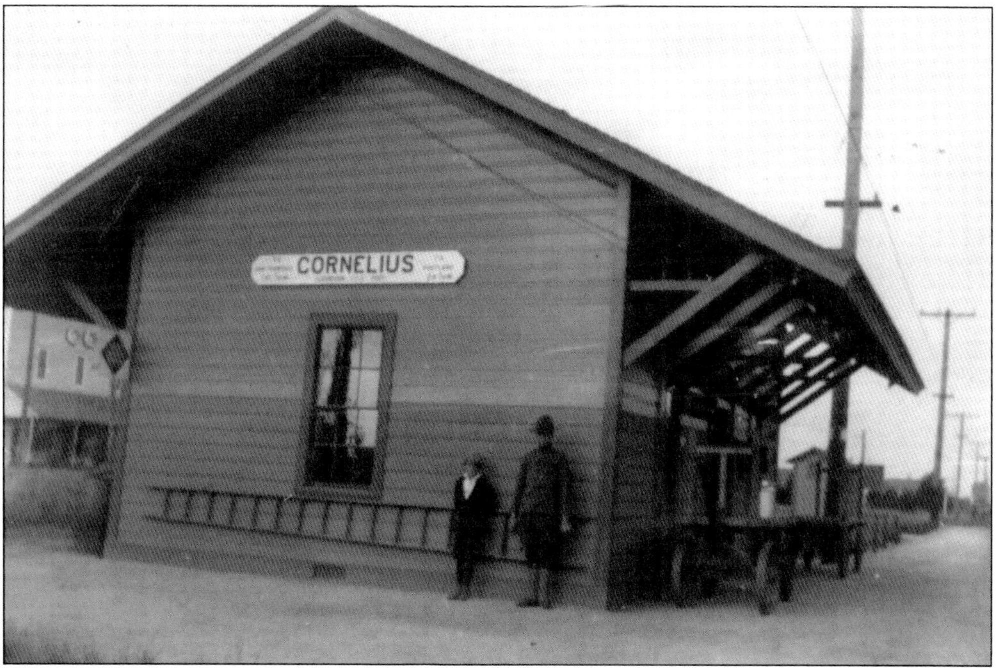

Lonely Vigil. A man in a World War I military uniform stands against the Southern Pacific station in Cornelius with a youngster—perhaps his son or a younger brother waiting with him before he returns to duty. The tracks through Cornelius, just three miles west of Hillsboro, were built by the Oregon & California Railroad in 1871. The route was taken over by Southern Pacific in 1887. (Collection of Washington County Museum.)

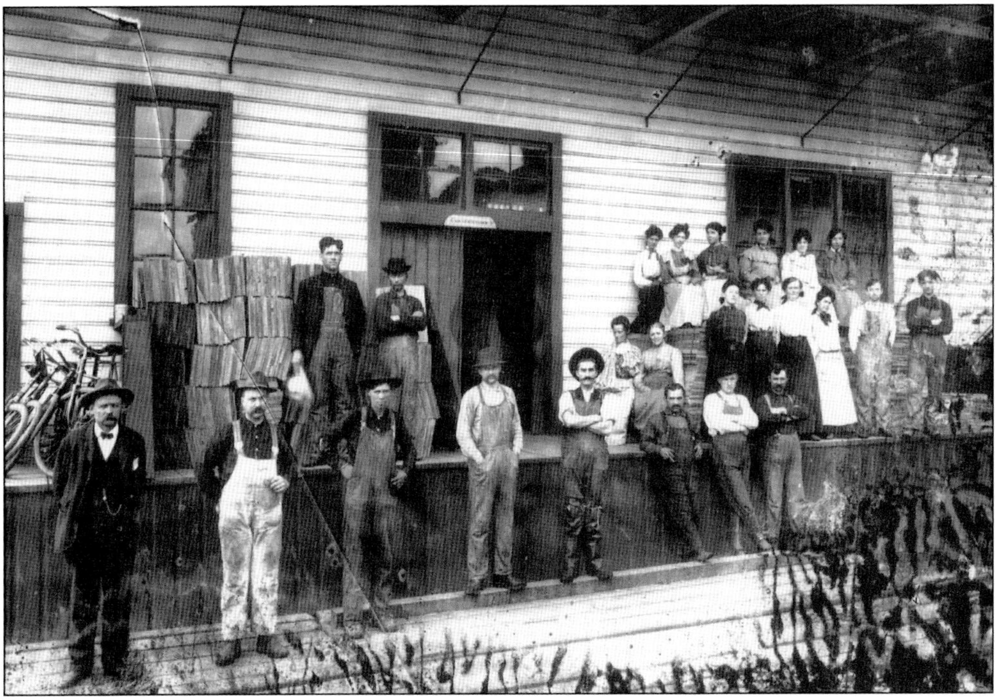

Hanging Out at the Station. This undated scene was salvaged from a cracked glass negative, and the photographer's notes do not give historians much to go on. The image was captured at the Oregon Electric depot in Hillsboro, and it appears to show a gathering of railroad employees for a group photograph, probably around 1910. (Collection of Curtis Culp.)

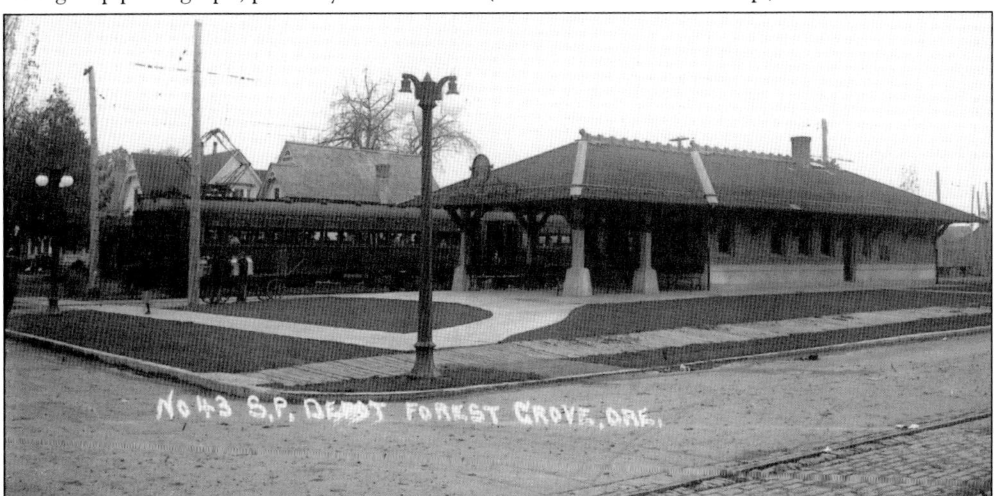

Ready for Boarding. An interurban train pauses at the Southern Pacific passenger depot at the corner of Main Street and Nineteenth Avenue in Forest Grove in the 1920s. The passenger cars are lettered for the Portland, Eugene & Eastern Railway, which Southern Pacific acquired in 1912. Note the milk containers on the baggage cart alongside the train. Milk was commonly transported by train to and from nearby communities in this era. SP's interurban passenger service to Forest Grove began in January 1914, more than five years after the Oregon Electric arrived here. (Collection of Friends of Historic Forest Grove.)

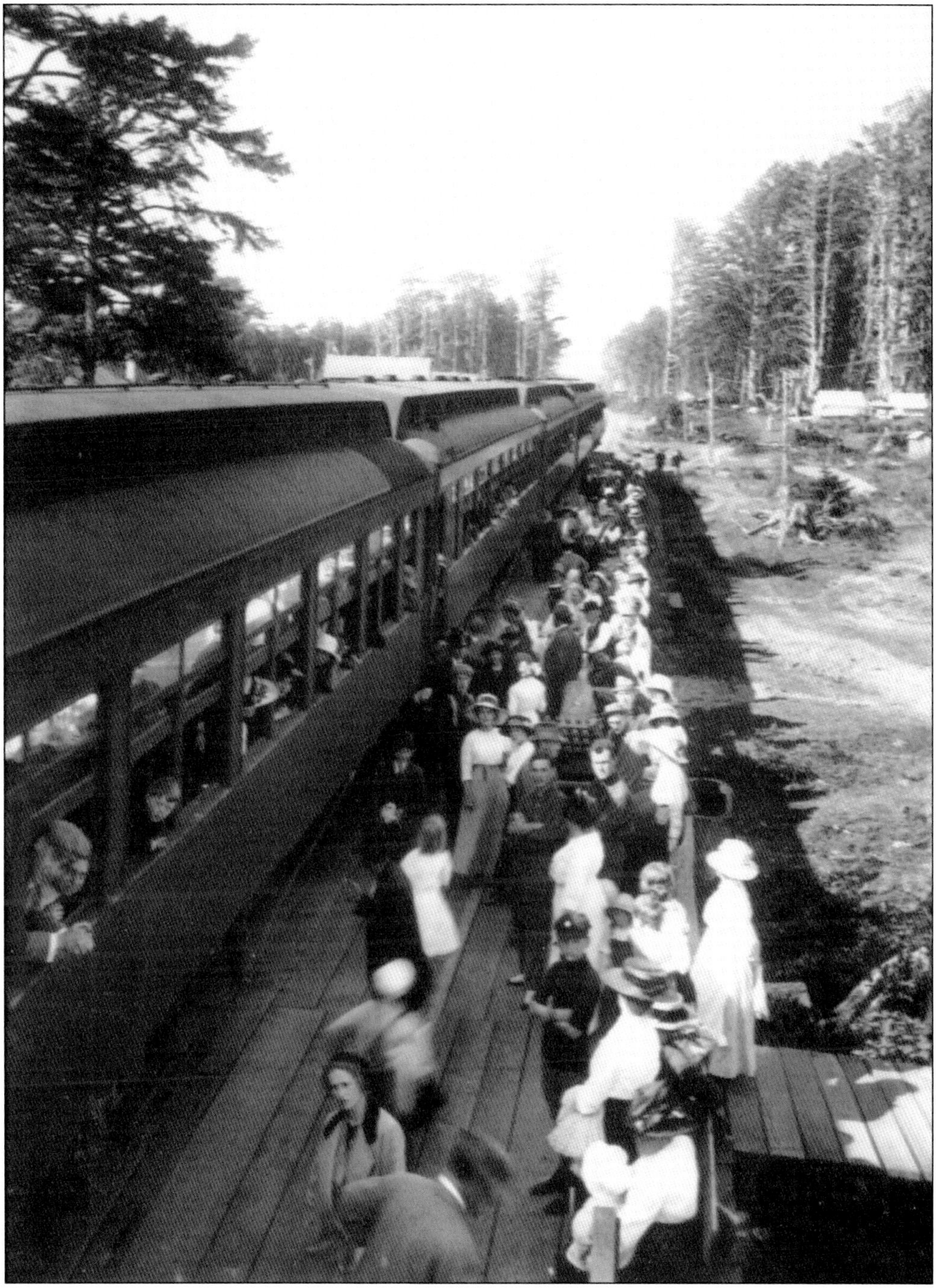

TO AND FROM HILLSBORO. Passengers are shown boarding a Pacific Railway & Navigation Company train at Rockaway Beach, a popular resort town on the Oregon coast about 15 miles north of the line's terminus in Tillamook. All trains carrying passengers to and from the coastal resorts served by the Tillamook Branch passed through Hillsboro. The PR&N began operating the route from Hillsboro to the coast in 1911, but by 1915, just four years after the PR&N opened the line, Southern Pacific took control. (Collection of Curtis Culp.)

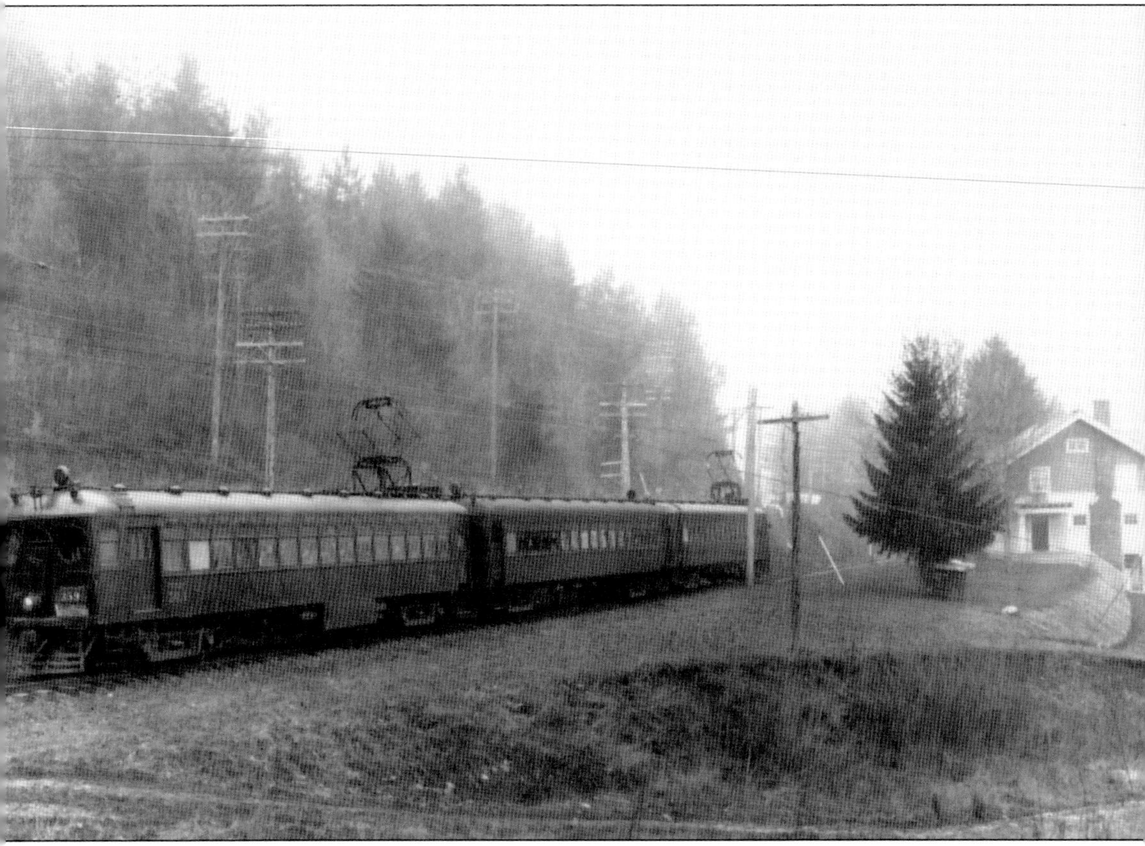

A Common Sight in 1920. A three-car Southern Pacific "Red Electric" interurban train rolls south on the way toward its southern terminus at Corvallis, situated about 75 miles south of Hillsboro, in this 1920 photograph. Three cars—two passenger coaches and a combination passenger-baggage car—were typical on SP's electric trains operating between Portland and Corvallis. SP ended its electric train service throughout the Willamette Valley in 1929. (Collection of Curtis Culp.)

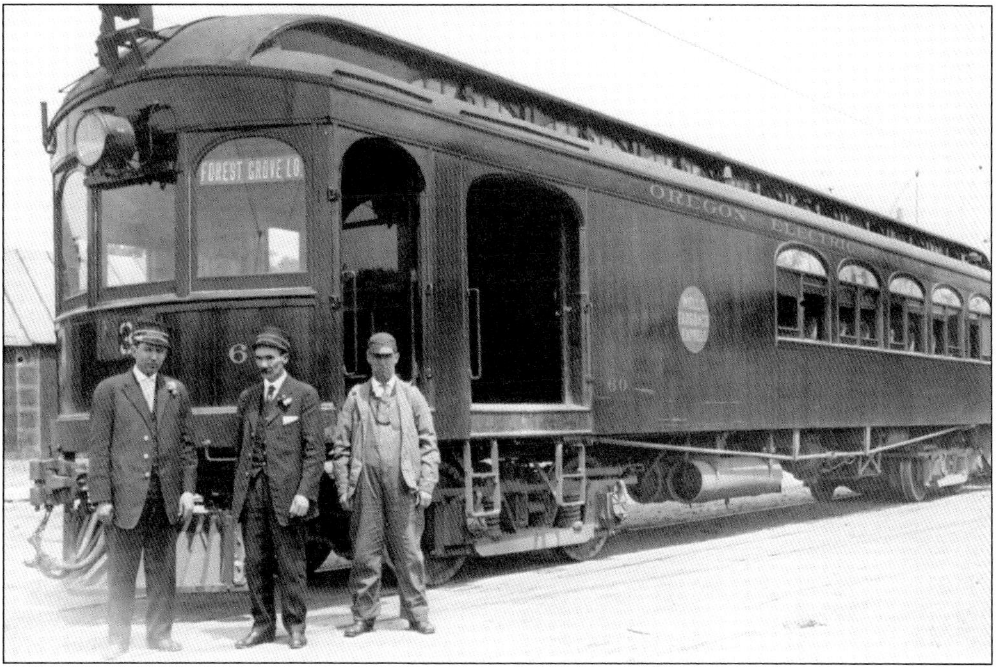

They'd Rather Get Back to Work. The crew of Oregon Electric's *Forest Grove Local*, which operated between Forest Grove and Portland, pauses for a photograph at a Forest Grove station stop in the photograph above, but the members of the crew do not look at all happy about it. In the photograph below, taken in 1912, a larger group of employees has stepped in for the shoot, and again, there appears to be no time for smiles. Note the wide sliding door near the front of the car in the top photograph, which was designed to make baggage handling a bit easier. Interurban service to Forest Grove was discontinued in 1932. (Above, collection of Curtis Culp; below, collection of Washington County Museum.)

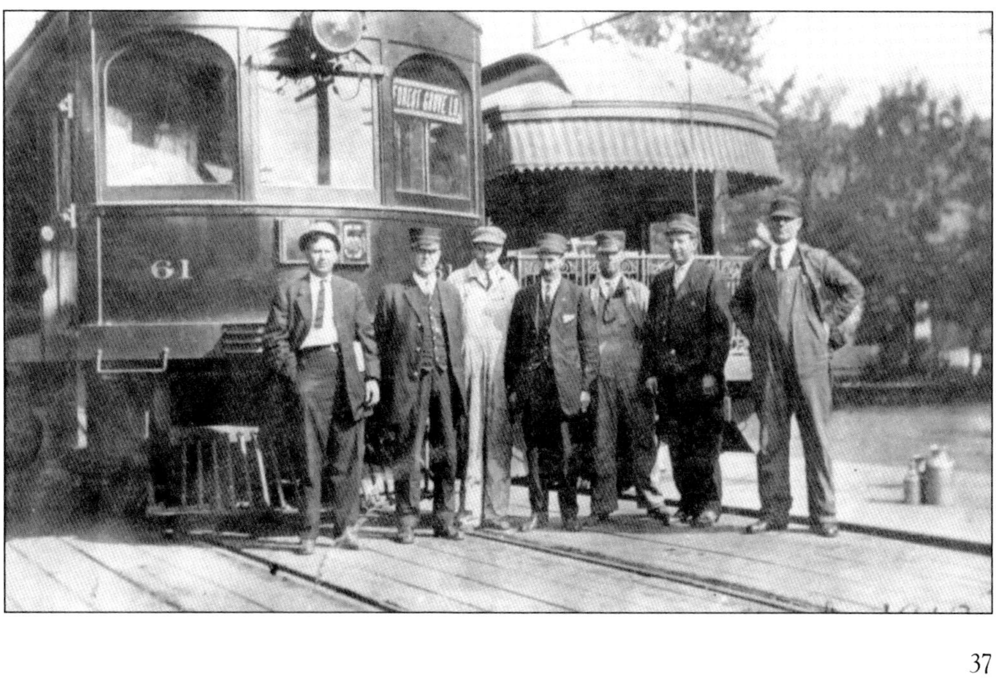

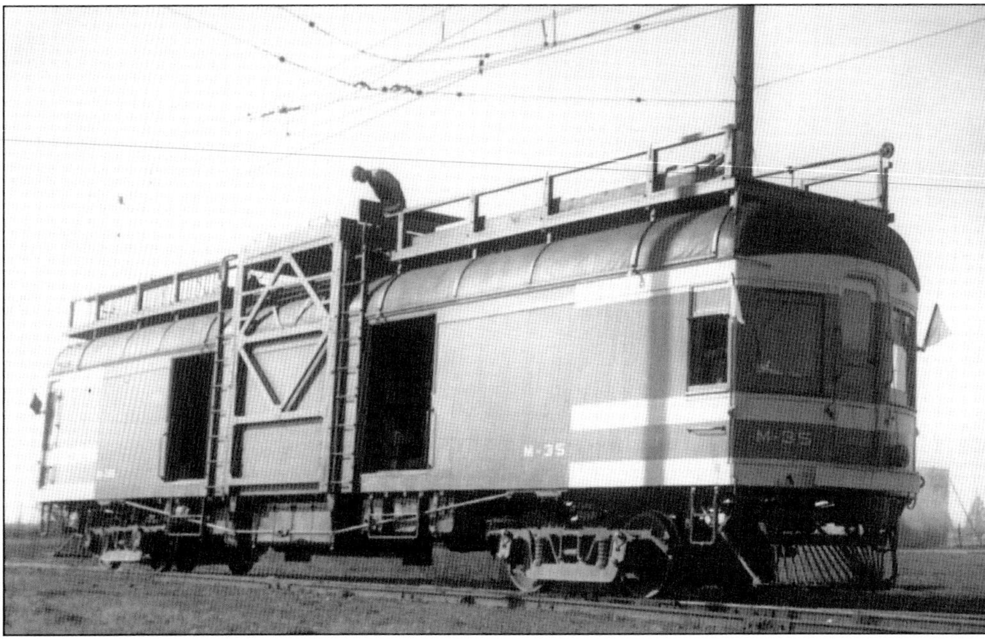

OVERHEAD MAINTENANCE. Oregon Electric Railway's M-35, known as a "line car," was designed to provide maintenance services for the railroad's electric lines. This 1928 photograph clearly shows the scaffolding atop the car, which extended upward to allow workers to reach overhead electric wires for repairs. M-35 was converted for this duty from a surplus OE baggage car. (Collection of Curtis Culp.)

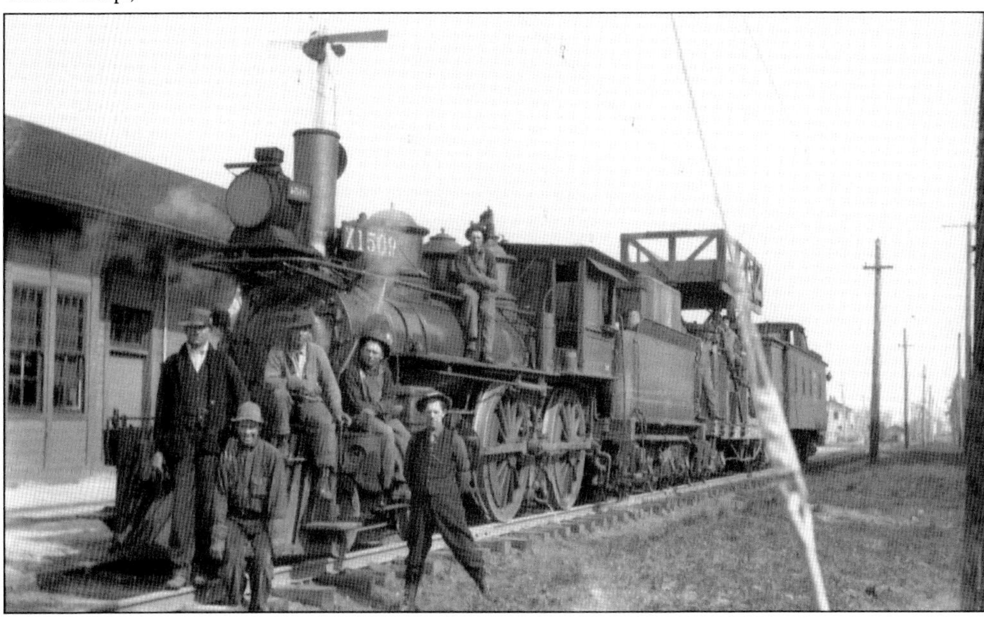

OUT FOR REPAIRS. In the 1920s, SP maintenance teams were on the job tackling repairs on the railroad's electric passenger train network. At their peak, SP's electrified lines stretched from Portland to Corvallis, with east side and west side routes and a total of 180 miles of track. With so many miles of outdoor wires, plenty of rainy weather, and wooden poles, crews like this one were kept busy. (Collection of Curtis Culp.)

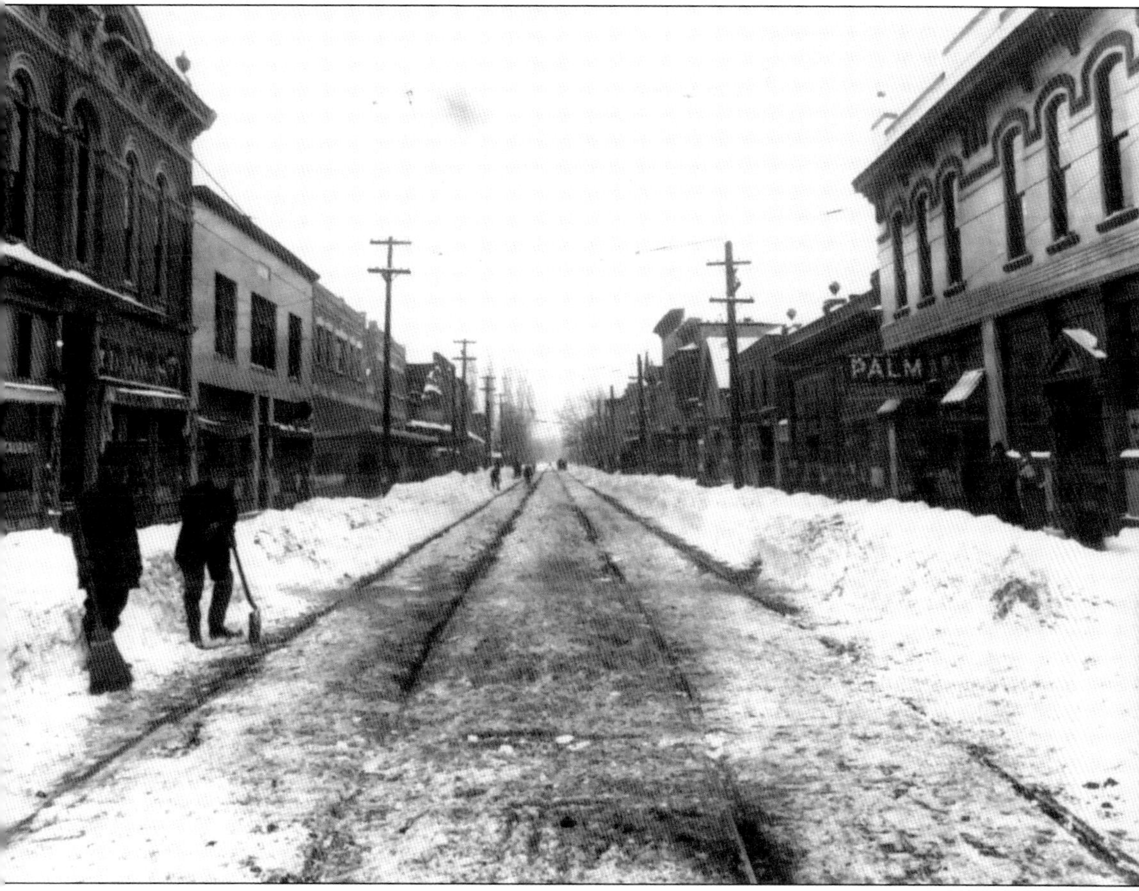

Keep the Lines Open. Workers armed with shovels and brooms are on the job in Hillsboro's downtown business district in this scene from December 1919. A heavy snowstorm created piles of snow deep enough to prevent Southern Pacific's "Red Electric" trains from getting through, so men were employed to keep the interurban rail line into Hillsboro open for business. (Collection of Washington County Museum.)

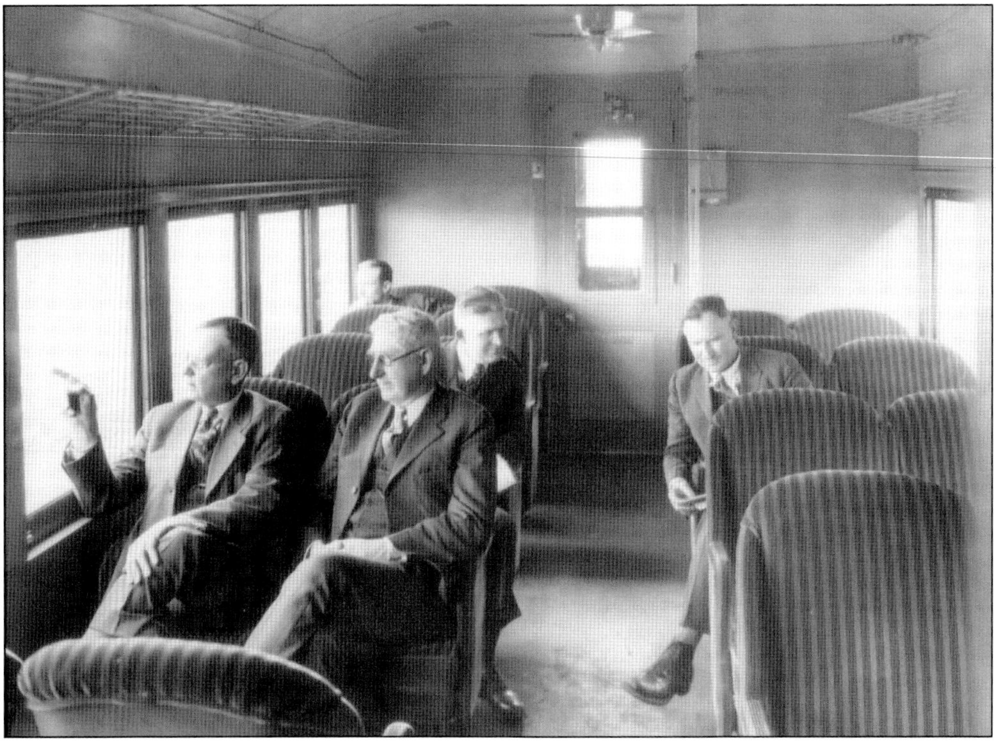

Along for the Ride. These two scenes show the interiors of trains operated by two competing railroad companies in Oregon's Willamette Valley. In the photograph above, several gentlemen appear to be enjoying the passing scenery as they roll along in one of Southern Pacific's "Red Electric" interurban coaches. The inside of a passenger coach on a Spokane, Portland & Seattle Railway passenger train in 1951 is shown below. The man seated in the foreground in this photograph is Edwin D. Culp, a Portland-based traveling freight agent for Southern Pacific at that time. Culp later wrote several books on the history of railroads in Oregon, including *Stations West*, which featured chapters on electric train operations in the Willamette Valley. (Both, collection of Curtis Culp.)

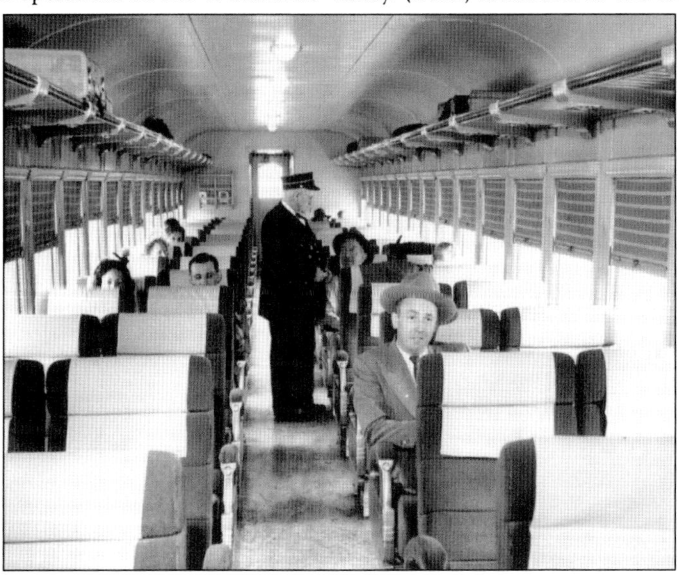

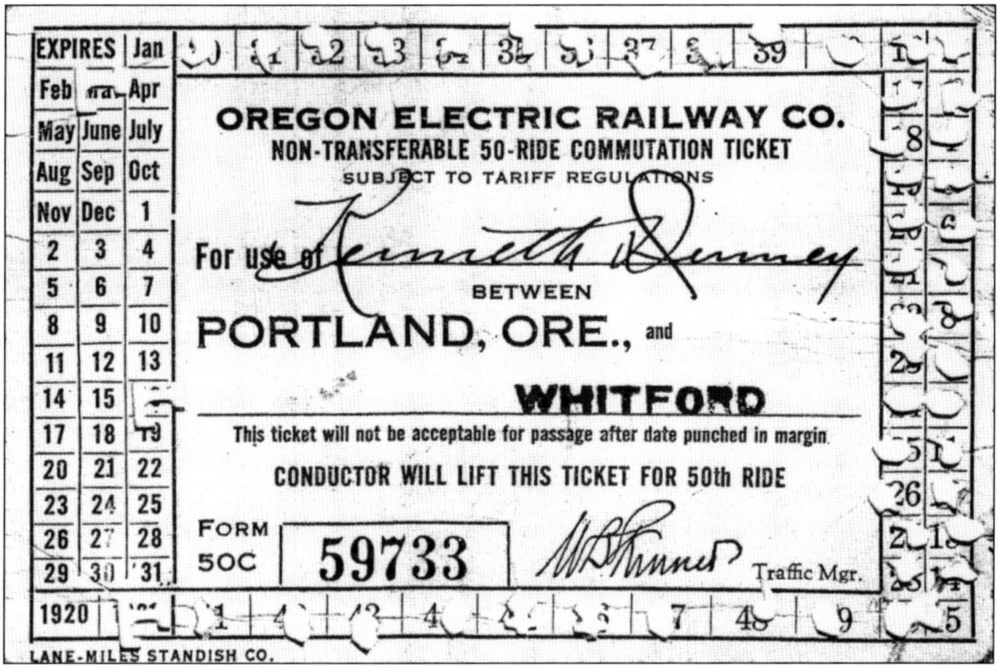

Good for 50 Rides. These well-worn tickets are an example of the passes issued by Oregon Electric Railway in the early 1920s that allowed the signee to move between Portland and whichever station was stamped in below. In this case, the traveler was going from Portland to Whitford. Whitford, a small community about 15 miles east of Hillsboro on the OE branchline from Garden Home to Forest Grove, essentially vanished when the Oregon Electric ceased operating on the branch in 1932. (Both, collection of Beaverton History Center.)

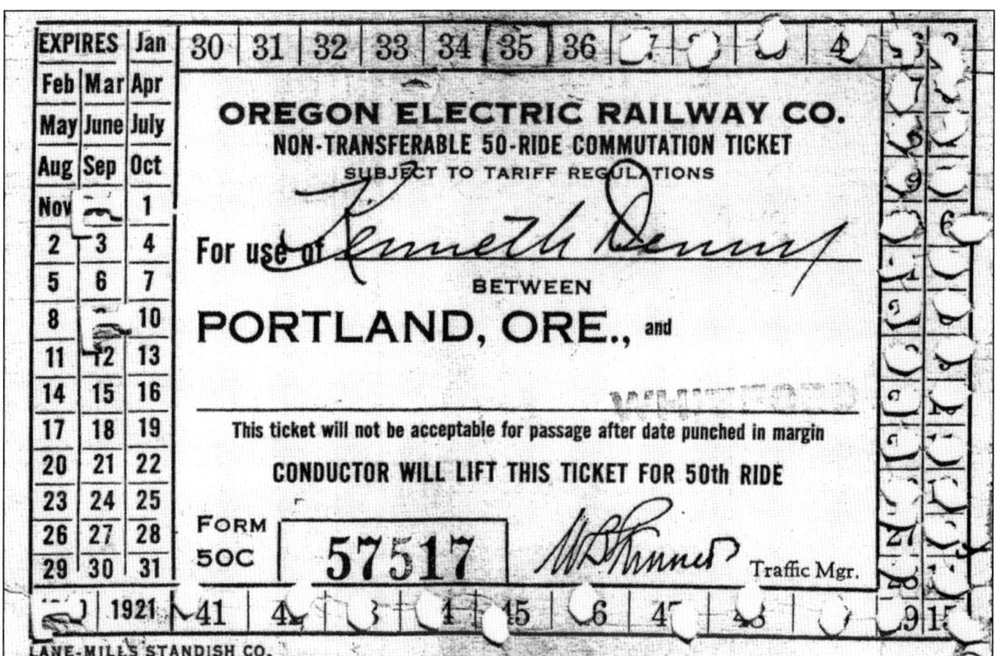

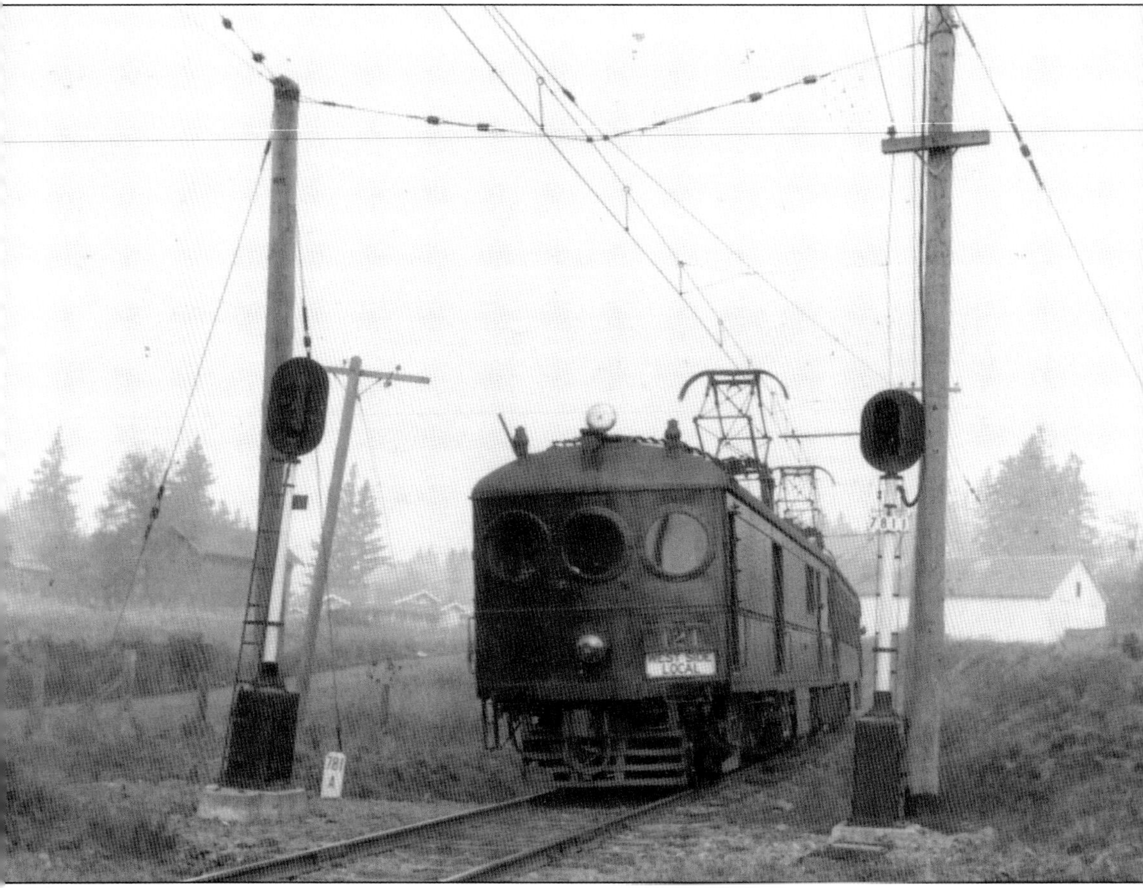

"Red Electric" on the Move. On September 30, 1928, the *West Side Local*, one of Southern Pacific's "Red Electric" passenger trains, cuts between two signal towers at Milepost (MP) 781 on the railroad's line through the town of Bertha, about 17 miles east of Hillsboro. The *West Side Local* rolled through Portland's West Hills to Beaverton, Hillsboro, and Forest Grove and then cut south to St. Joseph and eventually to Corvallis. The *East Side Local*, meanwhile, followed the Willamette River to Oswego and then turned west to Tualatin, Sherwood, Newberg, St. Joseph, and Corvallis. (Collection of D.C. Jesse Burkhardt.)

Southern Pacific Red Electrics

TO PORTLAND from Forest Grove, Hillsboro and Beaverton

CORRECTED TO JUNE 1, 1925
Light Face A. M. Dark Face P. M.
Subject to Change Without Notice

Stations	Miles	†120	†134	*126	*124‡	*128‡	*130	†122	Sun. Only	*136		
Lv. FOREST GROVE Tkt. Office	.0	......	6.05	6.50	8.41	12.25	3.30	5.15	6.15	......	......	......
Eddy (Masonic Home)	1.3	......	f.....	f.....	f.....	f.....	f.....	f.....	f.....	......	......	......
Catching	1.8	......	f 6.08	f 6.53	f 8.45	f12.29	f 3.33	f 5.18	f 6.18	......	......	......
Cornelius	2.7	......	6.10	6.55	8.48	12.32	3.35	5.20	6.20	......	......	......
Killgore	3.7	......	f.....	f.....	f.....	f.....	f.....	f.....	f.....	......	......	......
Jobe	4.6	......	f 6.13	f 6.58	f 8.51	f12.35	f 3.38	f 5.23	f 6.23		......	......
Hillsboro, Ticket Office	6.8	......	6.20	7.05	9.04	12.46	3.44	5.31	6.31	10.30	......	
Newton	8.8	......	f 6.25	f 7.10	f 9.09	f12.51	f 3.51	f 5.36	f 6.36	f10.35	......	
Matson	9.8	DlyExSun	f 6.27	f 7.12	f 9.11	f12.53	f 3.53	f 5.38	f 6.38	f10.37	......	
Hays	10.2	f.....	f.....	f.....	f.....	f.....	f.....	f.....	f.....	f.....	......	
Witch Hasel	10.5	......	f 6.28	f 7.13	f 9.12	f12.54	f 3.54	f 5.39	f 6.39	f10.38	......	
Reedville	11.9	5.55	6.31	7.16	9.15	12.57	3.57	5.42	6.42	10.40	......	
Tobias	12.6	f.....	f.....	f.....	f.....	f.....	f.....	f.....	f.....	f.....	......	
Aloha	13.4	f 5.58	f 6.35	7 20	9.17	f 1.00	f 4.00	f 5.45	f 6.45	f10.42	......	
Huber	14.0	f 6.00	f 6.38	7.22	9.19	f 1.01	f 4.02	5.47	6.47	f10.43	......	
St. Mary's	15.1	f 6.02	f 6.40	f 7.24	f 9.21	f 1.03	f 4.05	f 5.49	f 6.49	f10.45	......	
Beaverton	16.4	6.06	6.45	7.29	9.26	1.06	4.10	5.54	6.54	10.48	......	
Arrow	17.3	f.....	f.....	f.....	f.....	f.....	f.....	f.....	f.....	f.....	......	
Raleigh	18.5	6.10	6.49	7 35	f 9.31	1.10	4.15	5.58	6.58	10.52	......	
Olsen	19.5	f 6.12	f 6.51	f 7 37	f 9.33	f 1.12	f 4.20	f 6.00	f 7.00	f10.54	......	
Shattuck	19.8	f 6.13	f 6.53	f 7.38	f 9.34	f 1.13	f 4.21	f 6.01	f 7.01	f10.55	......	
Woodrow	20.4	f.....	f.....	f....	f.....	f.....	f.....	f.....	f...	f.....	......	
Pine	20.9	f.....	f.....	f.....	f.....	f.....	f.....	f.....	f.....	f.....	......	
Dosch	21 4	f 6.15	f 6.56	f 7 40	f 9.35	f 1.16	f 4.23	f 6.03	f 7.03	f10.57	......	
Bertha	21.9	6 20	7.01	7.45	9.41	1.19	4.28	6.07	7.07	10.59	......	
Third and Miles Streets	23.1	f 6.22	f 7.03	f 7.50	f 9.45	s.....	f 4.30	f 6.12	f 7.12	f11 01	......	
Bancroft	24.7	f 6 26	f 7.09	f 7.53	f 9.49	f 1.26	f 4.35	f 6.16	f 7.16	f11.04	......	......
Fourth and Jefferson	26.3	6 34	7.18	8.01	9.58	1.34	4.43	6.26	7.26	11.11	......	....
4TH & STARK ST. (Tkt. Office)	26 5	6.38	7.23	8.08	10.03	1.39	4.47	6.32	7.32	11.15	......	......
Ar. PORTLAND Union Station.	27.4	——	7.30	8 15	10.10	1.45	4.55	6.40	7.40	....	......	......

†Daily Except Sunday

‡Connects with Tillamook Branch train at N. Range and Main Street Hillsboro

f Flag Stop. Trains stop at Salmon, Morrison, Burnside and Flanders Streets, Portland, and flag at 3rd and 5th Sts. and 3rd Ave. Forest Grove; N. Range and Fir, N. Range and Main, 6th and Main, 6th and Fir, 10th St., Hillsboro; Ware; Hays, Hefter; Archer; Hooker St., Portland, Mile Post 779.9 between Woodrow and Dosch. All trains inbound stop 4th and College Sts. except 122 and 124 stop on flag. *Daily.

Forest Grove to Portland. Southern Pacific's 1925 timetable for its "Red Electric" trains running between Forest Grove and Portland via Hillsboro. At this time there were eight trains in daily operation and another one running Sunday only. Note that Hillsboro has the distinction of being a ticket office, one of only three along the route. The other two were at the end terminals of the branchline: Portland and Forest Grove. (Collection of D.C. Jesse Burkhardt.)

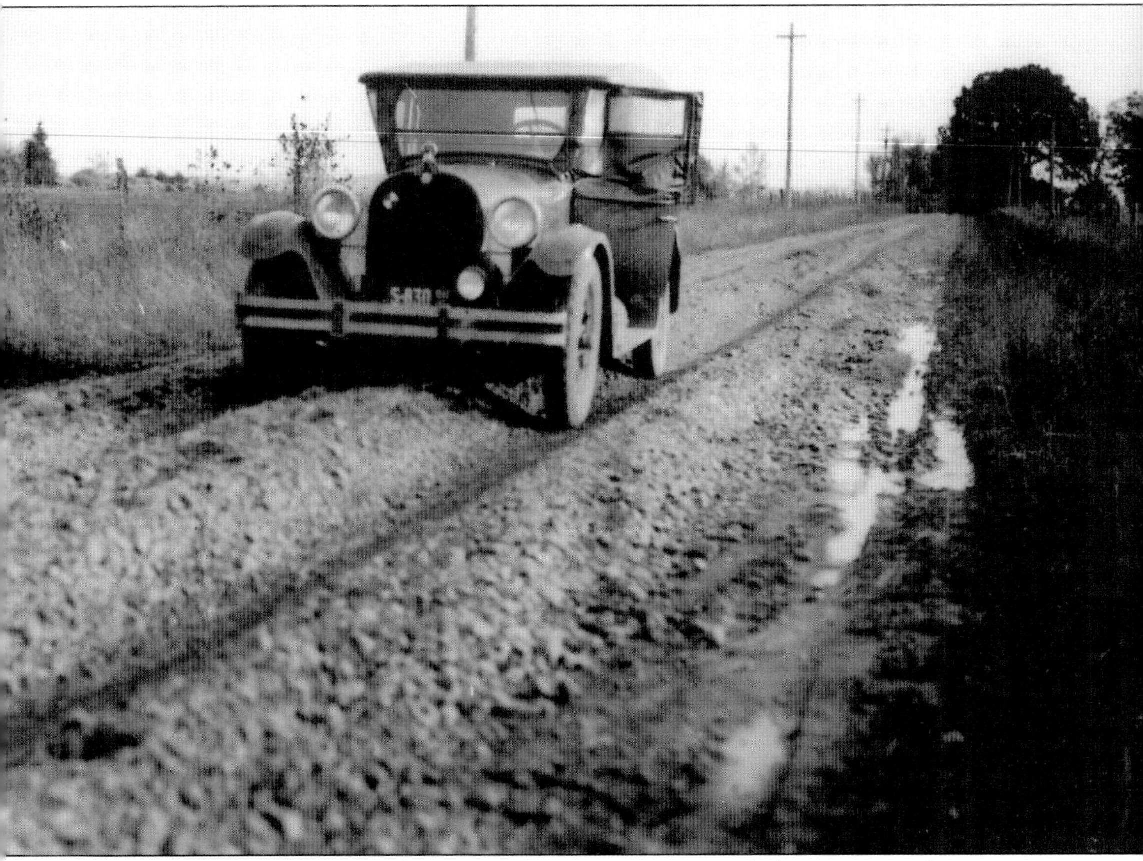

MUDDY TRAVEL. Although early automobiles were starting to grab the attention of citizens across the nation in the 1920s, the first roads might have been better suited for the horse and buggy. This scene shows a car on a gravel road near Banks, and it does not look like a pleasant ride. However, once the roads began to be improved and cars became increasingly prevalent, the demand for interurban passenger trains slowly faded away. The last interurban electric passenger trains in the Willamette Valley ceased operations on May 13, 1933. (Collection of Banks Historical Society.)

Another Money Saver!

the Red Electric

ONE DAY ROUND TRIP TICKET

A new ticket on sale daily that entitles you to make the round trip to any Red Electric station Portland to Amity inclusive at the regular

One Way Fare

Plus One Tenth

Note these examples:

To / From ☞	Huber	Aloha	Reedville
Forest Grove	.60	.55	.50
Hillsboro	.30	.30	.25
McMinnville	1.55	1.50	1.45
Portland	.55	.60	.65
Yamhill	1.10	1.10	1.05

Return portion of ticket will be honored on any train leaving prior to midnight on day of purchase

The popular 10-Ride ticket continues on sale--good for one or more traveling together and for sixty days

Southern Pacific

S. E. ANZALONE, Agt., Huber J. H. BUCK, Agt., Aloha E. J. LOWRY, Agt., Reedville

a-43 5-25-27 1M

MONEY SAVER. During the interurban passenger era, Southern Pacific was fairly aggressive with advertising campaigns to support its "Red Electric" services, especially as the number of passengers began declining. In this flier from 1927, the railroad offers a good deal on round-trip tickets from a number of stations in the northern Willamette Valley, including Forest Grove and Hillsboro—a growing town of about 3,000 residents in the late 1920s. (Collection of D.C. Jesse Burkhardt.)

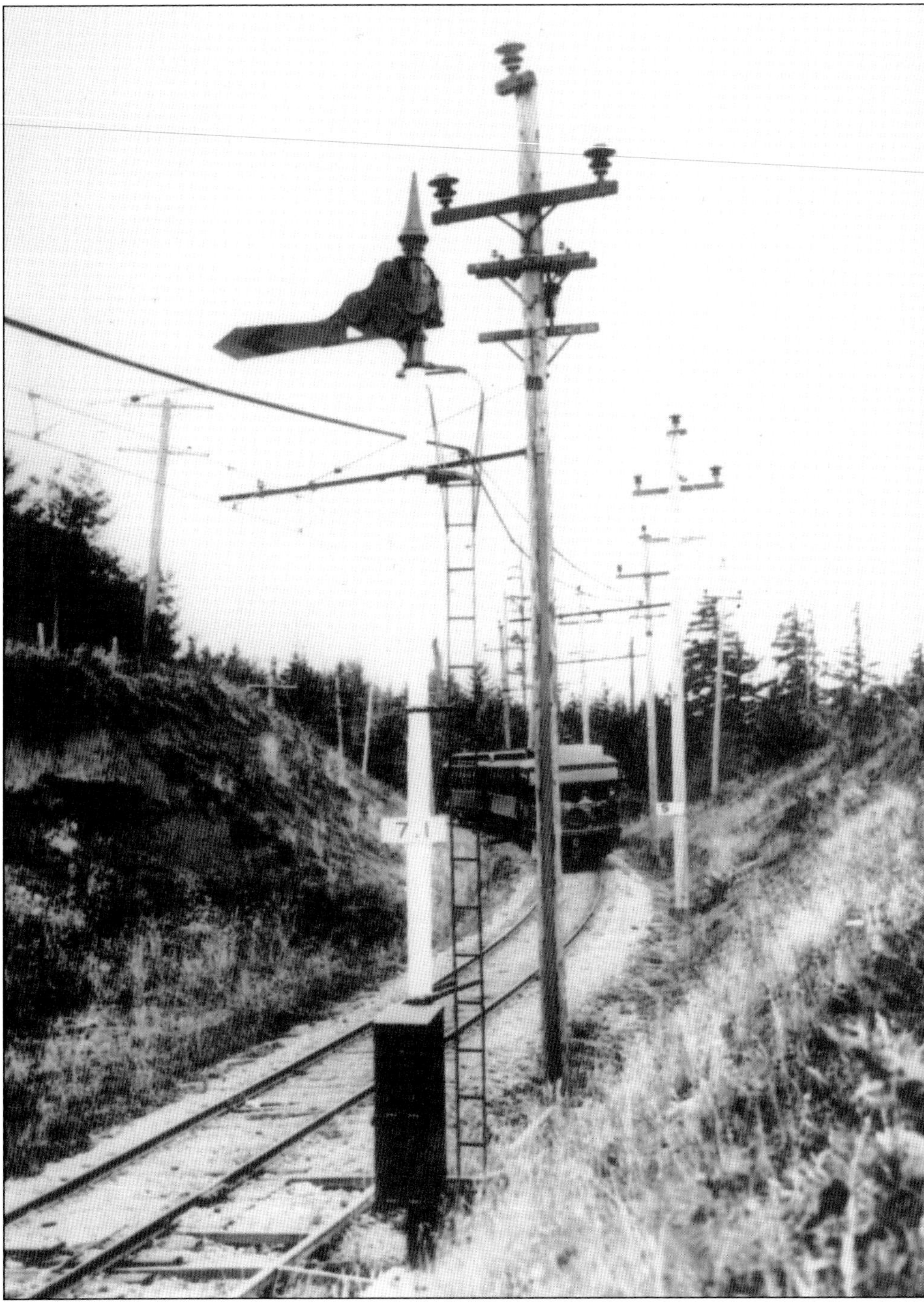

Signal Towers. An Oregon Electric interurban train rolls west past a semaphore signal tower at MP 7.1 on the OE's trackage from Garden Home through Beaverton, Hillsboro, and Forest Grove. Passenger service on the branchline to Forest Grove started in 1908 and continued until 1932. (Collection of Curtis Culp.)

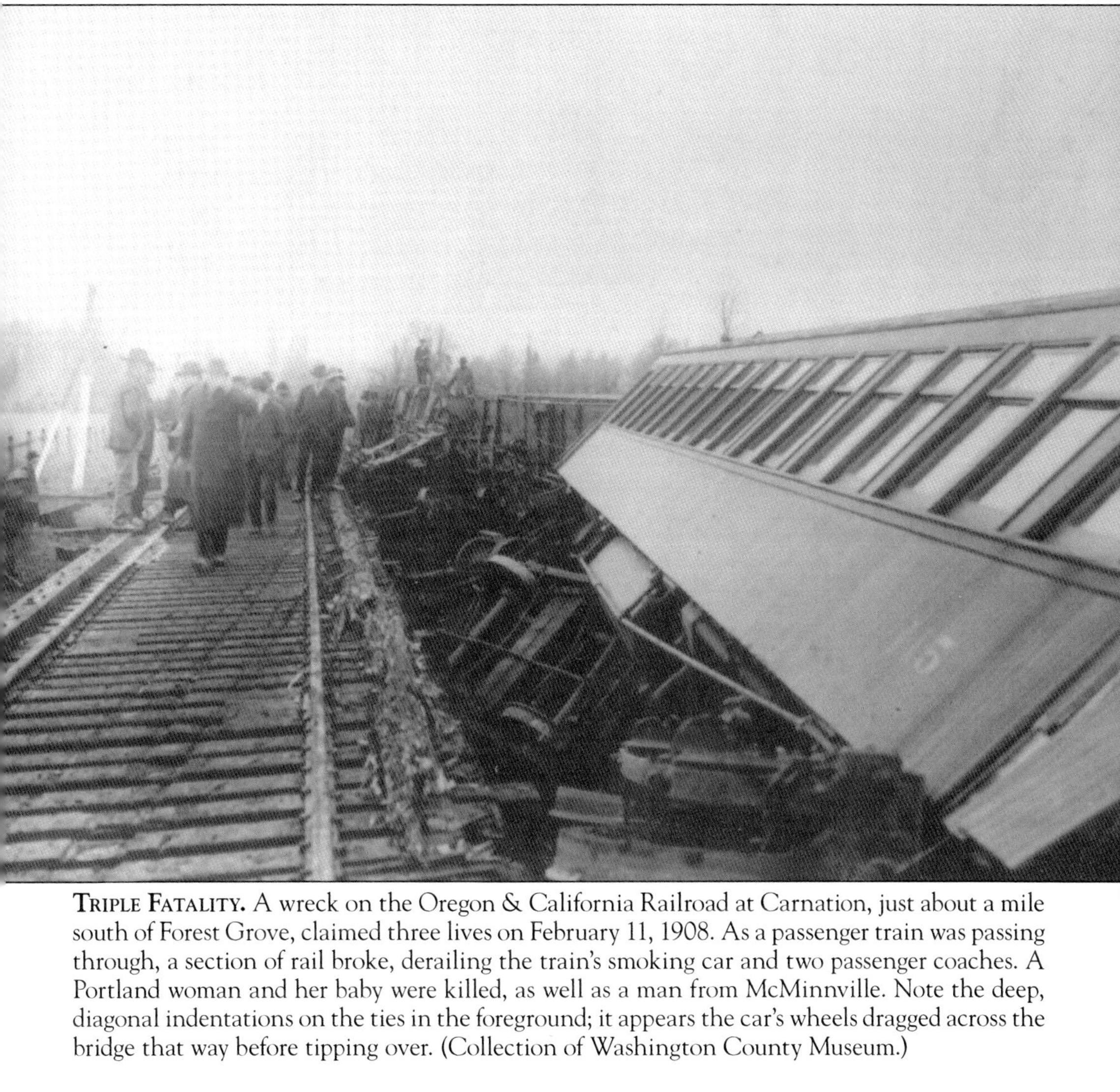

TRIPLE FATALITY. A wreck on the Oregon & California Railroad at Carnation, just about a mile south of Forest Grove, claimed three lives on February 11, 1908. As a passenger train was passing through, a section of rail broke, derailing the train's smoking car and two passenger coaches. A Portland woman and her baby were killed, as well as a man from McMinnville. Note the deep, diagonal indentations on the ties in the foreground; it appears the car's wheels dragged across the bridge that way before tipping over. (Collection of Washington County Museum.)

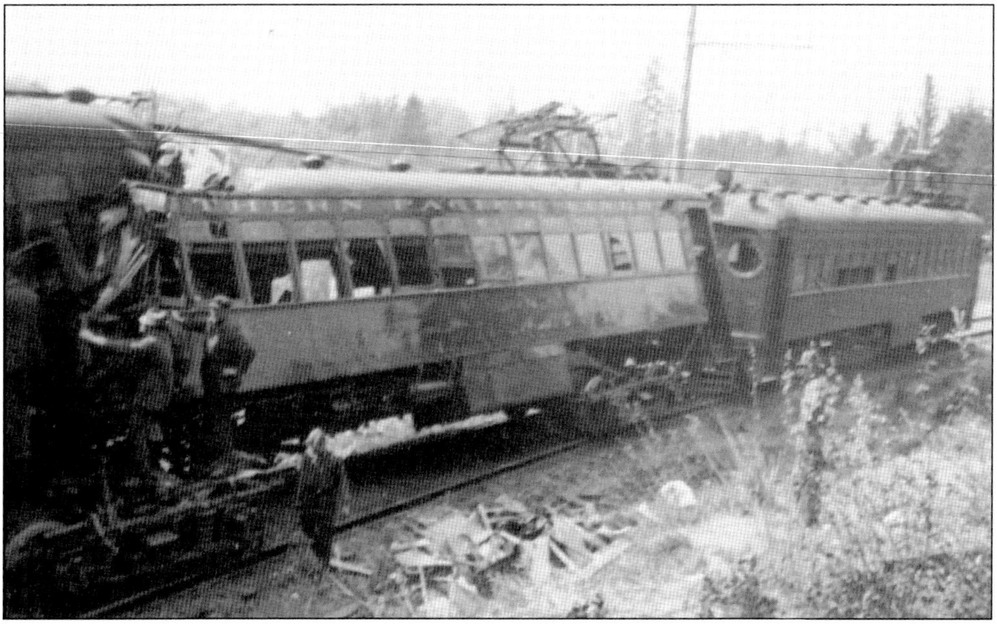

Tragedy on the "Red Electric" Line. On the morning of May 9, 1920, two of Southern Pacific's "Red Electric" passenger trains collided head-on near Bertha, a station six miles west of Portland. The wreck was deadly: eight people were killed and more than 100 injured when a Portland-bound train coming east out of Hillsboro hit a westbound train that had just left Portland headed for McMinnville. The eastbound train's engineer was among those who died in the wreck. In the photograph below, note how part of one passenger car has wrapped around a utility pole in the derailment. According to the unidentified photographer's notes, these photographs were taken roughly an hour after the tragedy. (Both, collection of Washington County Museum.)

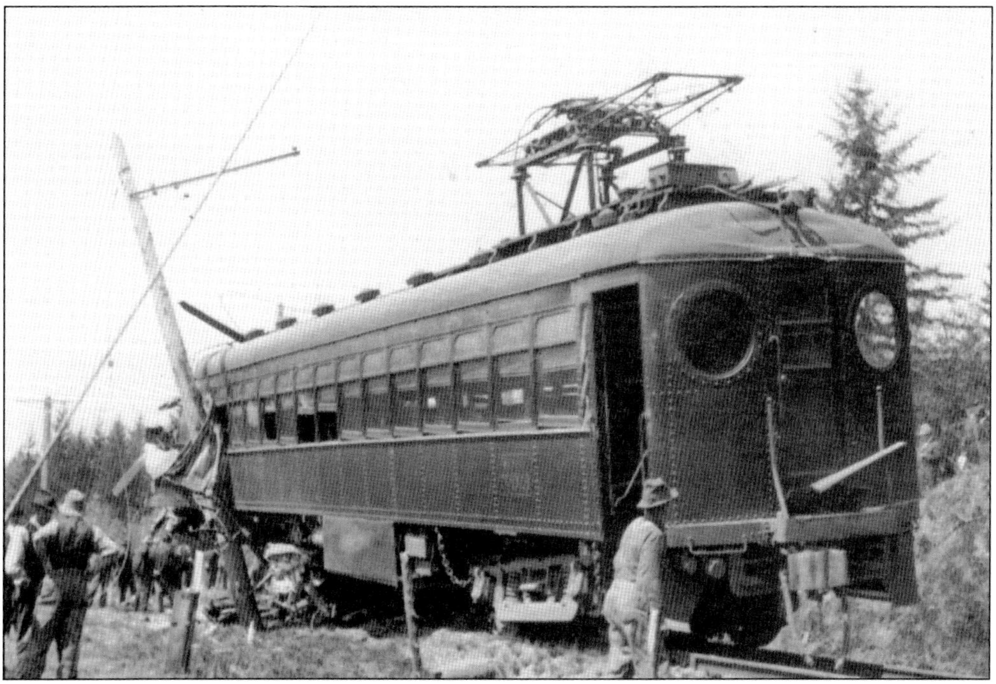

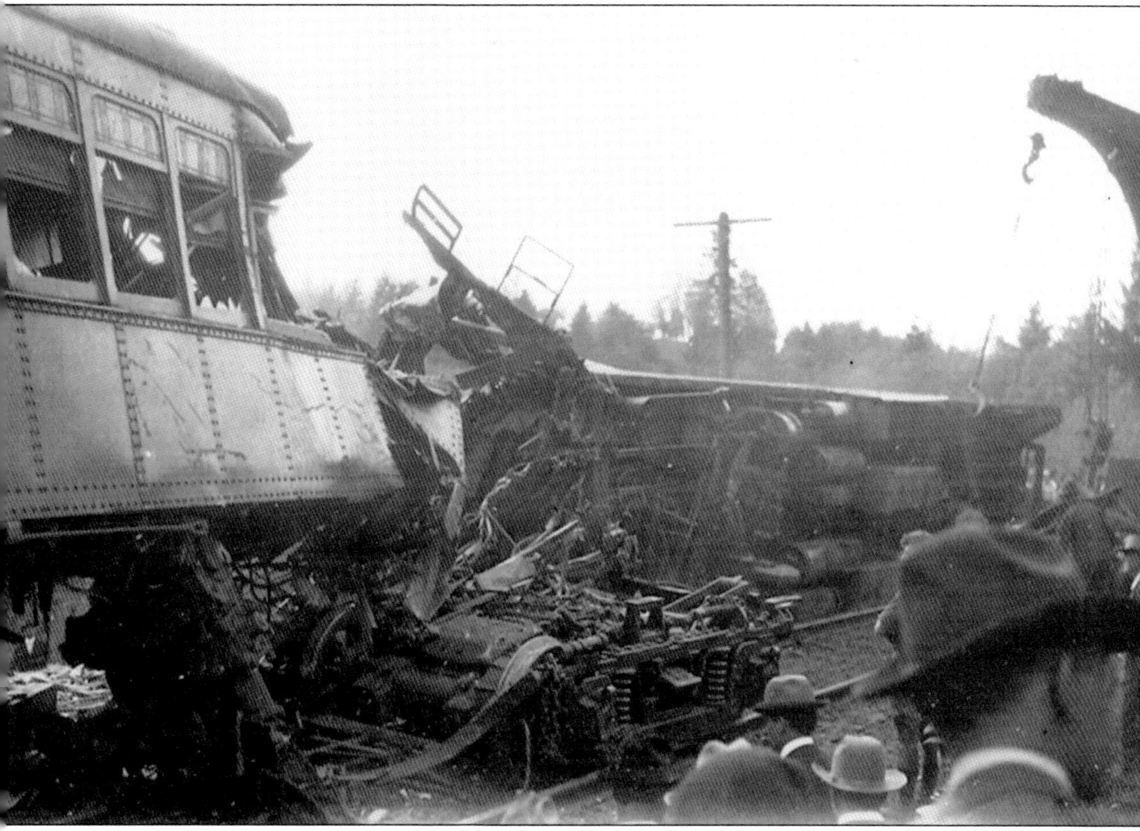

Heavy Lifting. A crane has arrived at the scene and is preparing to lift the twisted passenger cars in the aftermath of the wreck of the two SP interurban trains near Bertha in May 1920. The subsequent investigation into the cause of the crash determined that the engineer and conductor on the Portland-bound train had not heeded a train order that called for their train to take a siding at Bertha to allow the westbound train to pass. As shown in this photograph, a large group of spectators at the accident scene was allowed to get surprisingly close to the wreckage. (Collection of D.C. Jesse Burkhardt.)

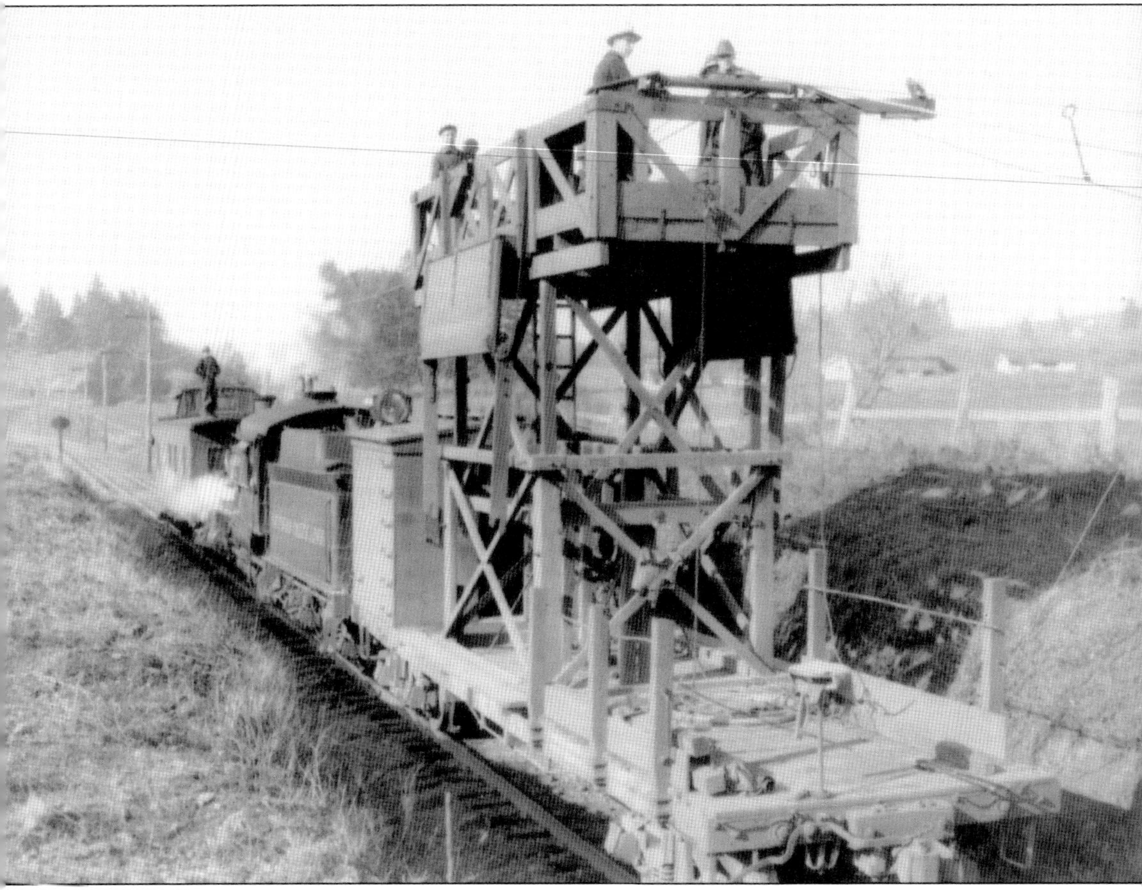

Pulling Them Down. After Southern Pacific "Red Electric" trains ceased operations in 1929, there was no longer any reason for SP to maintain the overhead electric wiring that had powered the interurban runs. In the early 1930s, SP crews went down the line removing the wires. This work team takes down the wires near Sherwood on the Newberg Branch, about 15 miles south of Hillsboro. (Collection of Curtis Culp.)

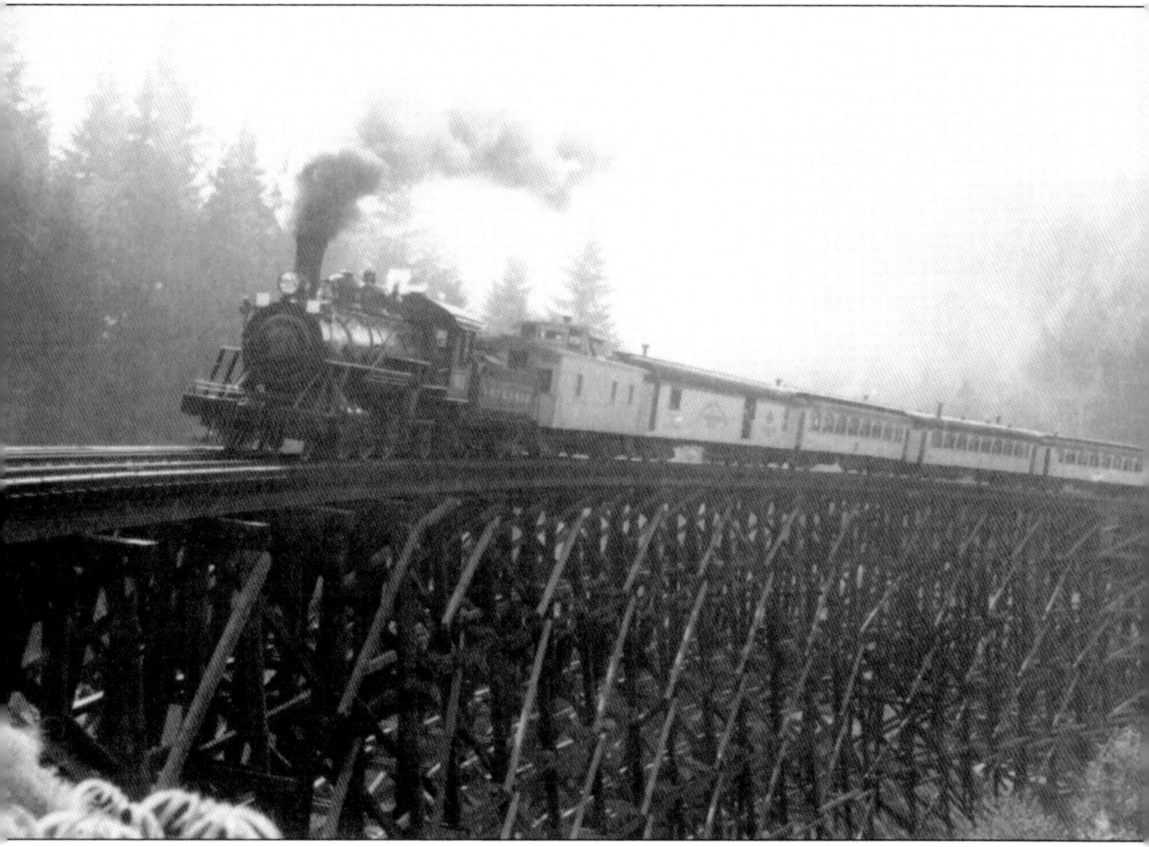

SIXTIES STEAM. Long after Spokane, Portland & Seattle Railway had ended passenger train service on its line between Banks and Vernonia, the Vernonia, South Park & Sunset Steam Railroad operated steam-powered excursion trains on the 21-mile-long route, using passenger cars from the Oregon Electric Railway and locomotive No. 105, a 1925 Baldwin 2-6-2 formerly rostered by the Oregon-American Lumber Company in Vernonia. The operation ran from 1965 to 1969. Here, the excursion train is crossing the Horseshoe Trestle near Vernonia on its way south toward Banks, a rural community nine miles west of Hillsboro. (Collection of Washington County Museum.)

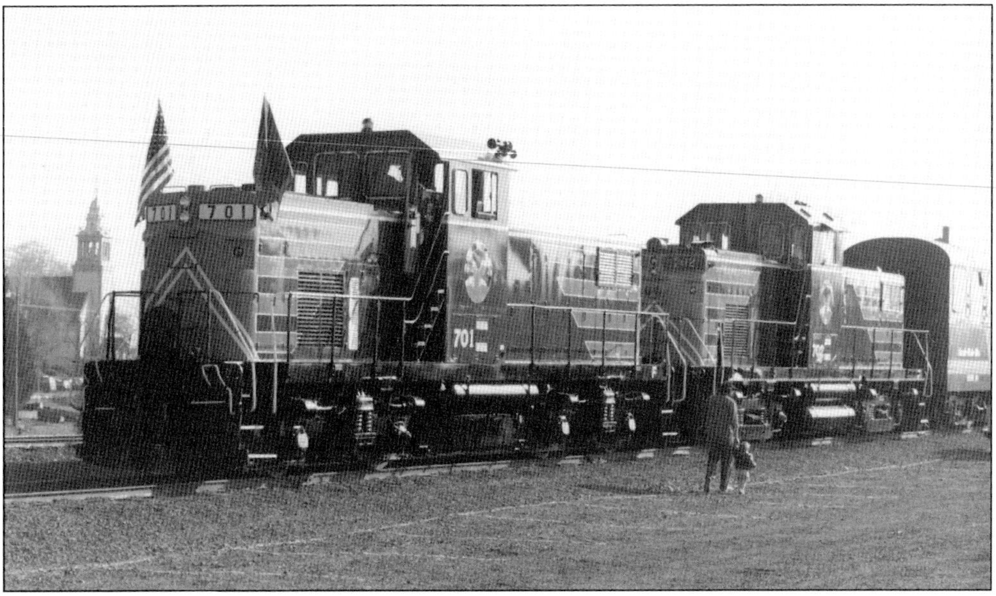

ROLLING DINER. Entrepreneur Bob Steele launched the *Spirit of Oregon* dinner train service out of Roy, a farming community seven miles west of Hillsboro, with an inaugural run on February 14, 1993—Valentine's Day. The trains operated on a portion of the ex–Southern Pacific Tillamook Branch between Roy and Cochran, a scenic, 54-mile-long round trip. In the photograph above, note the wonderful bell tower on the St. Francis Catholic Church, which was built in 1912, in the background. Below, the colorful dinner train crosses a trestle west of Buxton on March 27, 1994, as it reaches the foothills of the Coast Range while on the way to Cochran. Two former Columbia & Cowlitz Railway Alco C415s pull the four-car train. The *Spirit of Oregon* trains stopped running in August 1996. (Photographs by D.C. Jesse Burkhardt.)

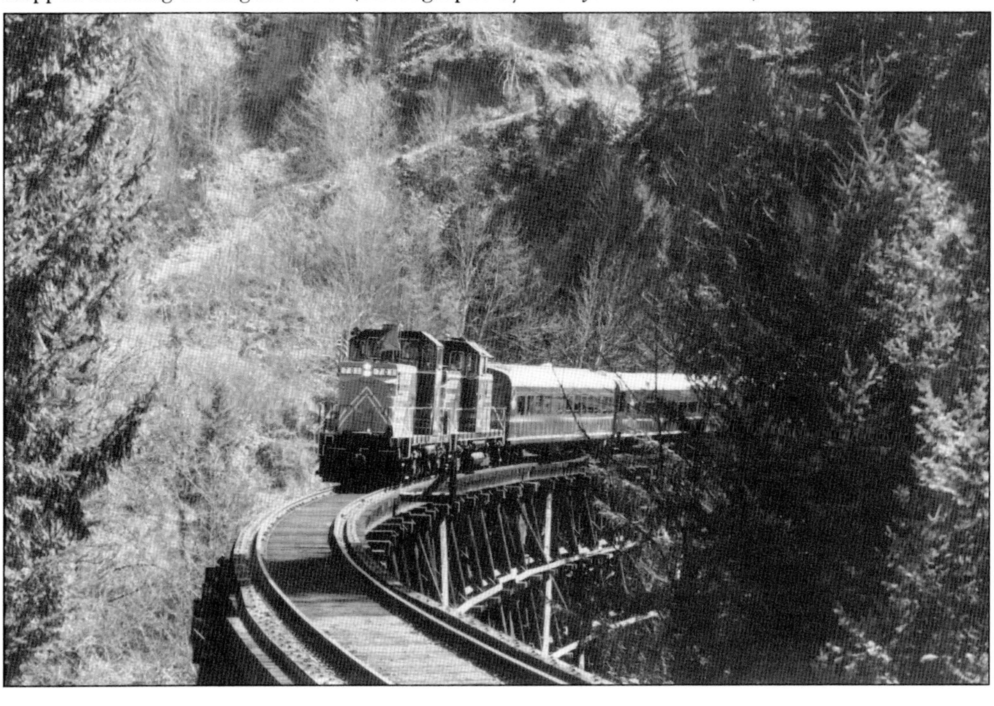

Three

Hauling Hillsboro's Goods

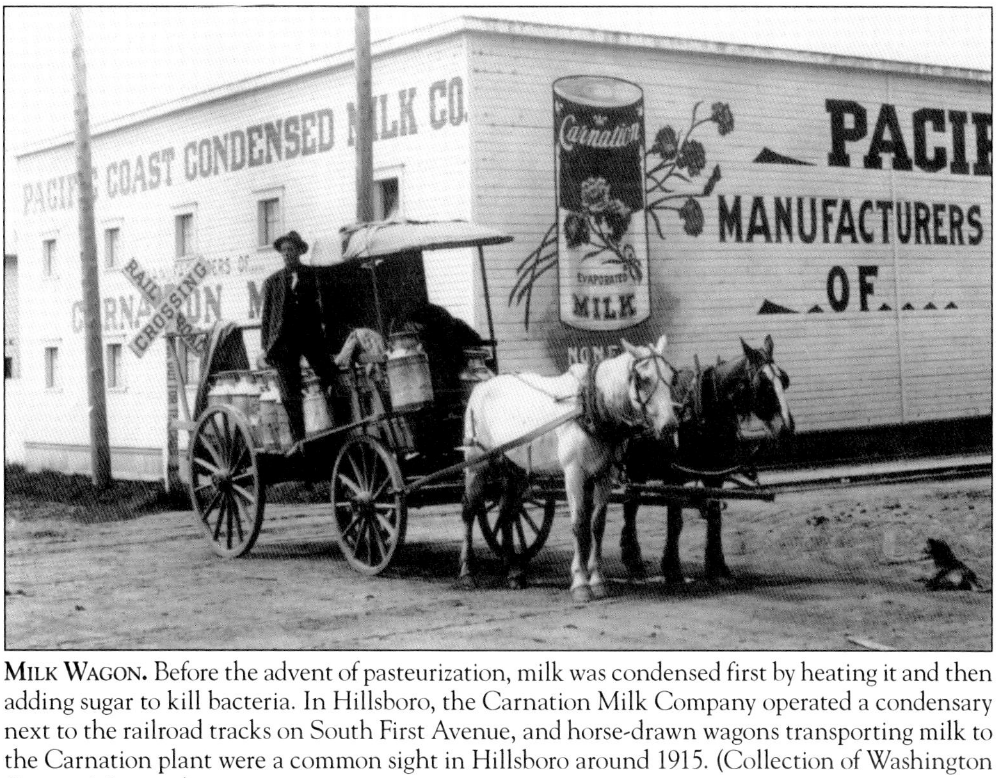

Milk Wagon. Before the advent of pasteurization, milk was condensed first by heating it and then adding sugar to kill bacteria. In Hillsboro, the Carnation Milk Company operated a condensary next to the railroad tracks on South First Avenue, and horse-drawn wagons transporting milk to the Carnation plant were a common sight in Hillsboro around 1915. (Collection of Washington County Museum.)

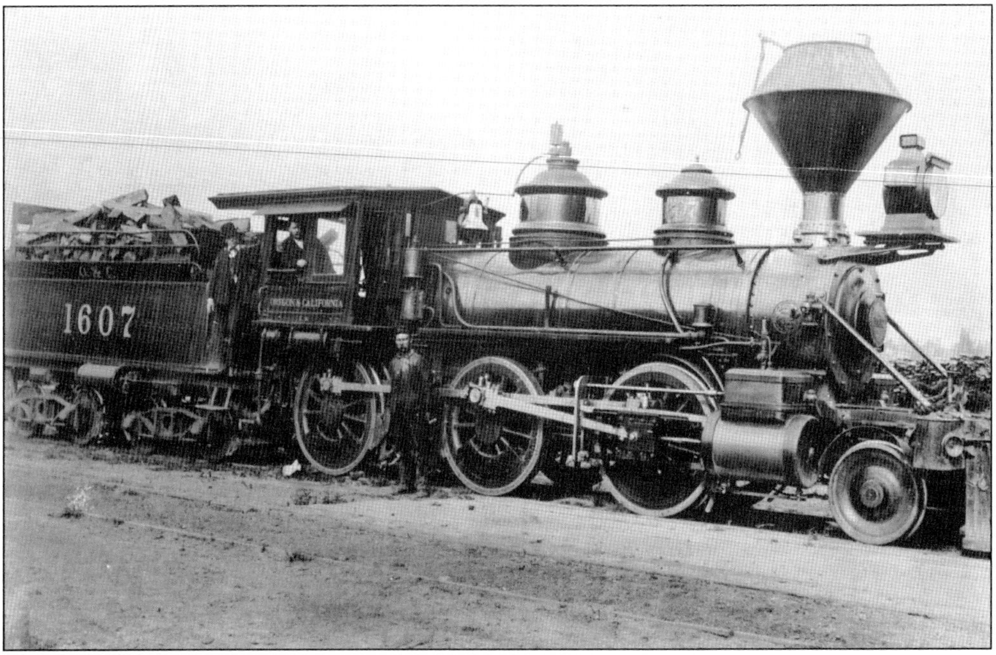

Early Power. The first railroad to reach Hillsboro, the Oregon & California, moved freight trains through town with locomotives such as O&C No. 1607, a Civil War–era 2-6-0. The O&C laid track just south of Hillsboro in 1871 as it built a route from Portland that extended to Corvallis and eventually all the way to the California border just south of Ashland, Oregon. (Collection of Curtis Culp.)

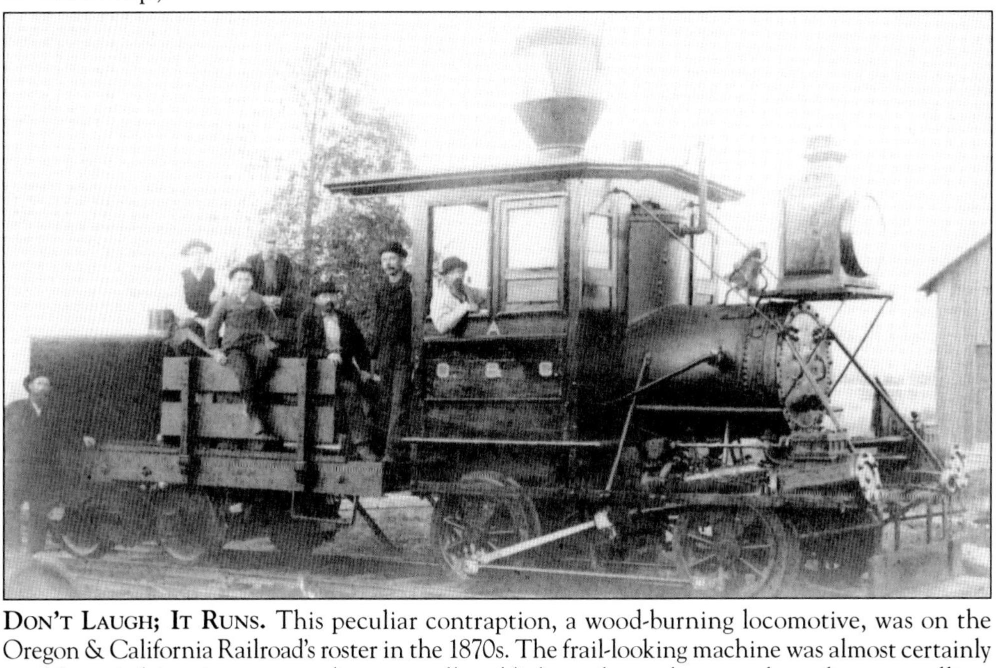

Don't Laugh; It Runs. This peculiar contraption, a wood-burning locomotive, was on the Oregon & California Railroad's roster in the 1870s. The frail-looking machine was almost certainly used for switching; it appears to be too small and light to do any heavy or long-distance pulling. But compared to moving goods with horses and a wagon, there is little doubt this device was considered a huge upgrade in its time. (Collection of Curtis Culp.)

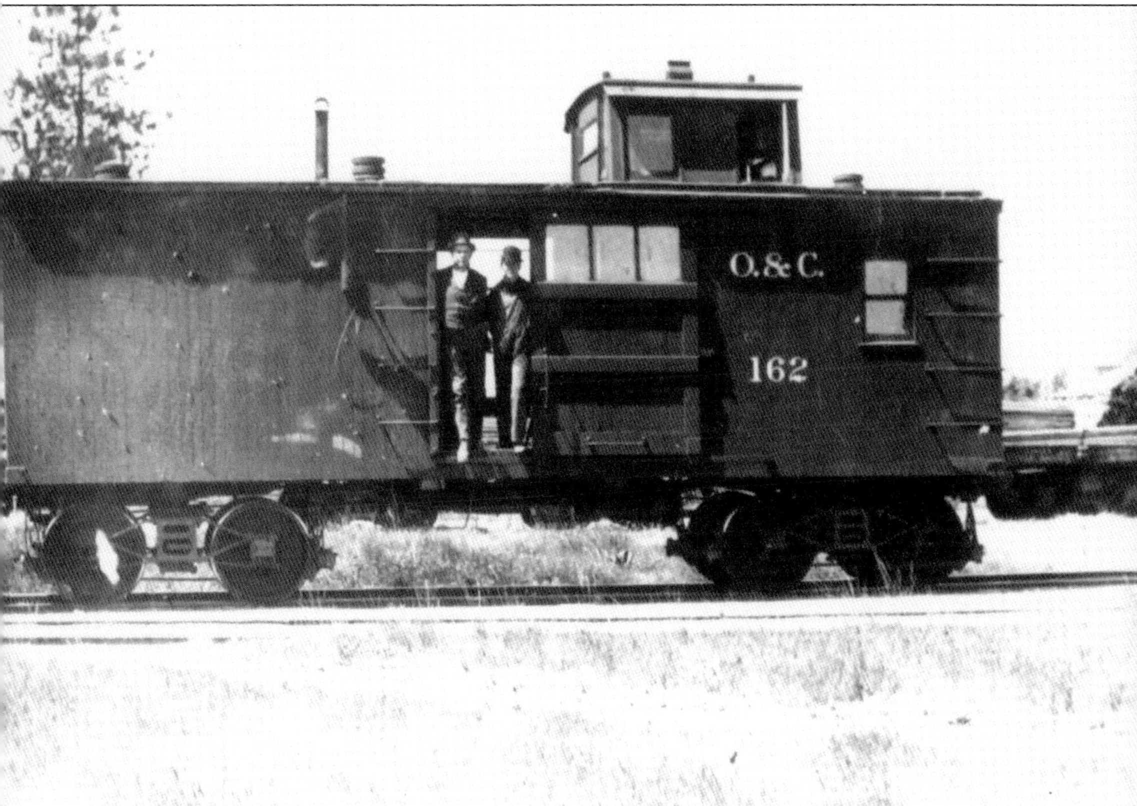

View from the Doorway. Two employees of the Oregon & California Railroad hang out in O&C No. 162, an odd, sliding-door cupola caboose at rest in Oregon's Willamette Valley. The O&C's time serving the Hillsboro area was relatively short; the railroad through Hillsboro had been in place for only 16 years before Southern Pacific took over all the O&C's lines in 1887. (Collection of Curtis Culp.)

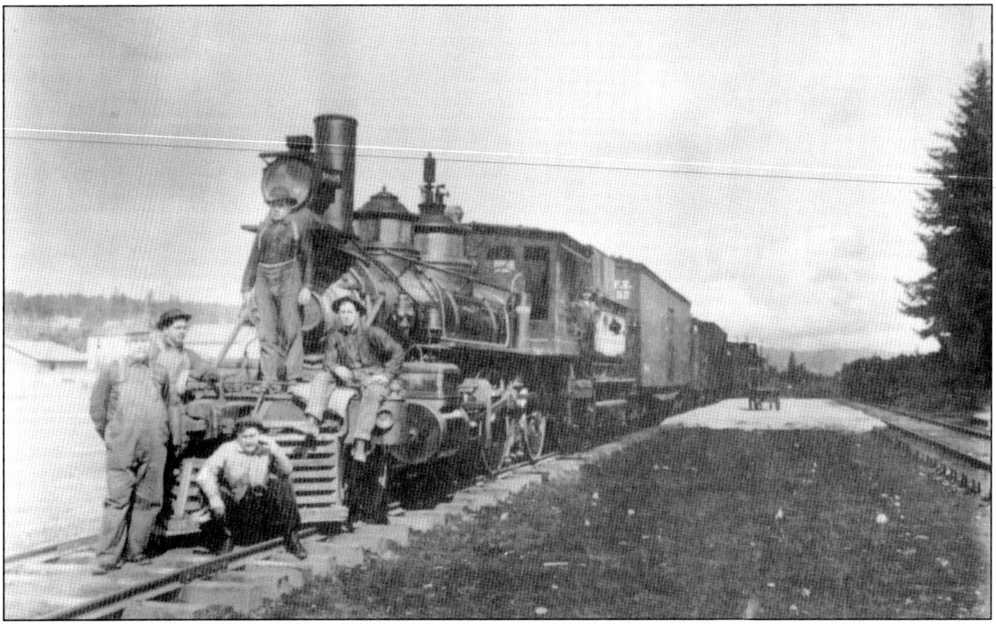

Timeout in Cornelius. The crew of a Southern Pacific freight train takes a break for a photograph in this 1905 scene from Cornelius, located three miles west of Hillsboro. This track was built in 1871, and in 2014—more than 140 years later—trains still run through Cornelius on their way to and from a lumber mill at Seghers, another seven miles down the line from Cornelius. (Collection of Washington County Museum.)

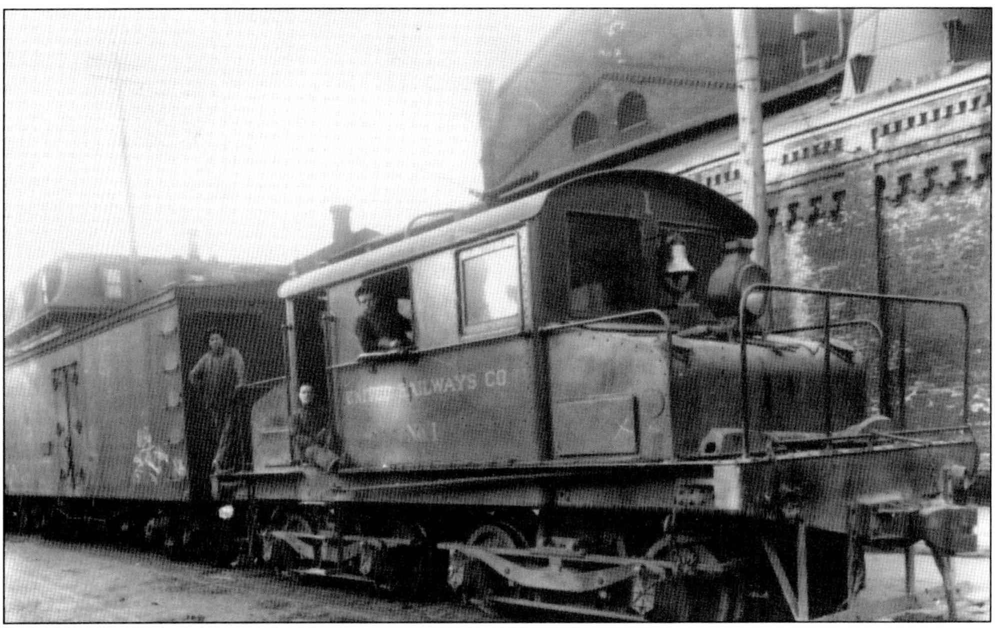

Early Roots. United Railways No. 1, built by Baldwin Locomotive Works in 1908, is seen here moving freight in Portland in 1909. The United Railways line between Portland and Banks was envisioned as an electrified interurban passenger railroad, but freight was moved as well. In 1909, the company came under the ownership of the Spokane, Portland & Seattle Railway, even before its route to Banks was completed. (Collection of D.C. Jesse Burkhardt.)

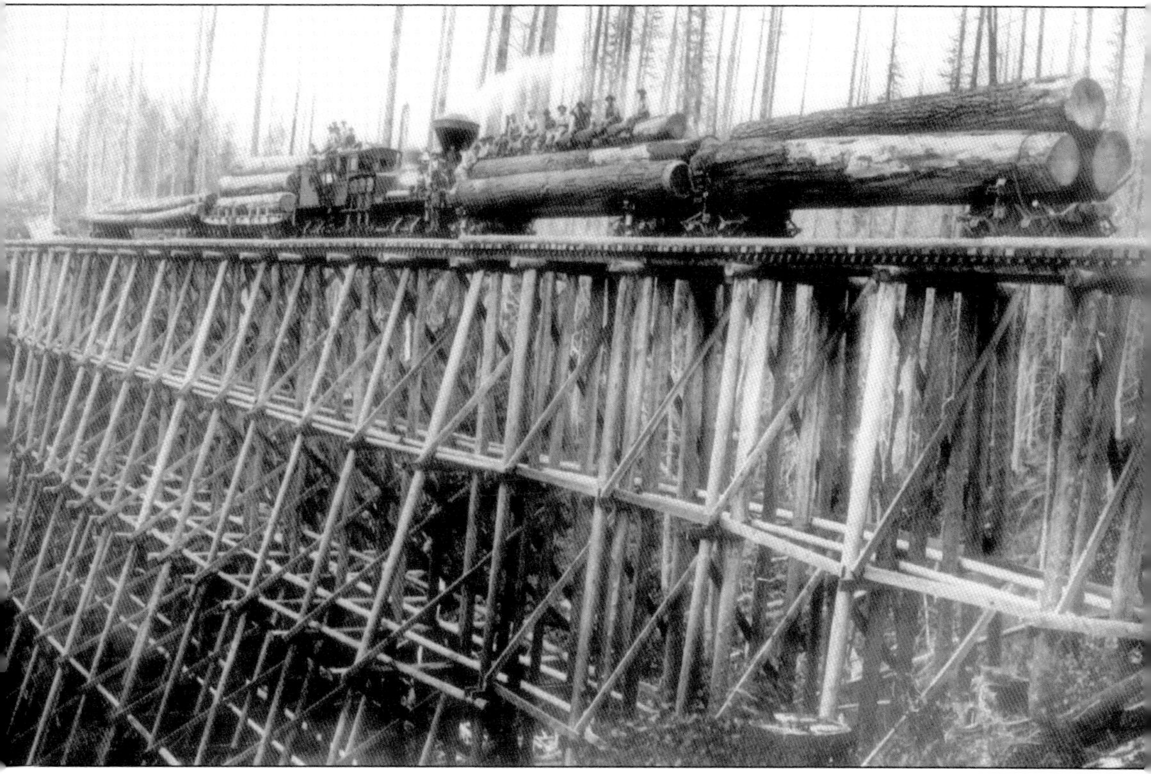

BIG STICKS. A logging crew working with a Shay locomotive poses for a photograph on the Big Baldwin trestle about 30 miles west of Hillsboro. Logs and lumber have always been among the primary commodities hauled by railroads moving through the Hillsboro area. (Collection of Curtis Culp.)

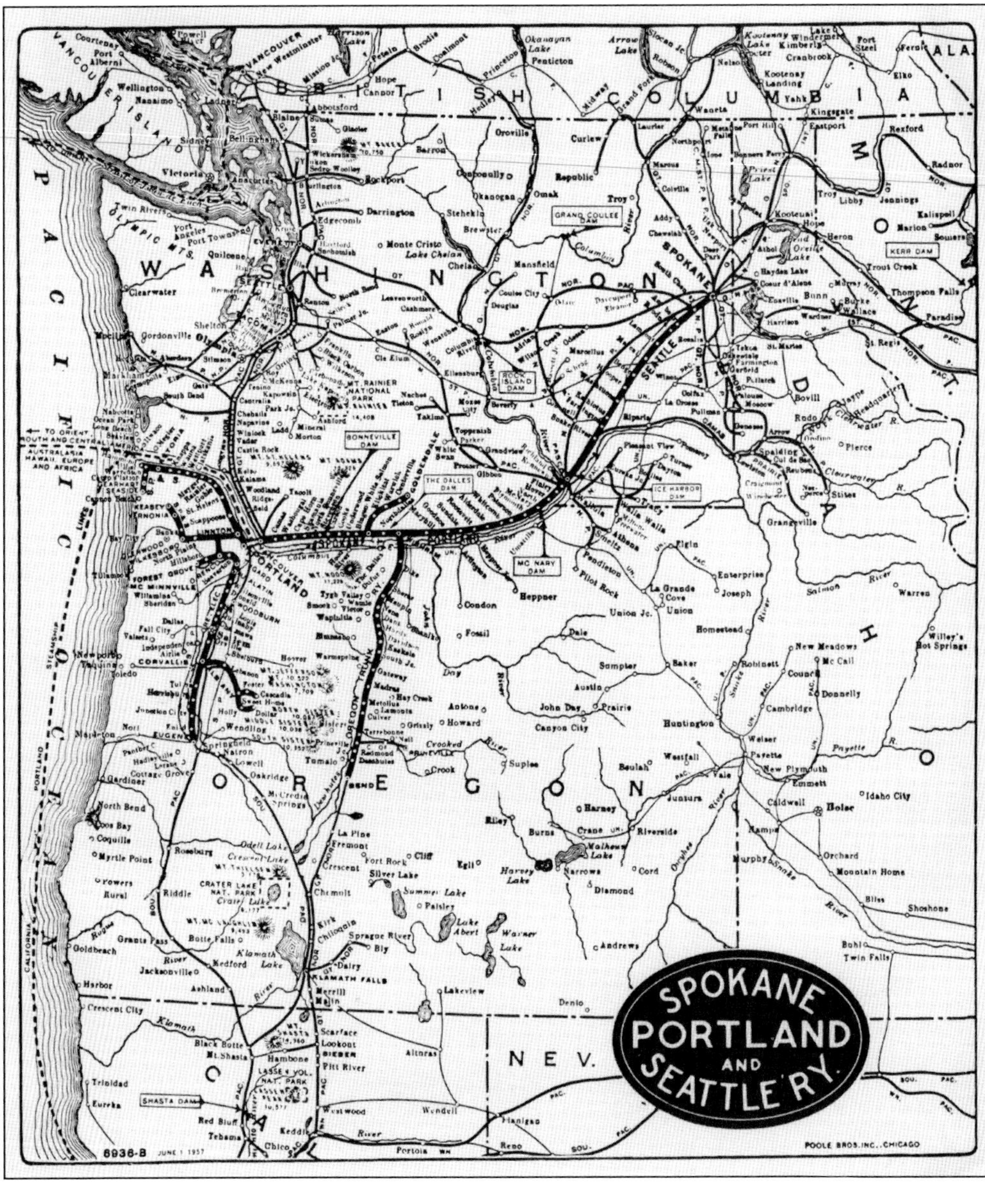

Northwest Railway. The Spokane, Portland & Seattle Railway's branchline into Hillsboro was part of a much larger rail network, as this 1957 map of the SP&S system illustrates. The railroad stretched from Spokane, Washington, to Portland, Oregon, with secondary lines extending south to Eugene as well as west to Astoria and Seaside on the Oregon coast. Hillsboro appears as a station near the end of a somewhat isolated branchline that ended in Forest Grove, about six miles to the west. The SP&S was merged into Burlington Northern Railroad in 1970. (Collection of D.C. Jesse Burkhardt.)

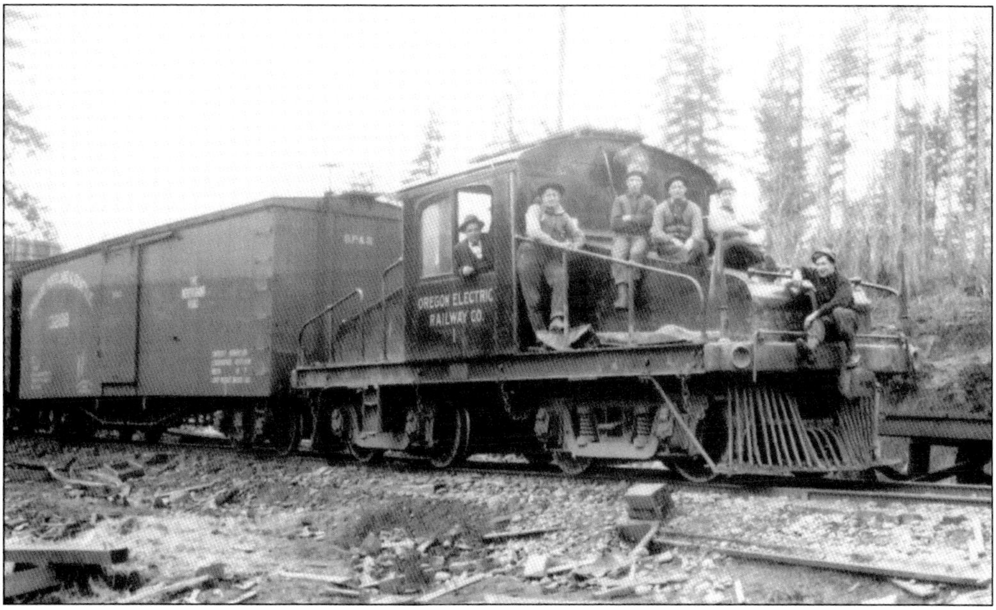

WILLAMETTE VALLEY ROUTE. The Oregon Electric Railway was designed to be a passenger railroad, but moving freight ultimately proved to be a more lucrative business. In the photograph above, an OE crew pauses near Wilkesboro, eight miles northwest of Hillsboro. The Oregon Electric became a subsidiary of the Spokane, Portland & Seattle in 1910, the same year this photograph was taken. Note the SP&S boxcar behind the engine with its iconic "North Bank Road" slogan. Oregon Electric No. 1 was built by the American Locomotive Company in 1907. Below, a freight train led by OE No. 50 rolls north along the Willamette Valley mainline. The Oregon Electric's main track ran between Eugene and Portland, with a busy branchline to Hillsboro that cut west off the main trunk at Garden Home, south of Portland. (Both, collection of Curtis Culp.)

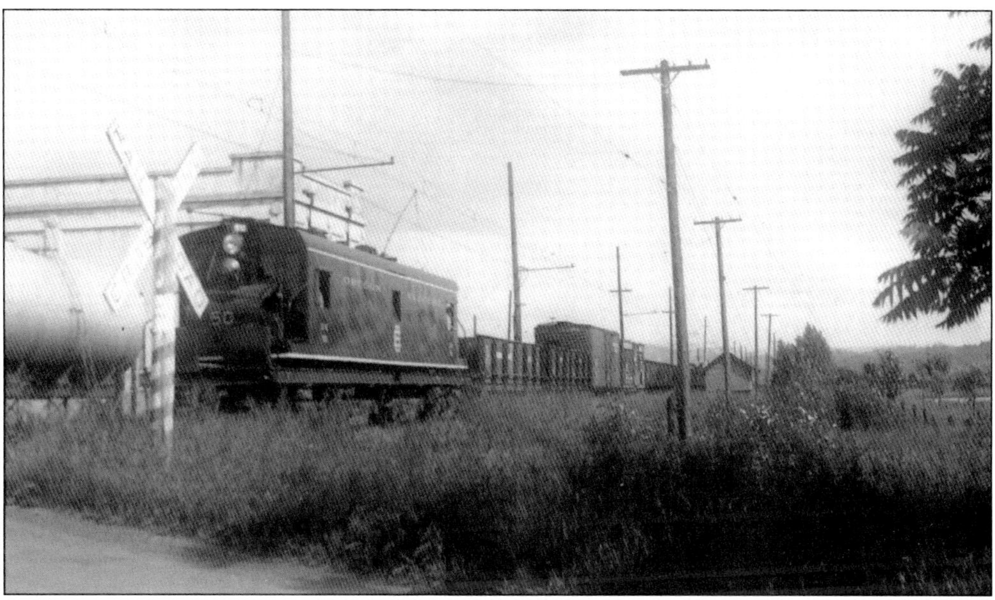

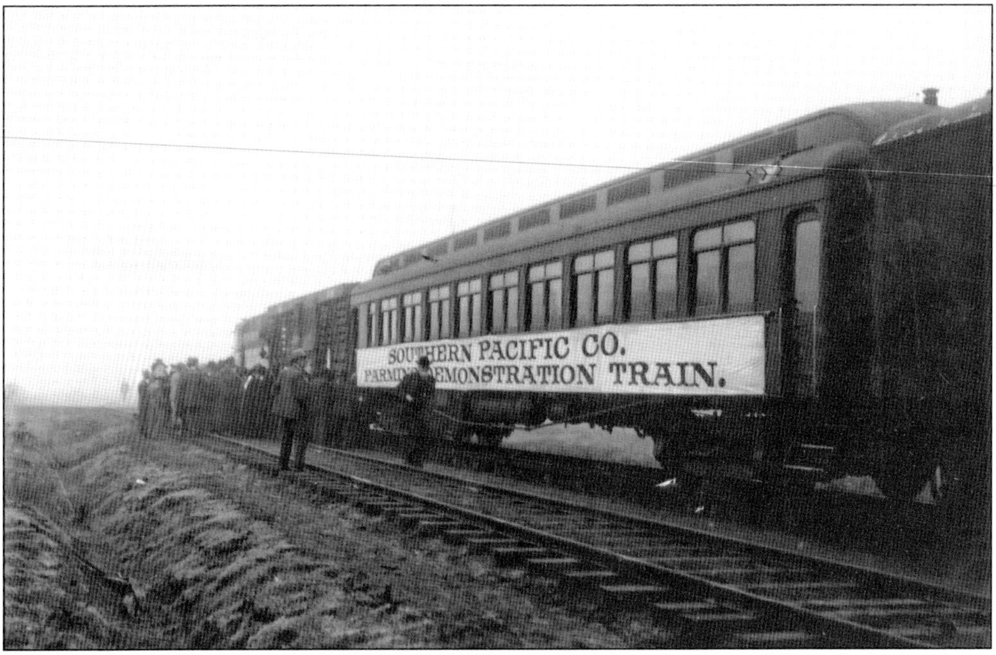

Help with the Harvest. In the early 1900s, Southern Pacific hosted a series of "Farming Demonstration Trains" that traveled throughout the SP system to help farmers boost their yields. If this crowd at Hillsboro is any indication, the visits were appreciated. These special trains carried farm-related exhibits and experts to assist with soil surveys and irrigation—a shrewd way to ensure the region's shippers would continue to move large volumes of agricultural goods by rail. (Collection of Washington County Museum.)

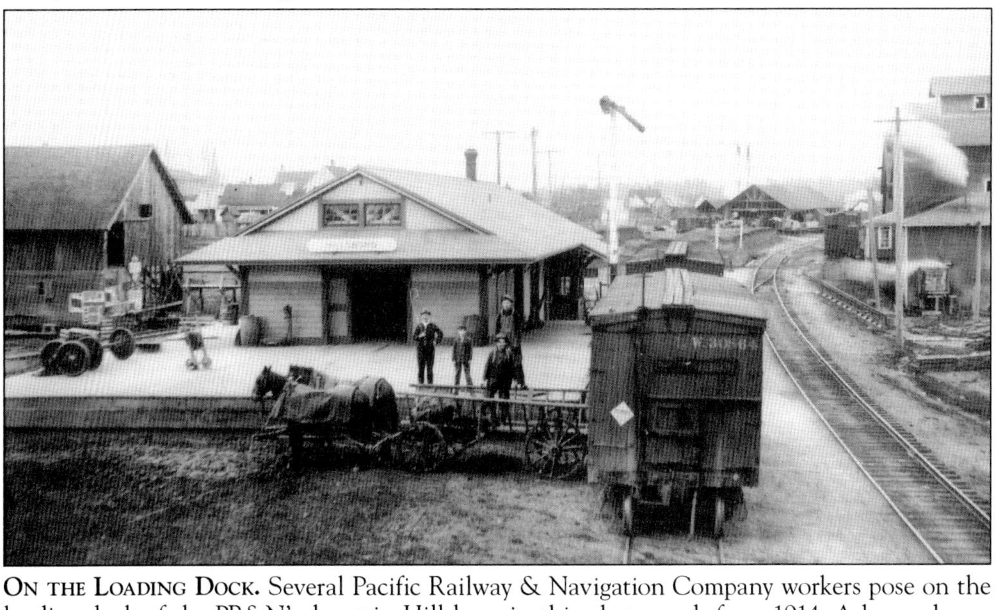

On the Loading Dock. Several Pacific Railway & Navigation Company workers pose on the loading dock of the PR&N's depot in Hillsboro in this photograph from 1914. A horse-drawn cart has been backed up to one of the boxcars on the station's spur track to load or unload goods, while in the background, boxcars wait to be filled with lumber from a busy sawmill. (Collection of Curtis Culp.)

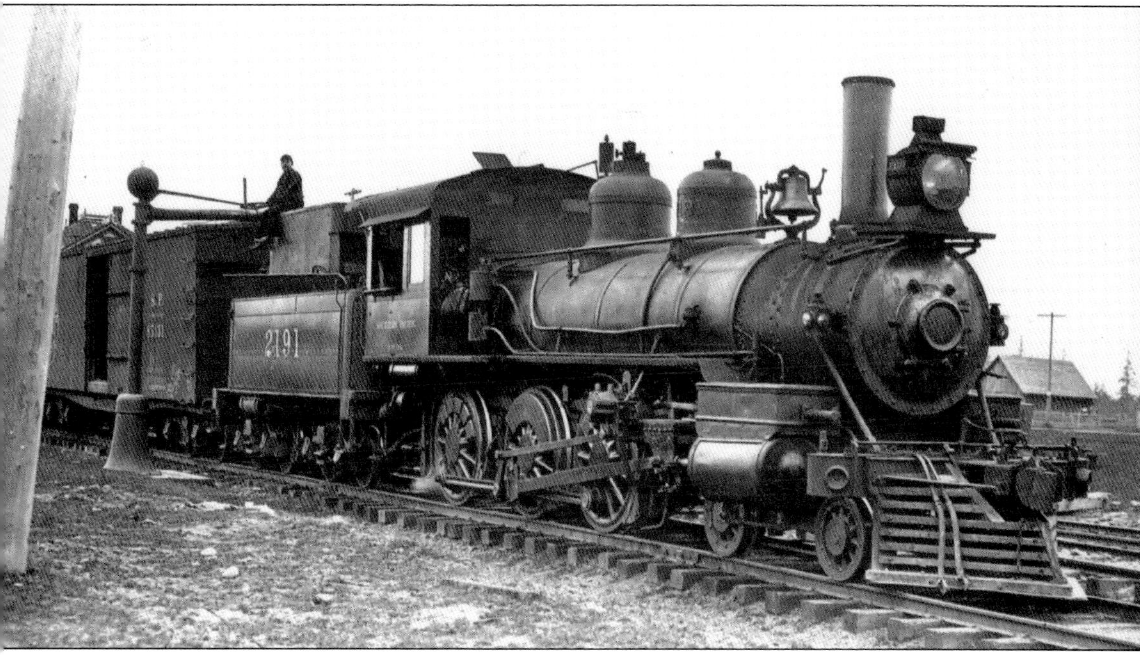

THIRSTY LOCOMOTIVE. A Southern Pacific freight train, led by locomotive No. 2191, pauses at Whiteson to take on water while on its way north to Hillsboro in this 1905 scene. Whiteson was located 34 miles due south of Hillsboro on SP's West Side Branch, which connected Hillsboro with McMinnville and Corvallis. At Whiteson, an SP branchline extended west to the mill towns of Sheridan and Willamina. (Collection of Curtis Culp.)

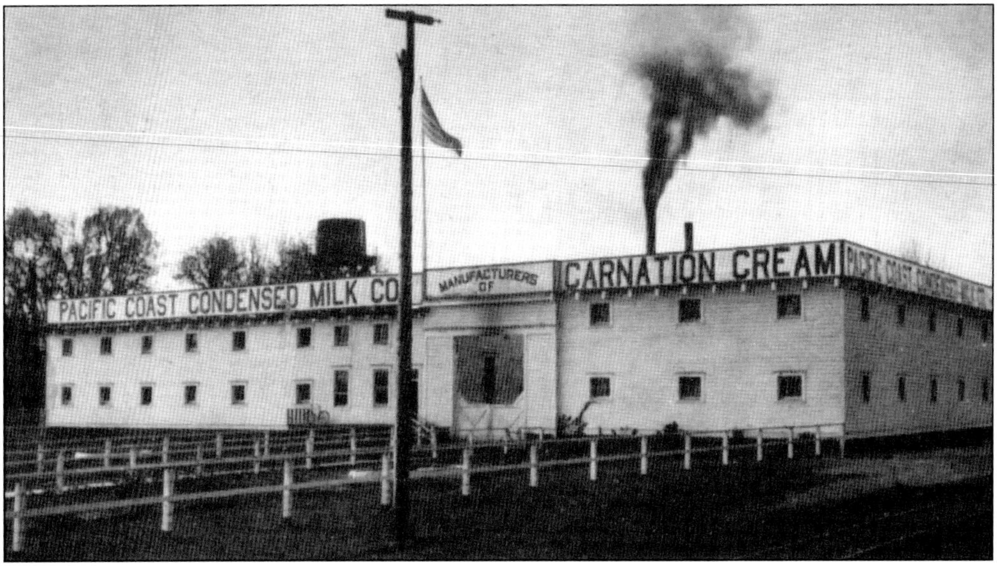

CARNATION. The huge Carnation Milk Products plant in Forest Grove, built in 1902, was known as a condensary—where milk was concentrated by evaporating some of its water. To show how important this business was to Southern Pacific, the railroad named the station where the plant was located "Carnation." Although the plant closed in 1929 and no shipper remains at Carnation, the station is still listed on contemporary railroad timetables. (Collection of Friends of Historic Forest Grove.)

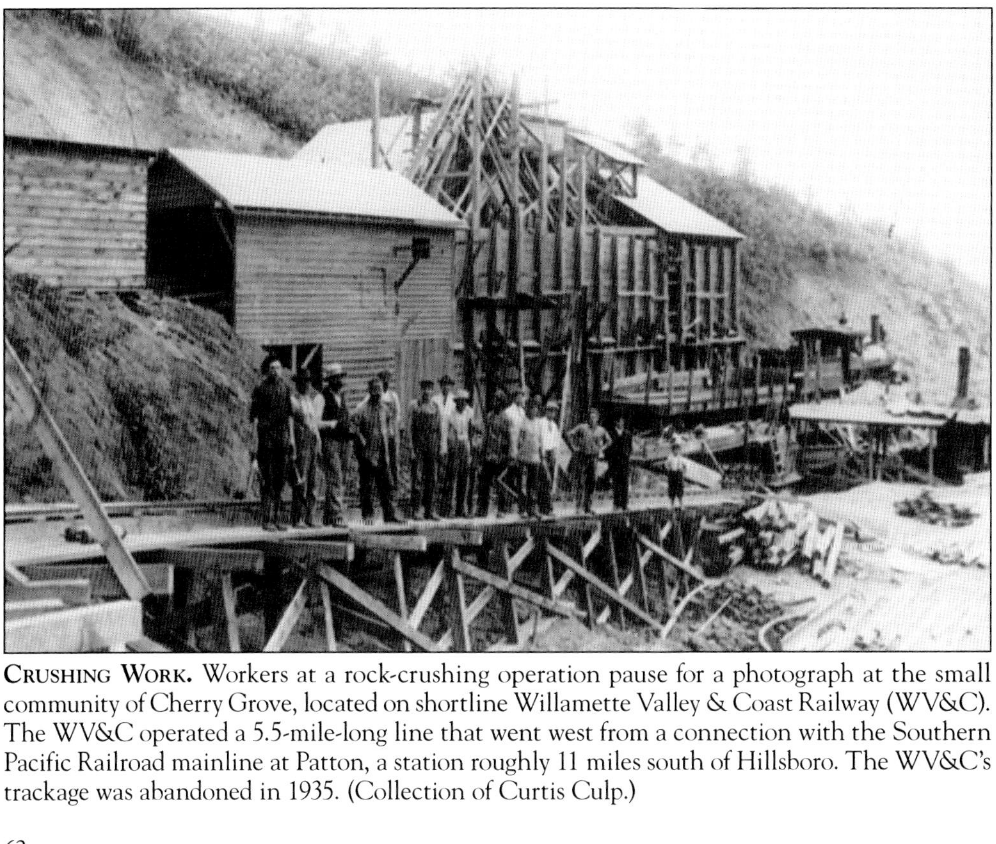

CRUSHING WORK. Workers at a rock-crushing operation pause for a photograph at the small community of Cherry Grove, located on shortline Willamette Valley & Coast Railway (WV&C). The WV&C operated a 5.5-mile-long line that went west from a connection with the Southern Pacific Railroad mainline at Patton, a station roughly 11 miles south of Hillsboro. The WV&C's trackage was abandoned in 1935. (Collection of Curtis Culp.)

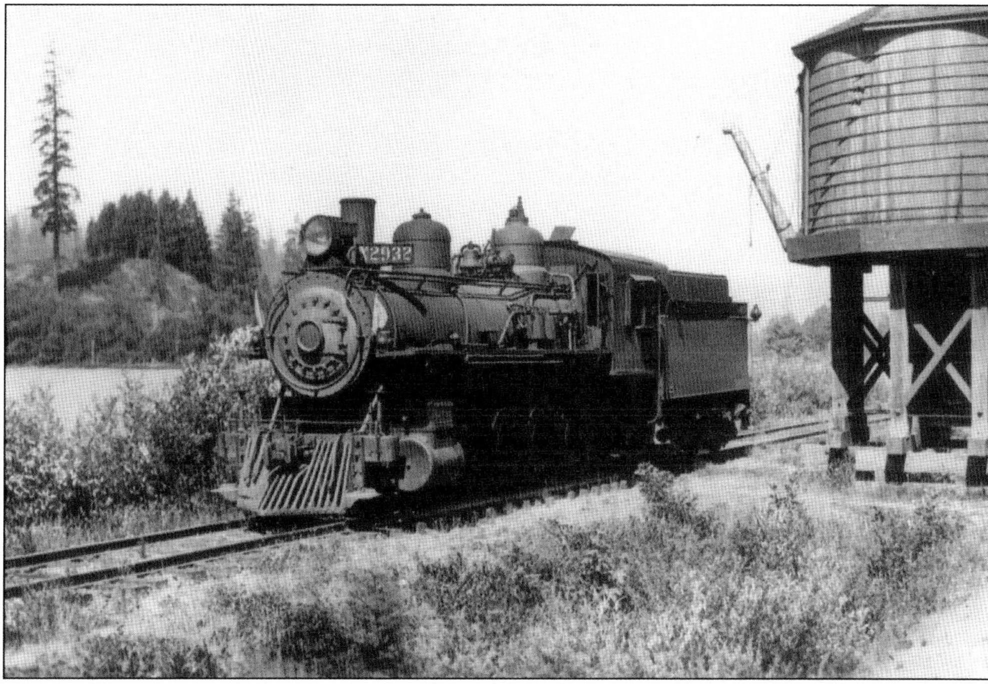

TANK TOWN. In the photograph above, Southern Pacific freight locomotive No. 2932 pauses at a water tank in Buxton, situated about 16 miles west of Hillsboro on the railroad's Tillamook Branch. In the photograph below, SP No. 237 rolls along the line somewhere between Buxton and Cochran, a stretch of track that has some of the mountain route's most rugged landscapes. (Both, collection of Washington County Museum.)

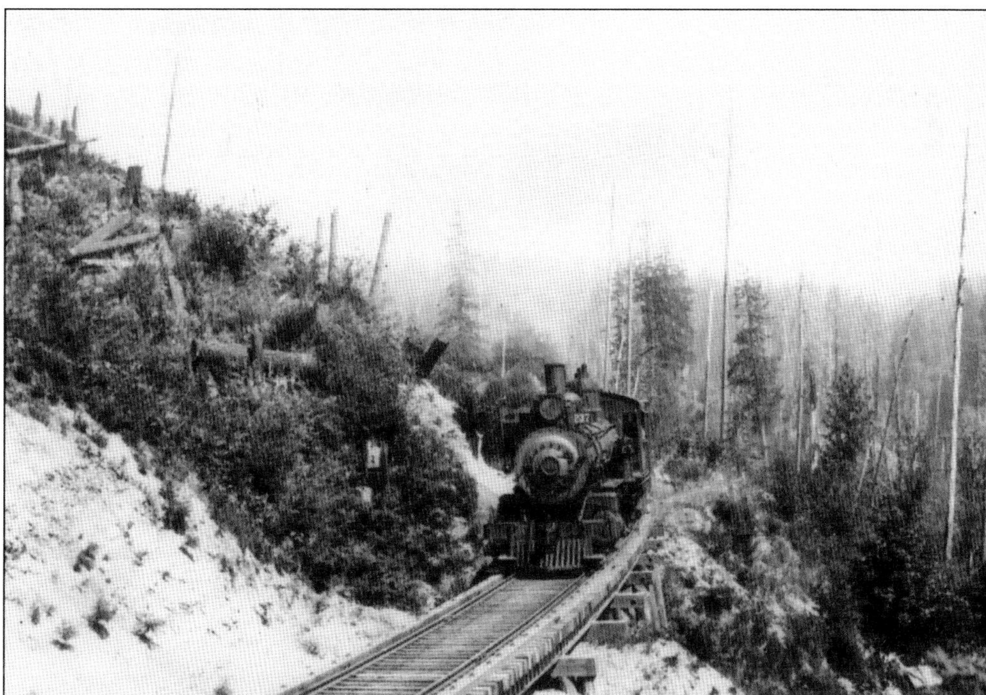

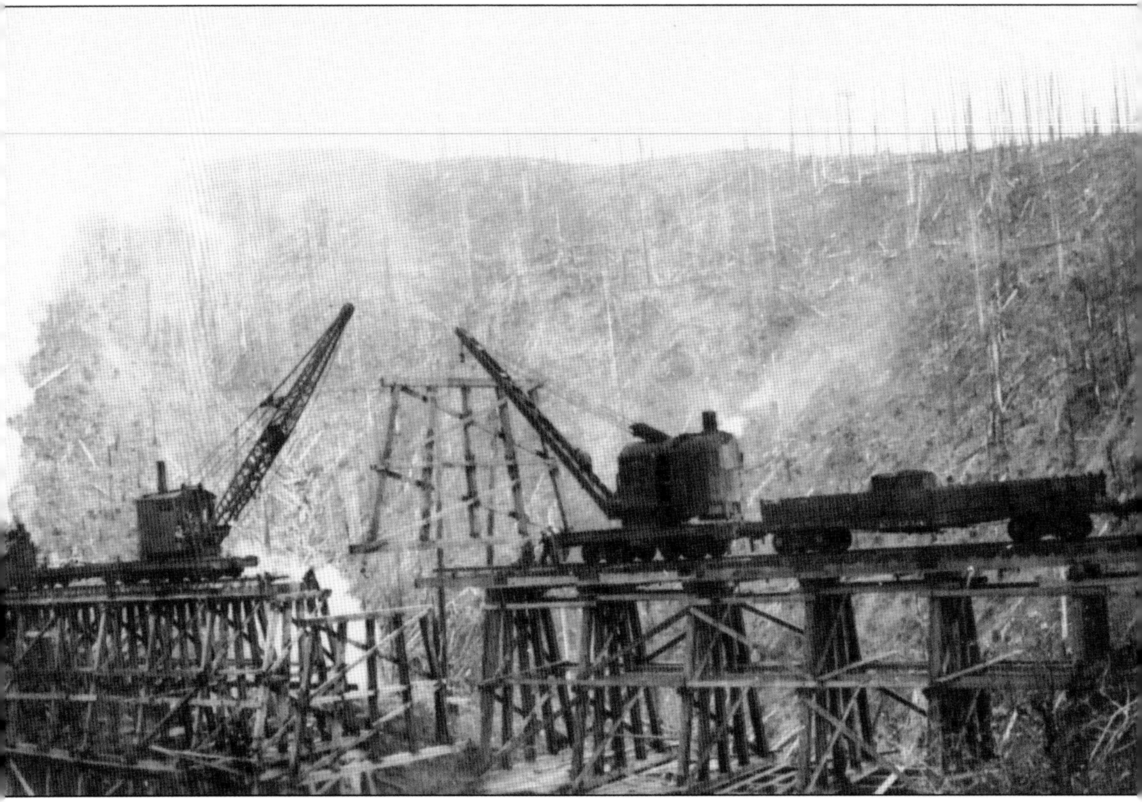

Fire's Aftermath. A Southern Pacific maintenance crew uses a pair of heavy-duty cranes—one at each end of the bridge segment that has been damaged—to lower new support trusses into place on a portion of the line between Hillsboro and Tillamook in 1935. The bridge has most likely been damaged in a forest fire; note the burned-over landscape. A series of massive forest fires known as the Tillamook Burn plagued the heavily forested areas of the Coast Range in the mid-1930s. Approximately 240,000 acres of prime timber were consumed in the most serious of these fires, which started in August 1933. (Collection of Curtis Culp.)

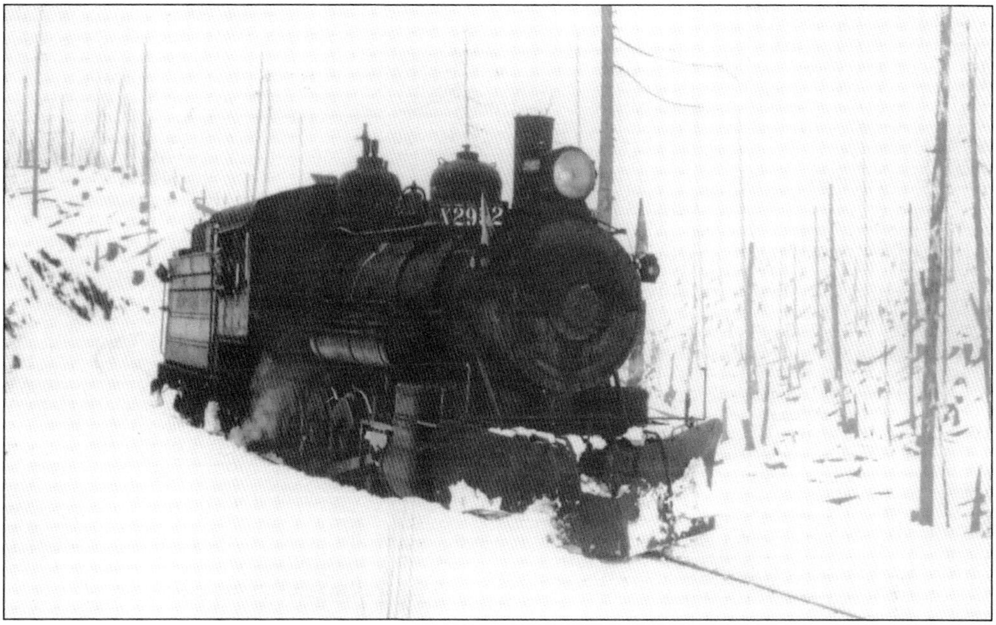

SOUTHERN PACIFIC POWER. In the photograph above, an SP locomotive rolls through a snowy landscape west of Hillsboro, while in the photograph below, SP No. 2679 is seen taking a spin on the turntable at Timber. For many years, Timber was a vital way station on the route from Hillsboro to the coast. In addition to the turntable, Timber—about 28 miles west of Hillsboro—boasted a passenger station and locomotive servicing facilities. Timber was also a helper station, and it was typical for extra locomotives to be added to trains at this location to ensure they had enough power to make it over the rugged Coast Range passes that waited on the route between Tillamook and Hillsboro. (Both, collection of Washington County Museum.)

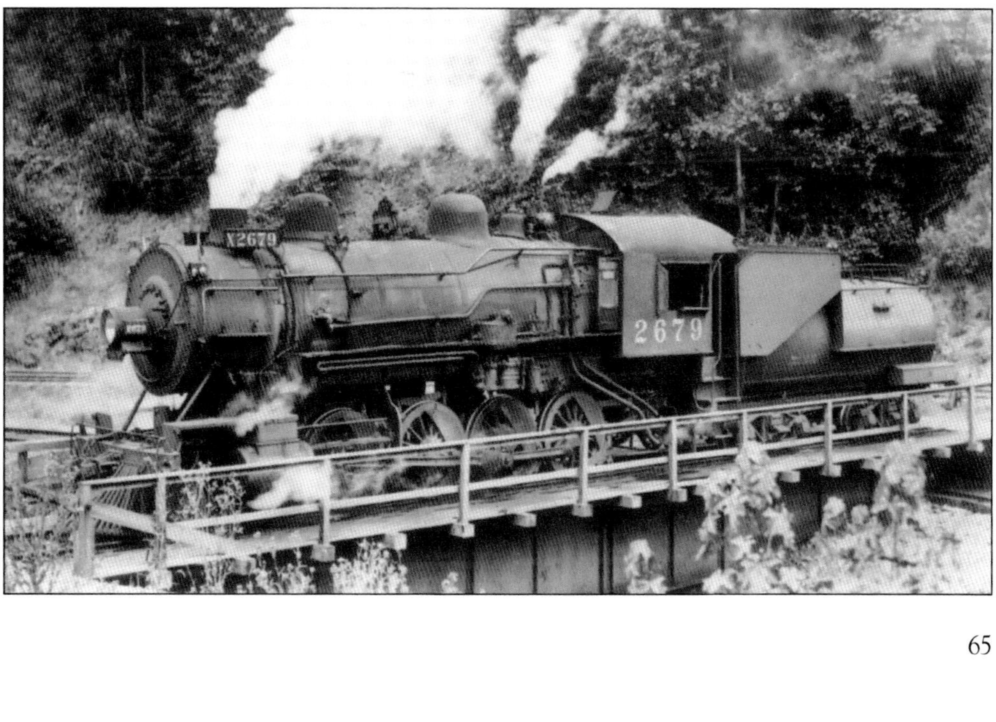

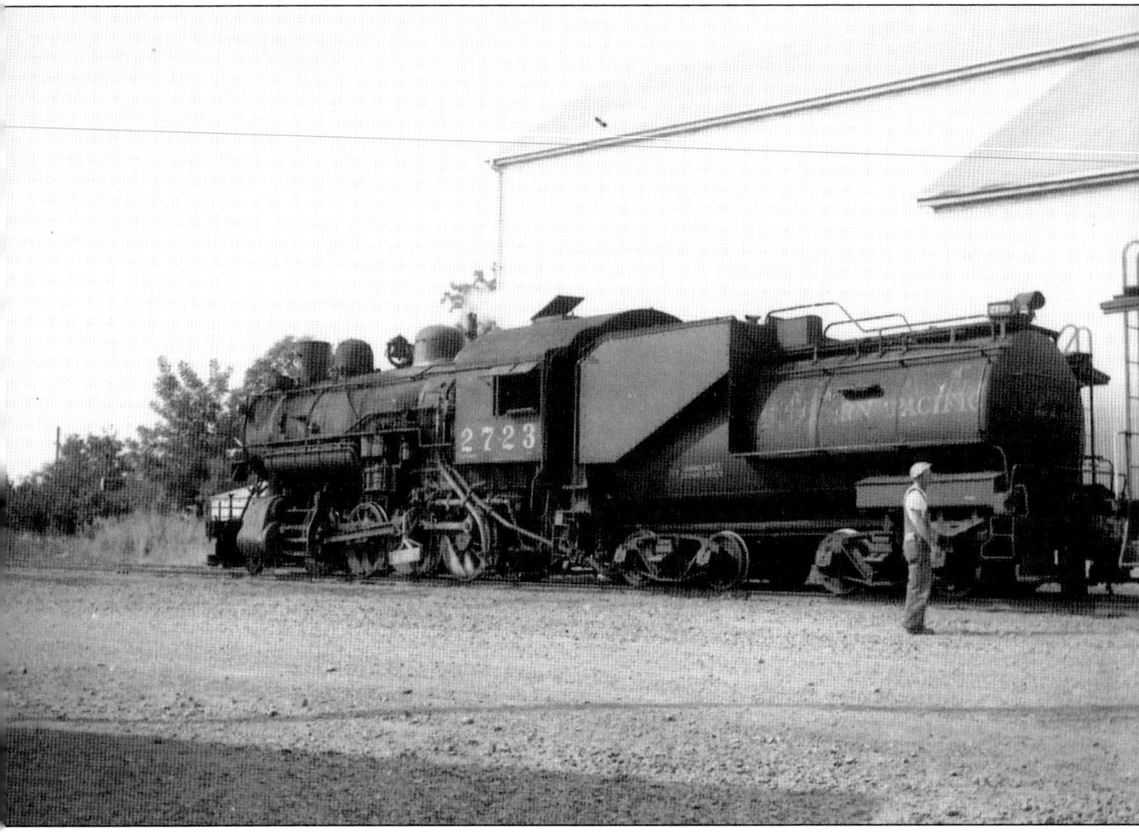

Fading Steam. Southern Pacific Consolidation-class 2-8-0 locomotive No. 2723 switches cars in Hillsboro in a photograph from the 1950s. Just a few years from when this scene was captured, steam locomotives would essentially vanish from the landscape and be replaced with the new diesel models. The last of the steam locomotives Southern Pacific used in regular service were retired in 1957. (Collection of Curtis Culp.)

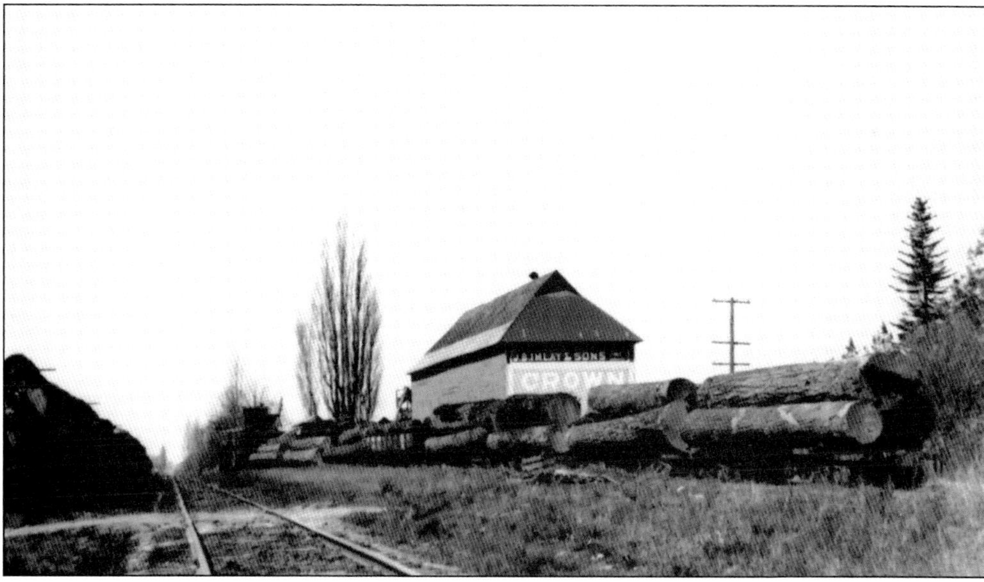

BUSY AT REEDVILLE. On April 8, 1951, long strings of flatcars carrying huge logs rest on sidings at Reedville, a small community about four miles east of Hillsboro on Southern Pacific's Tillamook Branch. The building behind the log cars is the J.B. Imlay & Sons granary, an active rail shipper at the time. (Collection of Washington County Museum.)

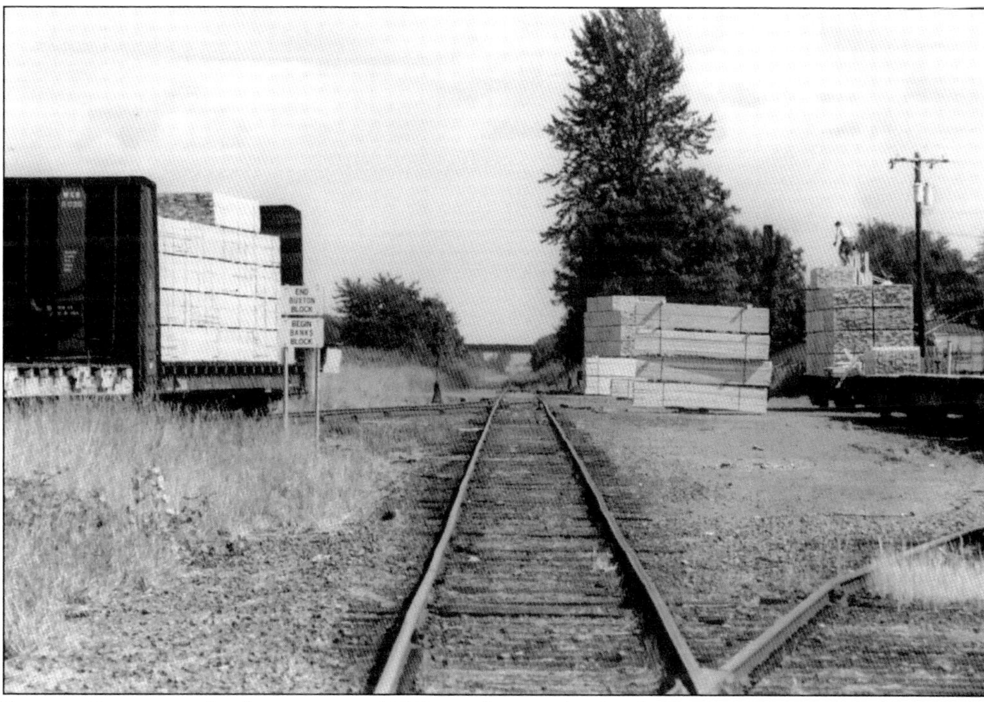

STEADY CUSTOMER. In the summer of 1991, workers at the Banks Lumber Company mill in Banks load fresh lumber onto flatcars during the time when the Port of Tillamook Bay Railroad (POTB) was serving the mill. After a severe storm knocked out sections of the port's rail line between Hillsboro and Tillamook in 2007, however, the Portland & Western Railroad eventually took over switching duties here. (Photograph by D.C. Jesse Burkhardt.)

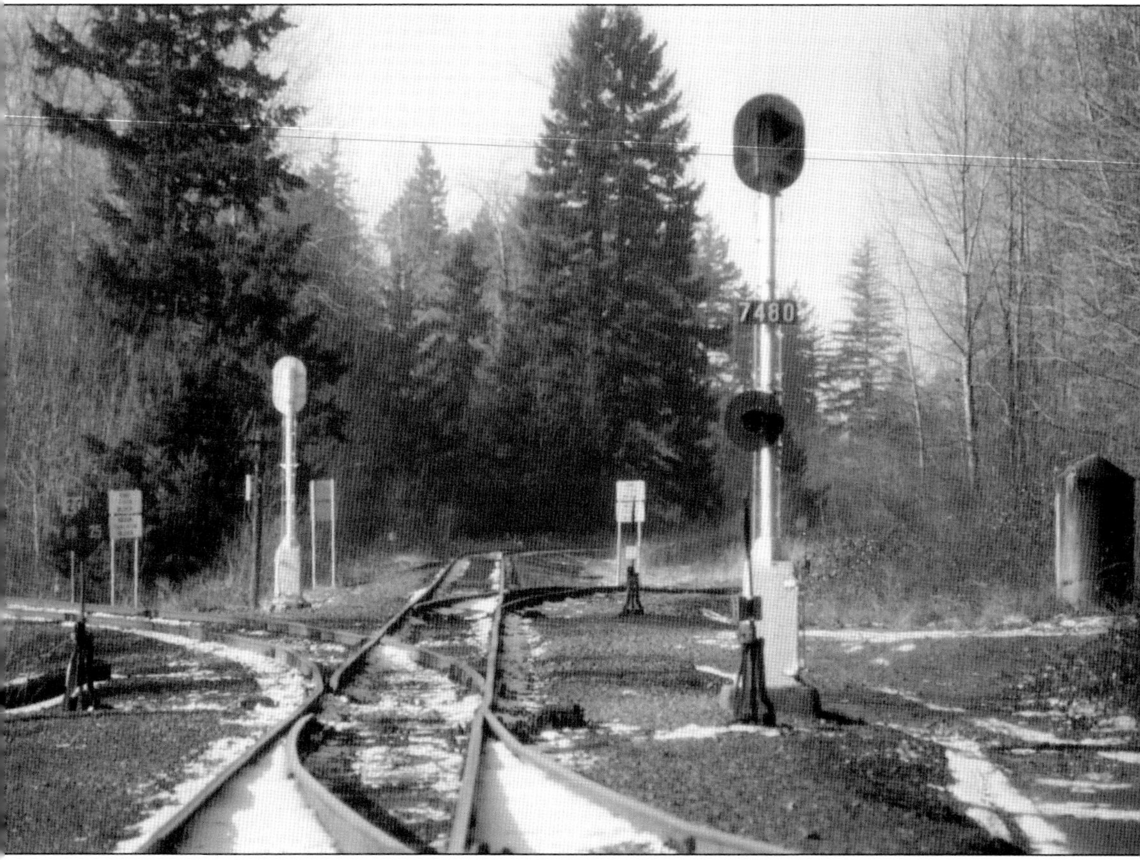

Gateway. In this February 1989 photograph, a light dusting of snow lines the tracks at Cook, an obscure station 17 miles southeast of Hillsboro where Southern Pacific's Newberg Branch and Tillamook Branch diverged. To the right, the tracks curve northwest to Tigard, Hillsboro, and Tillamook; to the left, the tracks head southwest to Newberg and McMinnville. The signal towers came down in 1990 as SP began controlling its Oregon Division branchlines by use of direct traffic control (DTC) blocks. Note the signs lining both tracks; these signs marked where specific DTC blocks began and ended. (Photograph by D.C. Jesse Burkhardt.)

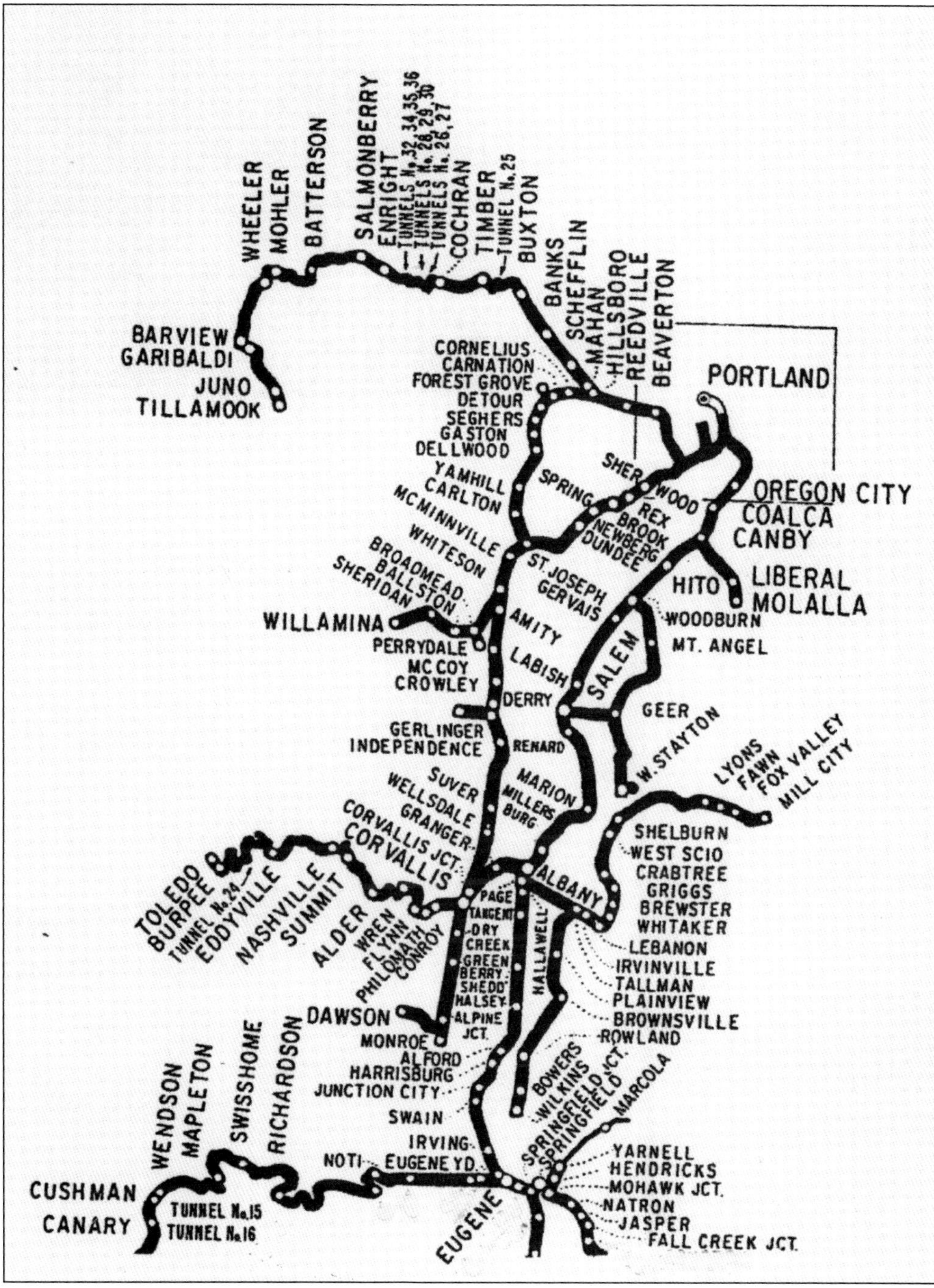

SP in the Willamette Valley. Southern Pacific's Oregon Division extended south from Portland, Oregon, to Dunsmuir, California, and Flanigan, Nevada. This detail of the Oregon Division map from SP's timetable, effective October 26, 1980, shows the Willamette Valley region of Oregon, which stretches from Eugene to Portland, a distance of 125 miles. (Collection of D.C. Jesse Burkhardt.)

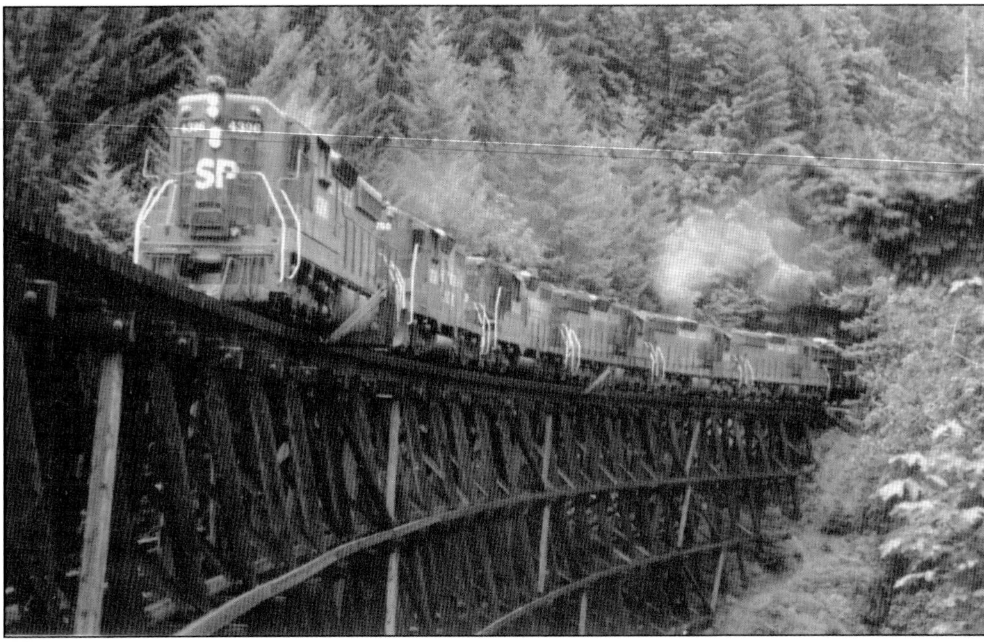

Batterson Turn. Southern Pacific's *Batterson Turn* crosses a bridge on the Tillamook Branch west of Buxton in September 1975. In the 1970s, westbound trains on the line came out of SP's Brooklyn Yard in Portland and ran through to Batterson, while another crew hauled eastbound cars out of Tillamook and met the westbound train at Batterson. The crews then exchanged their consists and returned to their respective home terminals. (Photograph by Randy Nelson.)

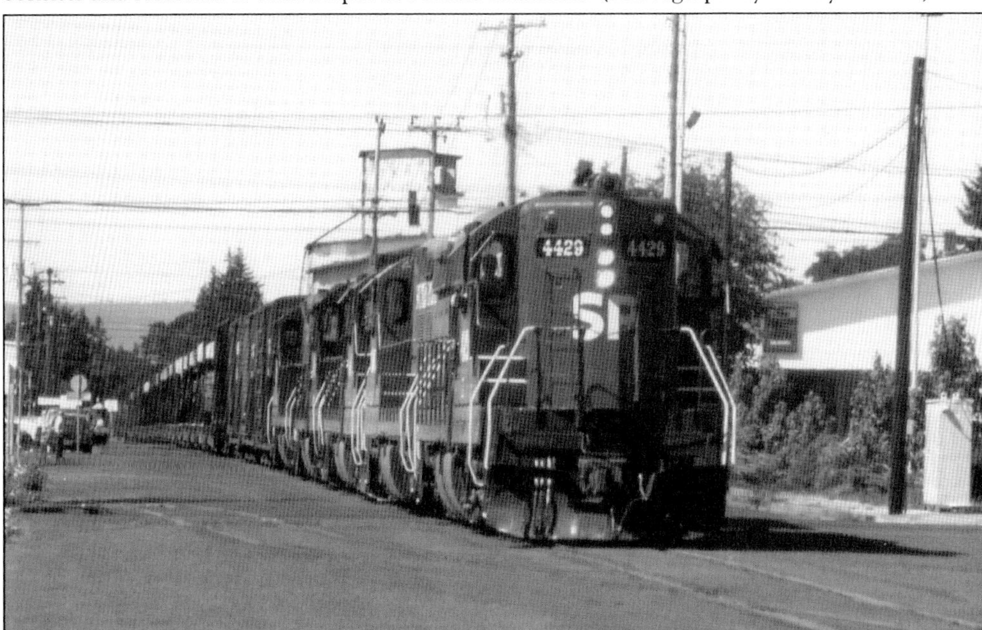

Rails in the Road. Powered by multiple SD9s, SP's *Batterson Turn* rolls down the middle of Adams Street in Hillsboro on its way back to Portland after a run out the Tillamook Branch to Batterson, 60 miles west of Hillsboro, in August 1985. The 1950s-era SD9s were commonplace on Oregon branchlines until the mid-1990s. (Photograph by Randy Nelson.)

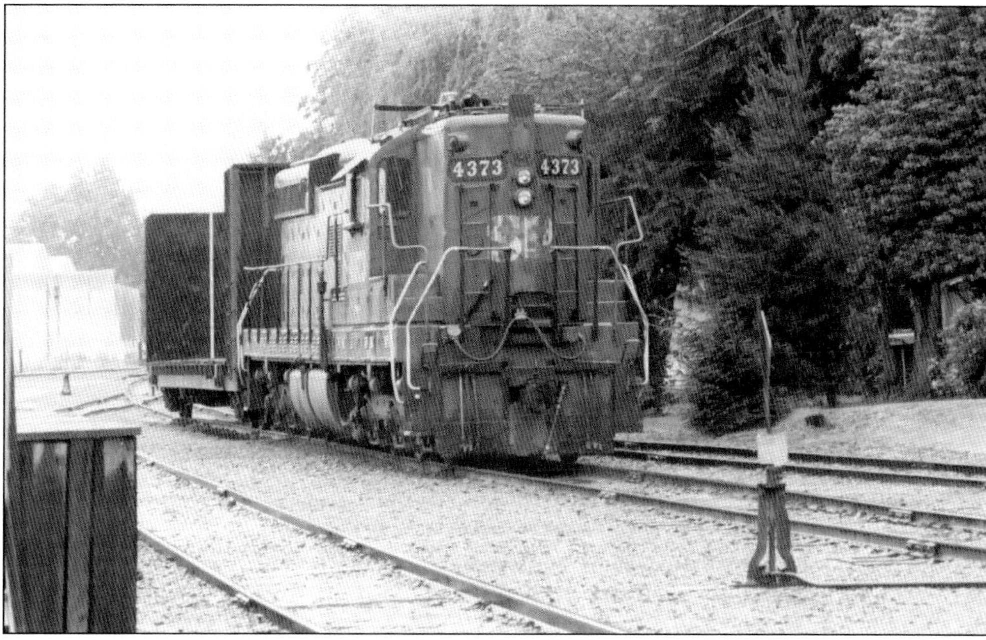

Waiting Out the Rain. Southern Pacific No. 4373, power for the *Hillsboro Roustabout*, rests next to the station in Hillsboro with one bulkhead flatcar on a rainy day in the June 1991 photograph above. In the early 1990s, the *Hillsboro Roustabout* was on the job five days a week, serving industries between Hillsboro and Cook, 17 miles away. In the photograph below, SD9s No. 4363 and No. 4323 idle in front of Hillsboro's Carnation Building on July 25, 1990. SP No. 4363 displays a paint scheme created in the early 1980s when SP anticipated merging with Santa Fe Railway; the initials "SF" were going to be added next to the "SP" once everything had been made official. However, the Interstate Commerce Commission quashed the merger in 1986, and the paint job became an obsolete reminder of what might have been. (Photographs by D.C. Jesse Burkhardt.)

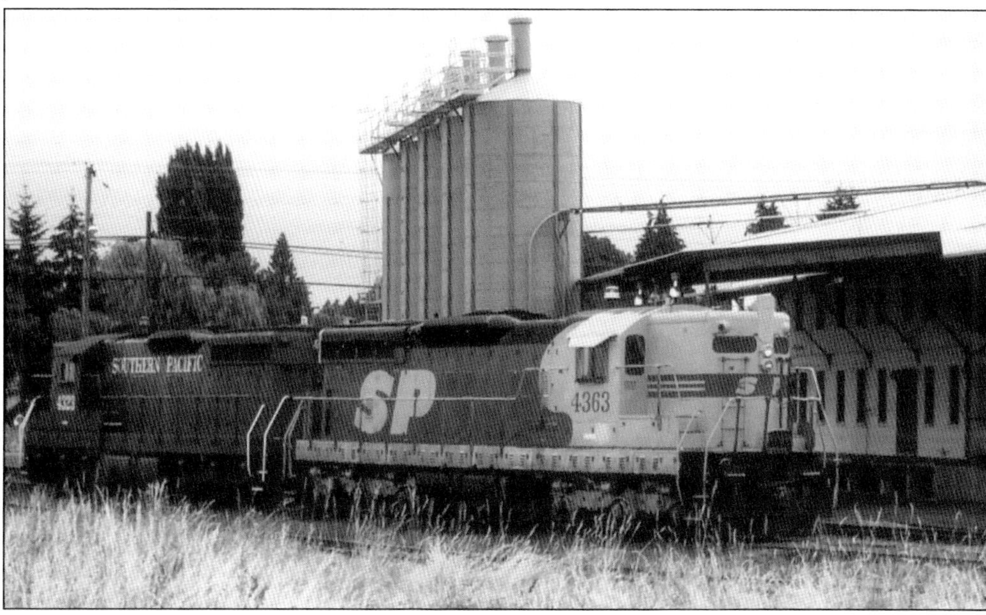

EASTWARD Mile Post		STATIONS SIDING CAPACITIES AND FACILITIES West Side Branch		Station Number	WESTWARD Distance
671.7		MONROE		02140	92.9
		1.3			
673.0	1280	ALPINE JCT.		02121	91.6
		8.3			
681.3		GREENBERRY		02111	83.3
		3.3			
684.6	2600	DRY CREEK		02105	80.0
		4.3			
688.9	Yd. Lmts.	CORVALLIS	PBY	02017	75.7
		1.0			
689.9	Yd. Lmts. R	CORVALLIS JCT.	Y	02014	74.7
		9.2			
699.1	1000	WELLSDALE		01434	65.5
		2.9			
702.0		SUVER		01427	62.6
		7.3			
709.3	Yd. Lmts.	INDEPENDENCE	P	01410	55.3
		1.2			
710.5	Yd. Lmts.	V. & S. JCT.		01408	54.1
		3.8			
714.3	Yd. Lmts. R	GERLINGER	PY	01330	50.3
		0.7			
715.0	Yd. Lmts.	DERRY		01220	49.6
		7.8			
722.8		McCOY		01210	41.8
		5.3			
728.1		AMITY		01205	36.5
		2.6			
730.7	Yd. Lmts. 1750	WHITESON	PY	01030	33.9
		4.2			
734.9	Yd. Lmts. 2910 TO-R	McMINNVILLE	BKQP	01020	29.7
		3.1			
738.0	Yd. Lmts. 825 R	ST. JOSEPH	PY	01005	26.6
		4.2			
742.2		CARLTON		00850	22.4
		3.4			
745.6		YAMHILL		00839	19.0
		6.7			
752.3		DELLWOOD		00835	12.3
		0.8			
753.1		GASTON		00832	11.5
		1.8			
754.9		SEGHERS		00825	9.7
		2.9			
757.8		DETOUR		00817	6.8
		0.7			
758.5 759.2		CARNATION		00811	6.1
		2.5			
761.7		CORNELIUS		00805	3.6
		3.6			
765.3 764.9	Yd. Lmts. TO-R	HILLSBORO	BKYPQ	00680	0.0

West Side Branch. Southern Pacific's 93-mile-long West Side Branch ran from Hillsboro south to "end of track" in Monroe, as shown in Southern Pacific's Oregon Division timetable, dated October 26, 1980. At one time, the line continued south from Monroe for roughly another 25 miles to reach Eugene, but the trackage between Monroe and Eugene was abandoned in the 1950s. The branchline was named "West Side" because the route ran down the western side of the Willamette Valley. (Collection of D.C. Jesse Burkhardt.)

EASTWARD Mile Post			STATIONS SIDING CAPACITIES AND FACILITIES Tillamook Branch		Station Number	WESTWARD Distance
855.8	Yd. Lmts	TO-R	TILLAMOOK	BKPQ	00798	114.9
			2.2			
853.6			JUNO		00796	112.7
			7.9			
845.7		1250	GARIBALDI		00787	104.8
			1.9			
843.8			BARVIEW		00786	102.9
			10.2			
833.6		540	WHEELER		00776	92.7
			2.4			
831.2		1020	MOHLER		00773	90.3
			6.1			
825.1		5400 Yd. Lmts.	BATTERSON		00767	84.2
			9.4			
815.7			SALMONBERRY		00758	74.8
			4.7			
811.0			ENRIGHT		00753	70.1
			11.0			
800.0		2055	COCHRAN		00742	59.1
			6.9			
793.1			TIMBER		00733	52.2
			11.9			
781.2		710	BUXTON		00721	40.3
			6.5			
774.7		R	BANKS		00715	33.8
			4.5			
770.2		1175	SCHEFFLIN		00710	29.3
			3.8			
766.4	Yard Limits	2340	MAHAN		00705	25.5
			0.9			
765.5		R	BN JCT.		....	24.6
			0.5			
765.0 764.8		TO-R	HILLSBORO	BKPQY	00680	24.1
			4.7			
760.1		820	REEDVILLE		00660	19.4
			4.5			
755.6	A-PB, Yd. Lmts.	780	BEAVERTON	P	00650	14.9
			0.6			
755.0		4400	BEBURG	YP	00640	14.3
			1.6			
753.4			FANNO		00630	12.7
			1.5			
751.9			GRETON	P	00620	11.2
			0.8			
751.1	Yard limits		TIGARD		00610	10.4
			3.1			
748.0	ABS	R	COOK	YP	00430	7.3
			0.5			
747.5		2270	BRYANT		00420	6.8
			3.3			
744.2	Yard Limits	3160	LAKE OSWEGO	P	00400	3.5
			0.3			
743.9			WILSONIA	P	00320	3.2
			0.9			
743.0		1560	MENEFEE		00315	2.3
			1.1			
741.9			MILWAUKIE		00300	1.2
			1.2			
740.7			WILLSBURG JCT.	IP	00275	0.0

Tillamook Branch. The stations of Southern Pacific's 115-mile-long Tillamook Branch are also from SP's Oregon Division timetable of October 26, 1980. The line officially began at Willsburg Junction, near Portland, and continued west to Tillamook via Hillsboro. The Hillsboro-Tillamook portion of the line was built by the Pacific Railway & Navigation Company, which completed the route in 1911. Just four years later, in 1915, SP took full control of the PR&N, and it continued to operate trains over the line for the next 80 years. (Collection of D.C. Jesse Burkhardt.)

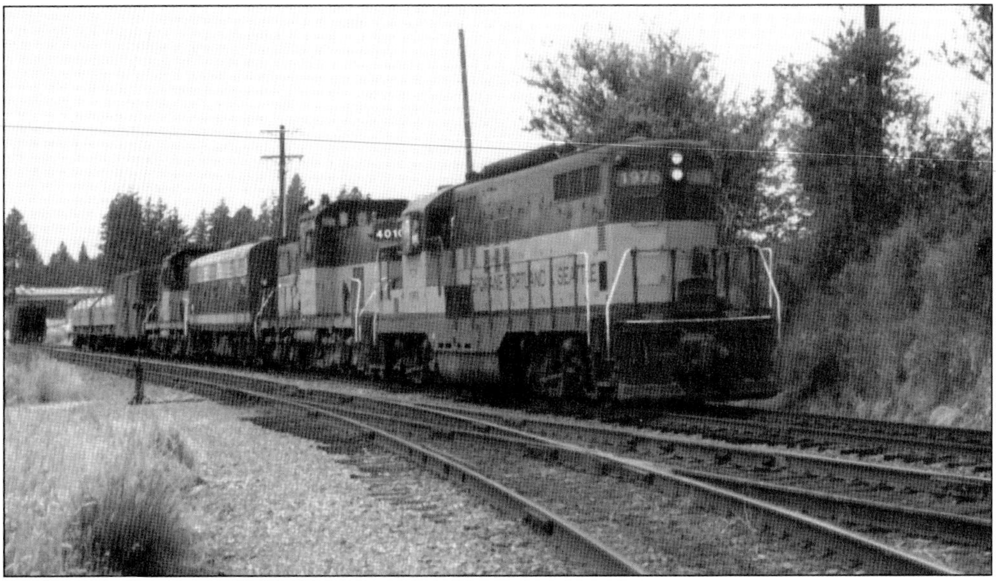

Alcos on the Main. A northbound train led by SP&S GP7 No. 1976 sets out cars on the Oregon Electric mainline near Beaverton in October 1970, just a few months after the railroad's merger into Burlington Northern. Note the two Alco C415s in the power consist. This was unusual, as the C415s had previously been used almost exclusively as yard switchers at Wishram, Washington, and Klamath Falls, Oregon. (Photograph by Randy Nelson.)

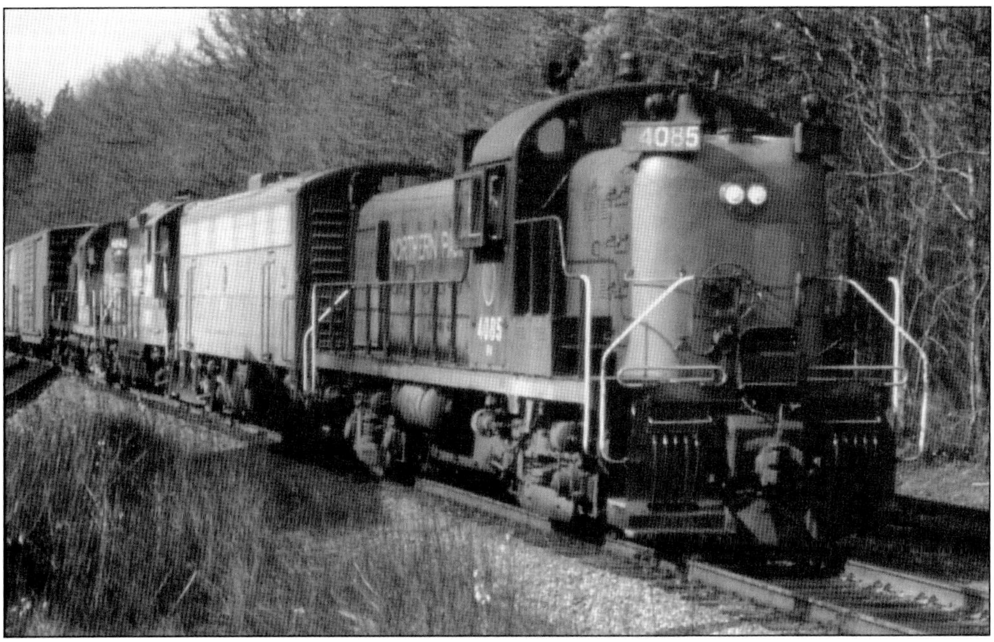

Northern Pacific Heritage. Burlington Northern (BN) westbound train No. 397, which operated daily between Albany, Oregon, and Vancouver, Washington, rolls along the Oregon Electric Branch a few miles east of Hillsboro in March 1973. The locomotive in the lead clings to its classic Northern Pacific paint scheme, three years after Burlington Northern merged the Northern Pacific; Great Northern; Spokane, Portland & Seattle; and Chicago, Burlington & Quincy into one company. (Photograph by Randy Nelson.)

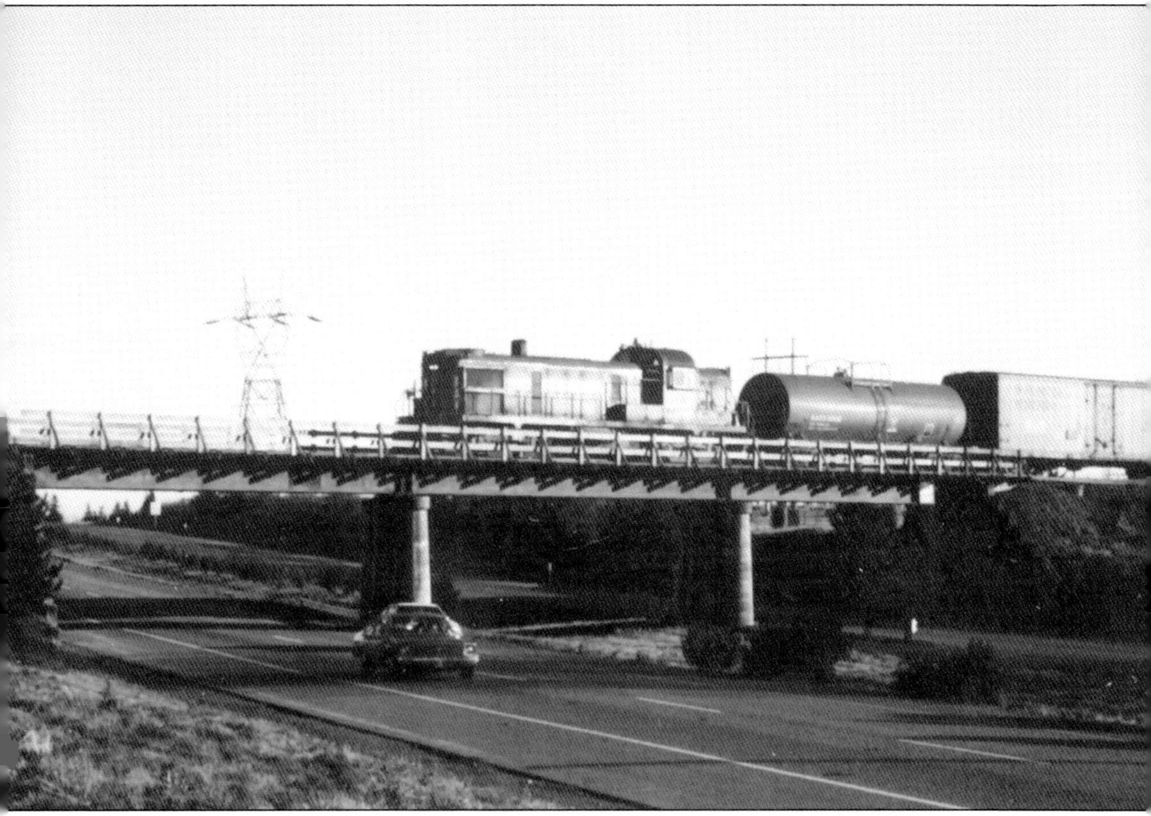

Highway Run. Burlington Northern's southbound *Beaverton Switcher* catches the rays of the morning sun as it crosses Highway 26 in February 1976. The train's locomotive is still dressed in the colors of the Spokane, Portland & Seattle Railway, which was merged into BN in 1970. In 1995, BN's trains were rerouted off this portion of the ex–Oregon Electric line to make way for a light rail system. Not long after that, the railroad's bridge over the highway was removed. (Photograph by Randy Nelson.)

Water, Wyes, Turn-tables, Fuel, Scales, Standard Clocks, Bulletin Boards, Register and Yard Limits	Station Numbers	Car Capacity: Sidings	Car Capacity: Other Tracks	Distance from Forest Grove Junction	Westward — Oregon Electric Ry.—SECOND SUB-DIVISION — TIME TABLE No. 130, October 25, 1959 — STATIONS	Distance from Forest Grove
JYPX	E22			0.0	.....FOREST GROVE JCT.....	10.6
					0.8	
X	F1	11	3E	0.8	..........ORENCO..........	9.8
					2.1	
	F3		7E	2.9	..........SEWELL..........	7.7
					1.6	
P	F5	5	36	4.5	D........HILLSBORO......BO	6.1
					3.4	
	F8		9	7.9	.........CORNELIUS.........	2.7
					2.7	
P	F11		65	10.6	D......FOREST GROVE.......	0.0
					Time Over District Average Speed per Hour	

Eastward 11

Eastward trains are superior to trains of the same class in the opposite direction.

Second Subdivision. The Oregon Electric Railway became a wholly owned subsidiary of Spokane, Portland & Seattle Railway in 1910, and this October 25, 1959, SP&S system lines timetable displays the stations along OE's Second Subdivision. All trains heading to and from Forest Grove on SP&S-subsidiary Oregon Electric Railway's Second Subdivision passed through Hillsboro, which was roughly midway on the 10.6-mile-long subdivision. The "Second Sub" began at Forest Grove Junction, 4.4 miles south of Bowers Junction on the OE's mainline, and went to Forest Grove via Hillsboro and Cornelius. (Collection of D.C. Jesse Burkhardt.)

Water, Wyes, Turn-tables, Fuel, Scales, Standard Clocks, Bul.-Bds., Register, Yard Limits	Station Numbers	Car Capacity: Sidings	Car Capacity: Other Tracks	Westward — SECOND CLASS 231 Freight Daily Ex. Saturday	Distance from Portland	S. P. & S. Ry., PORTLAND DIVISION—Third Sub-Division — TIME TABLE No. 130, October 25, 1959 — STATIONS	Distance from Vernonia	Eastward — SECOND CLASS 230 Freight
PXJ	A10			L10.15PM	10.0	N......UNITED JCT...... UJ	38.5	A 5.00AM
						1.0		
	U11A		31W	10.19	11.0	..........BAN SPUR..........	37.5	4.55
						0.7		
P	U12		4	10.22	11.7	........BURLINGTON........	36.8	4.52
						2.9		
P	U15		8W	10.31	14.6	Auto. Blk. .....TUNNEL SPUR.......	33.9	4.42
						2.5		
JXPR	U17		25 5E	A10.40PM	17.1	DN......BOWERS JCT.......BJ	31.4	L 4.30AM
						4.8		
P	U22	47	44		21.9	D......NORTH PLAINS....NP	26.6	
						1.4		
	U23		24		23.3	..........VADIS..........	25.2	
						2.2		
	U26		11E		25.5	..........CHRISTIE..........	23.0	
						6.2		
P	U32	24	7		31.7	.........MANNING.........	16.8	
						7.1		
P	U39	20	8E		38.8	..........TOPHILL..........	9.7	
						4.3		
P	U43	29			43.1	..........BRAUN..........	5.4	
						5.4		
BYK XPR	U49		Yard		48.5	D........VERNONIA.......VN	0.0	
								Daily Ex. Mon.
				0.25 17.0		Time Over District Average Speed per Hour		0.30 14.2

EASTWARD TRAINS ARE SUPERIOR TO TRAINS OF THE SAME CLASS IN THE OPPOSITE DIRECTION
At Bowers Junction all westward trains to and eastward trains from O.E. Ry. First Sub-division will register by Ticket per Rule 83(A).
Eastward trains from Third Sub-division will not register.

Third Subdivision. SP&S Railway's Portland Division/Third Subdivision timetable from October 25, 1959, shows the route of the Vernonia Branch, which went northwest from United Junction, about 10 miles west of Portland, to where the tracks came to an end in Vernonia, 38.5 miles away. Note the schedule for the way freight that operated on this line from United Junction to Bowers Junction, "daily except Saturday." For more than three decades, Vernonia was an important station for the railroad because a large Oregon-American Lumber Company sawmill located there in 1924. The sawmill closed in 1957, however, and the line's future suddenly turned dark. With the mill gone and not much other business on the branch west of Banks, the portion of the SP&S "Third Sub" between Vernonia and Banks was torn out in the early 1970s. (Collection of D.C. Jesse Burkhardt.)

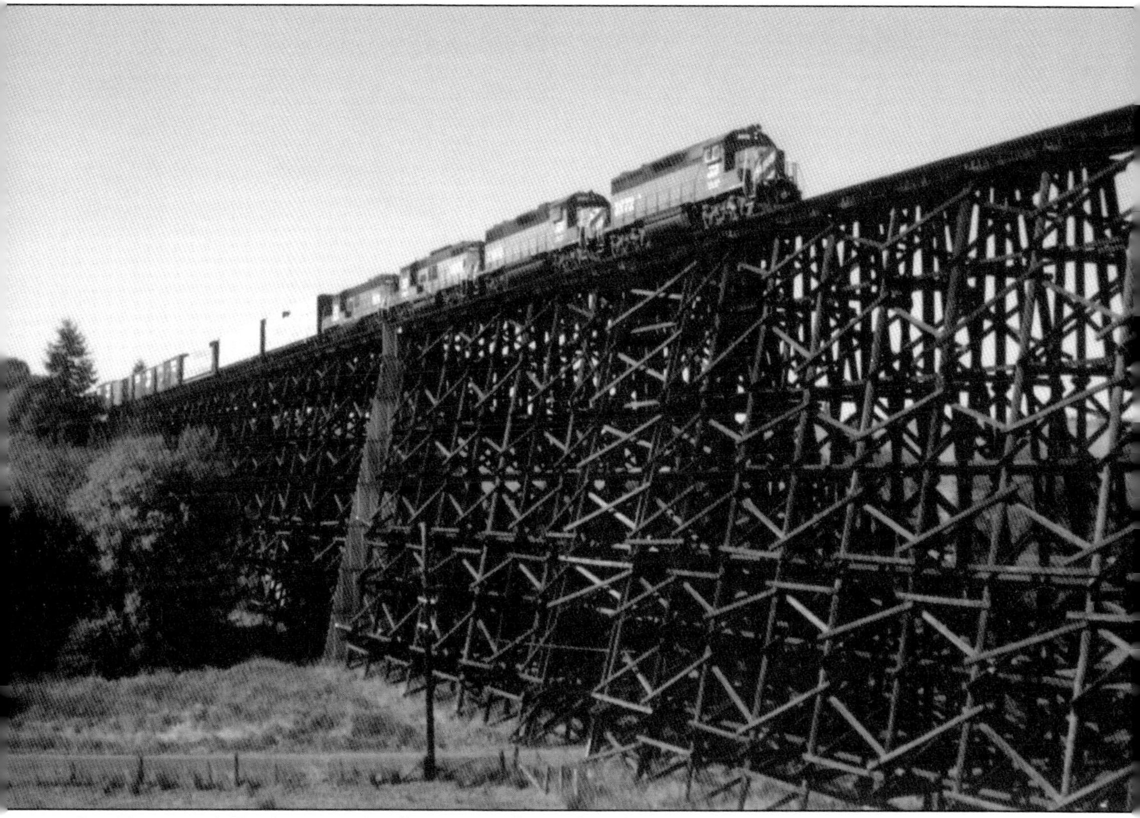

SKY BRIDGE. A Burlington Northern mixed merchandise train on its way to Pasco, Washington, crosses the Holcomb Creek trestle on Cornelius Pass near Bowers Junction in October 1986. The iconic timber trestle was built by United Railways in 1905 and is 1,168 feet long and about 90 feet high. The freight train crossing the tall bridge originated in Albany. (Photograph by Randy Nelson.)

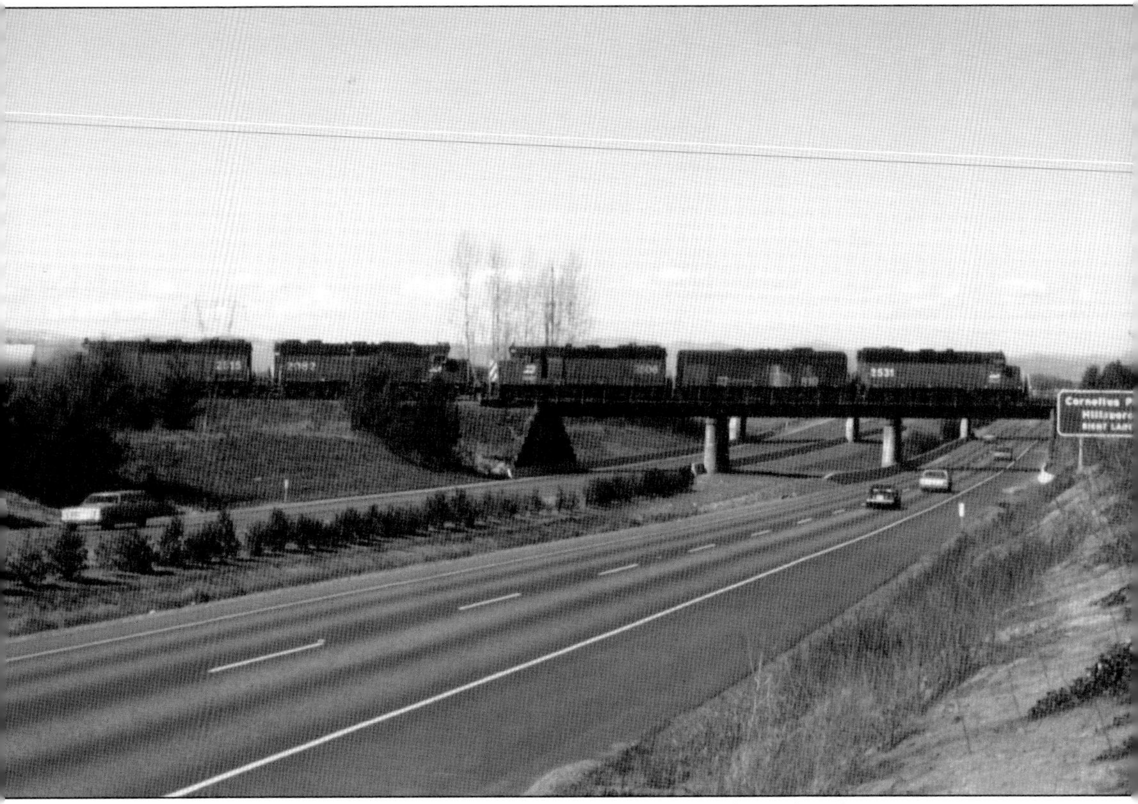

Cornelius Pass. Behind five locomotives, a Burlington Northern freight train powers across Highway 26 at Hillsboro as it heads northeast to Pasco, Washington, in April 1980. The impressive lineup of locomotives was necessitated by the relatively steep grades of Cornelius Pass, which waited just a few miles ahead, as well as the heavy tonnage of these long, daily trains. Note the highway sign advising motorists of the Cornelius Pass exit. (Photograph by Randy Nelson.)

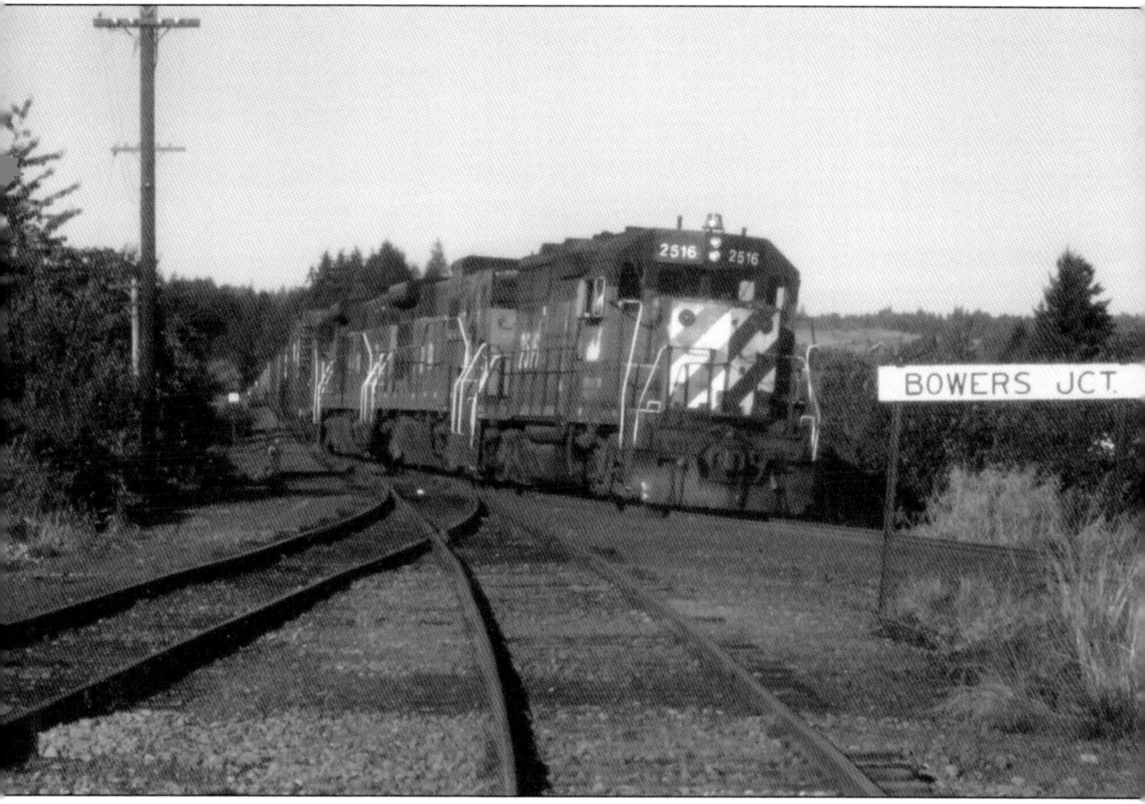

THROUGH THE JUNCTION. A long freight train led by Burlington Northern GP35 No. 2516 cuts south onto the Oregon Electric Branch at Bowers Junction in August 1988 on its daily run from Vancouver, Washington, to Albany, Oregon. Albany is another 79 miles from the junction. In the foreground are the tracks of the Vernonia Branch, which goes west for 10 miles from here to reach Banks. (Photograph by Randy Nelson.)

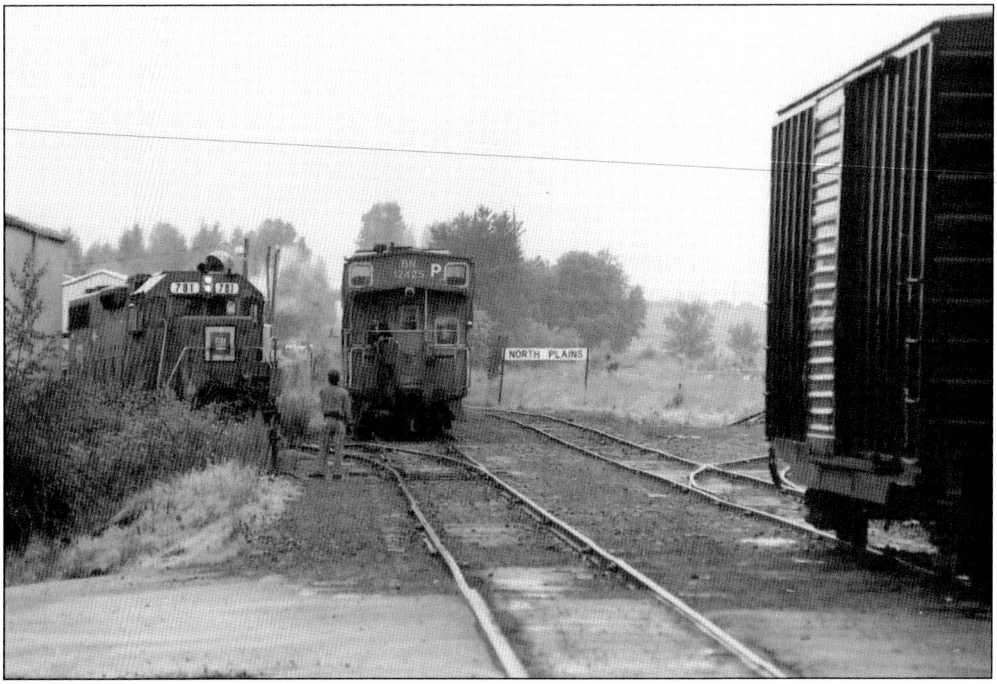

Three Times a Week. Burlington Northern's *North Plains Local*, which operated three times a week in the early 1990s, switches in North Plains with leased GP38 No. 781 and BN caboose No. 12425 on June 20, 1991. In the early 1990s, BN interchanged cars with the Port of Tillamook Bay Railroad in North Plains, and an agricultural business, Van Dyke Grain Elevators, Inc., took inbound carloads of cottonseed at this location. After completing switching duties here, the train and its crew will head east to Bowers Junction and from there cut south to the crew's home base in Beaverton to tie up for the night. (Photographs by D.C. Jesse Burkhardt.)

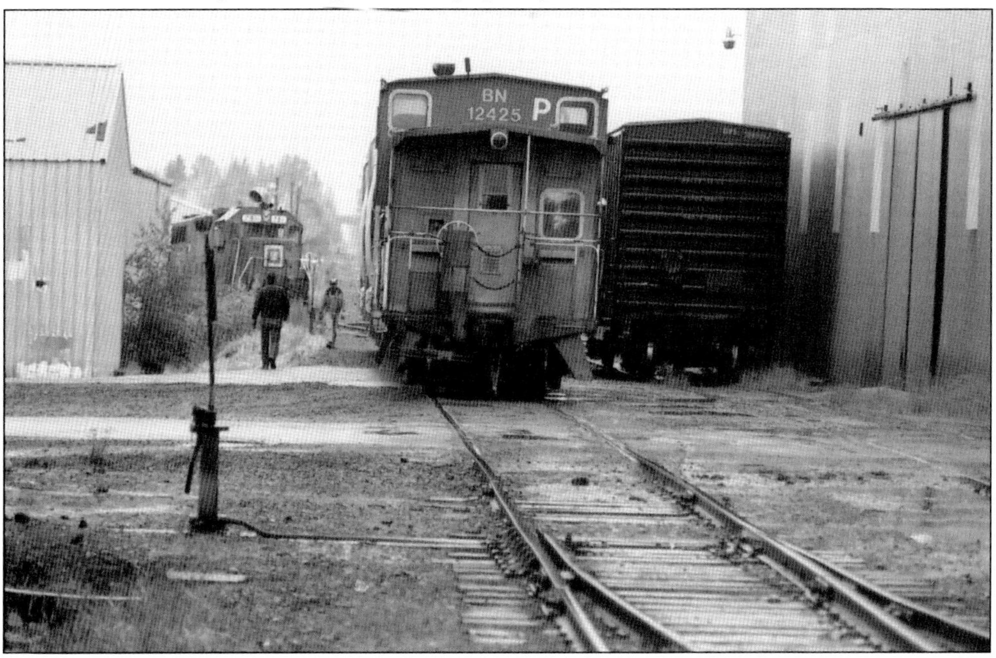

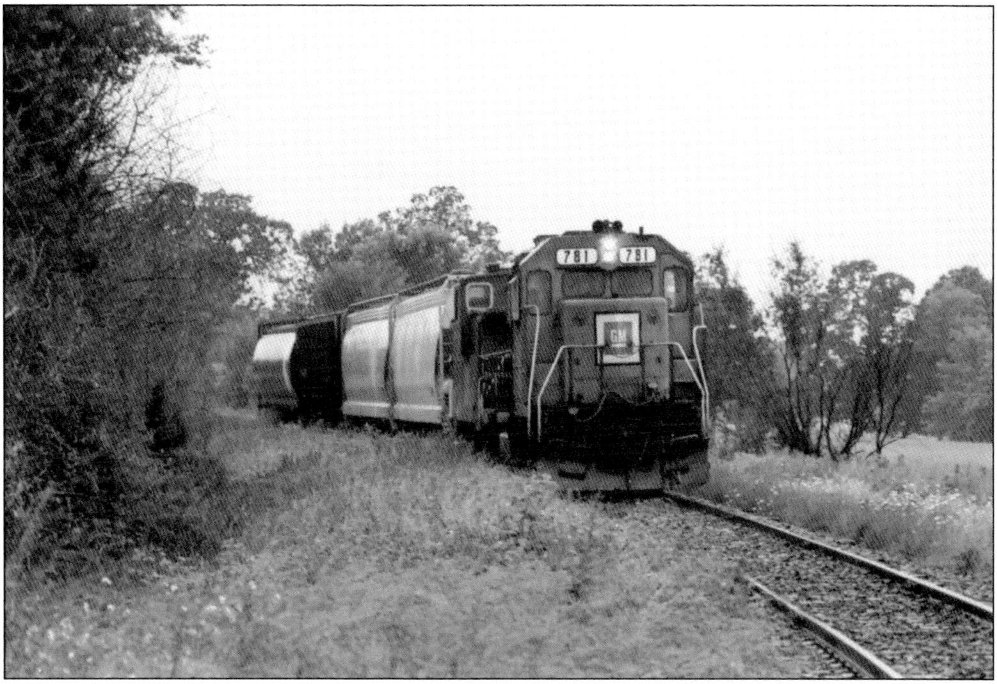

COMING AND GOING. The *North Plains Local* comes around a corner a mile east of North Plains as it heads to Bowers Junction with four covered hoppers in tow on June 20, 1991. At Bowers Junction, five miles from North Plains, the train will cut onto the mainline of the Oregon Electric Branch and head south to Beaverton, where the freight cars will be left on a siding at St. Marys Junction for pickup by one of BN's through trains operating between Albany, Oregon, and Pasco, Washington. In the photograph below, the short train has just crossed Jackson School Road north of Hillsboro and is slowly pulling away into the foggy distance, running at about 10 miles per hour on a stretch of aging track that is truly in need of some tender loving maintenance. (Photographs by D.C. Jesse Burkhardt.)

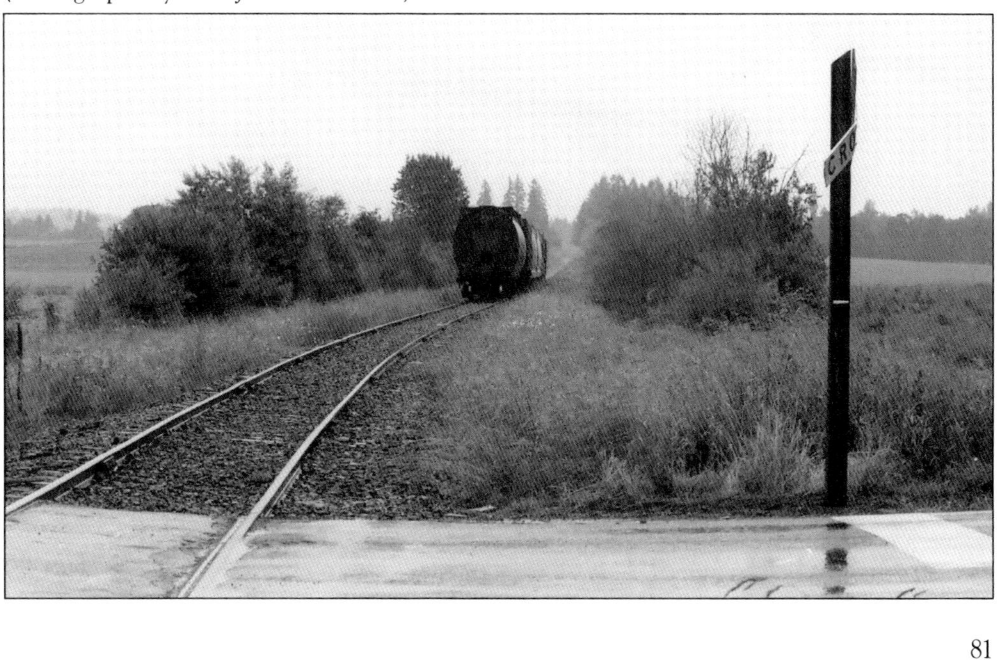

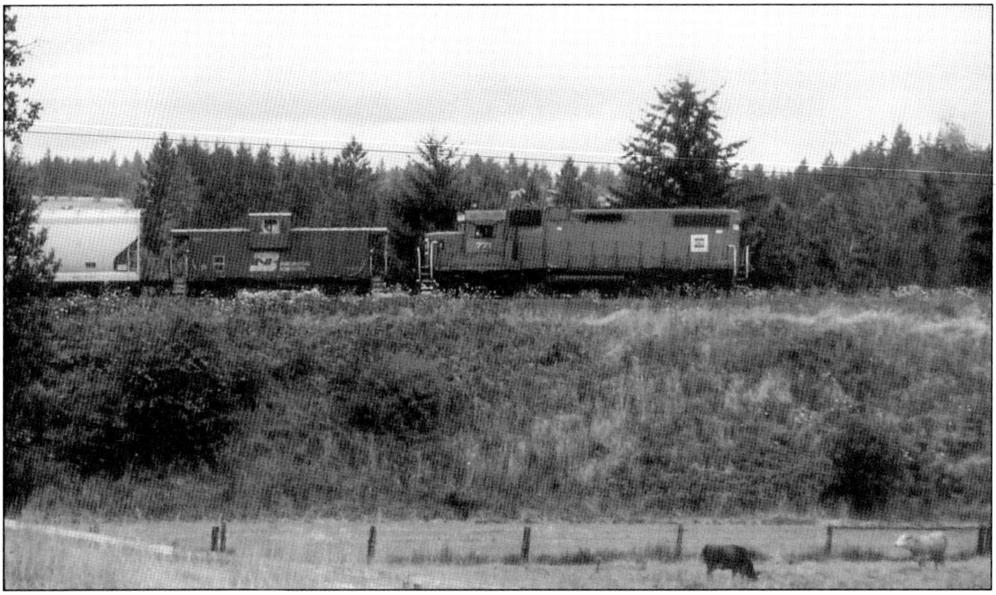

ALMOST DONE FOR THE DAY. After completing the day's switching chores on July 26, 1990, Burlington Northern's *North Plains Local* rolls east through Helvetia on the Vernonia Branch behind leased General Motors GP38-2 No. 771. Just one mile ahead, the short train will reach Bowers Junction and proceed south for another 10 miles on BN's Oregon Electric Branch to the train's home station at Beaverton. (Photograph by D.C. Jesse Burkhardt.)

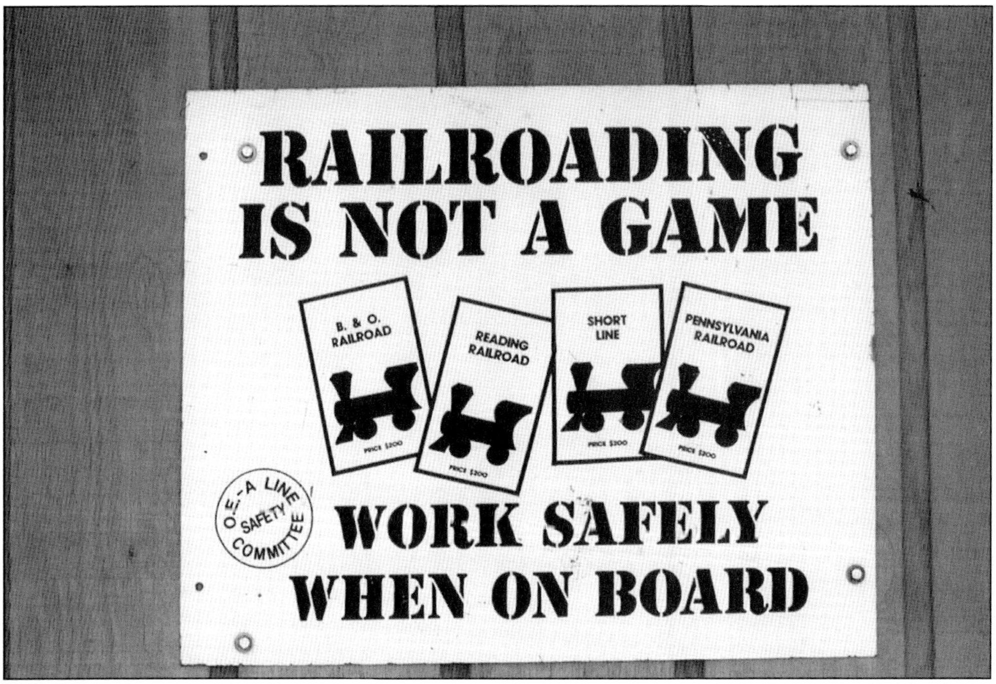

FOCUS ON SAFETY. A sign attached to Burlington Northern's station at Beaverton in August 1993 cleverly displays a message tied to cards in a game of Monopoly as part of a safety awareness campaign. BN's Oregon Electric–Astoria Line Safety Committee created the sign. (Photograph by D.C. Jesse Burkhardt.)

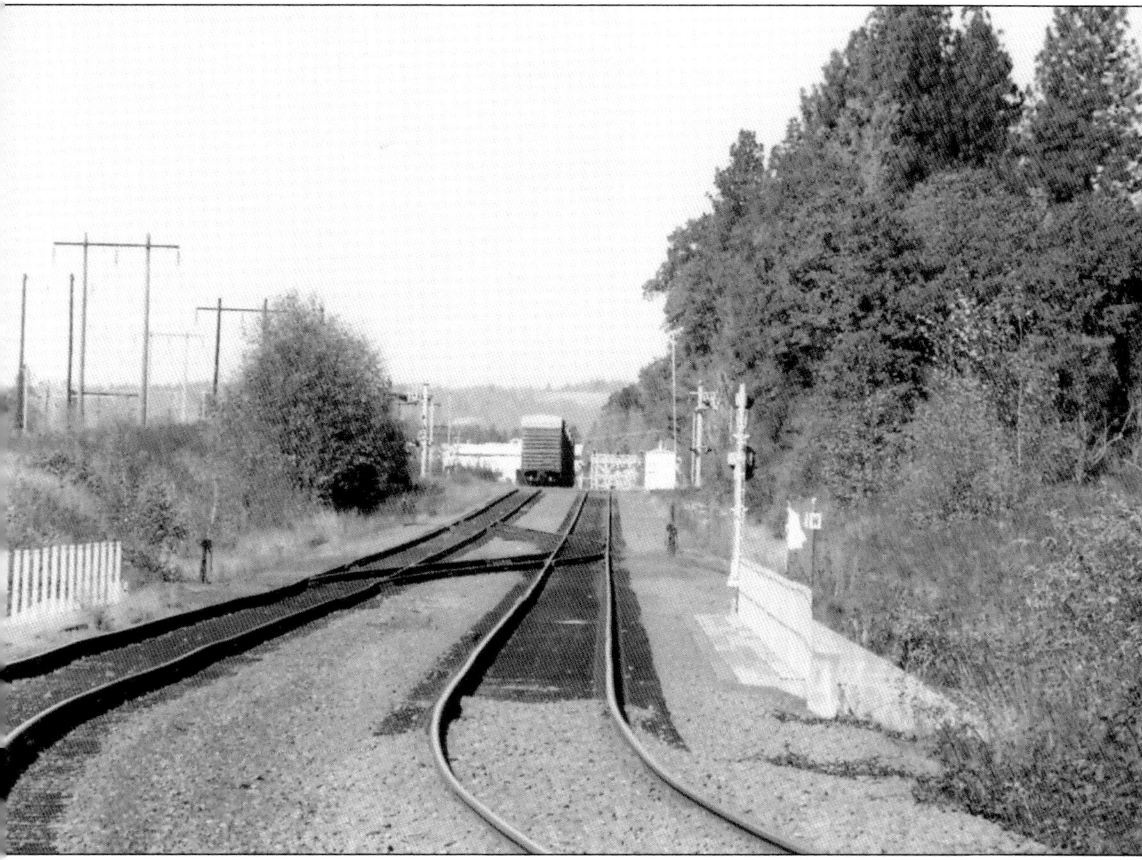

Grand Trunk at St. Marys. A cut of Grand Trunk Western boxcars wait on the siding in this view looking north along the Burlington Northern mainline at St. Marys in September 1995. This stretch of track was built in 1984 to allow BN to connect with SP's Tillamook Branch, because the nearby city of Beaverton wanted BN's mainline routed away from its downtown as part of an urban redevelopment project. To compensate, a deal was worked out that granted BN trackage rights over the Tillamook Branch between St. Marys (MP 756.9) and Greton (MP 751.9). However, just 10 years later, in January 1995, the BN mainline a mile north of this location was severed to make way for a new light rail system that took more of BN's trackage in the area. BN was again forced to move, this time to SP's adjacent Valley Line. From St. Marys, BN also operated a short industrial spur to a General Motors auto parts warehouse about two miles away. Service to the GM facility continued until the plant closed in 2010. (Photograph by D.C. Jesse Burkhardt.)

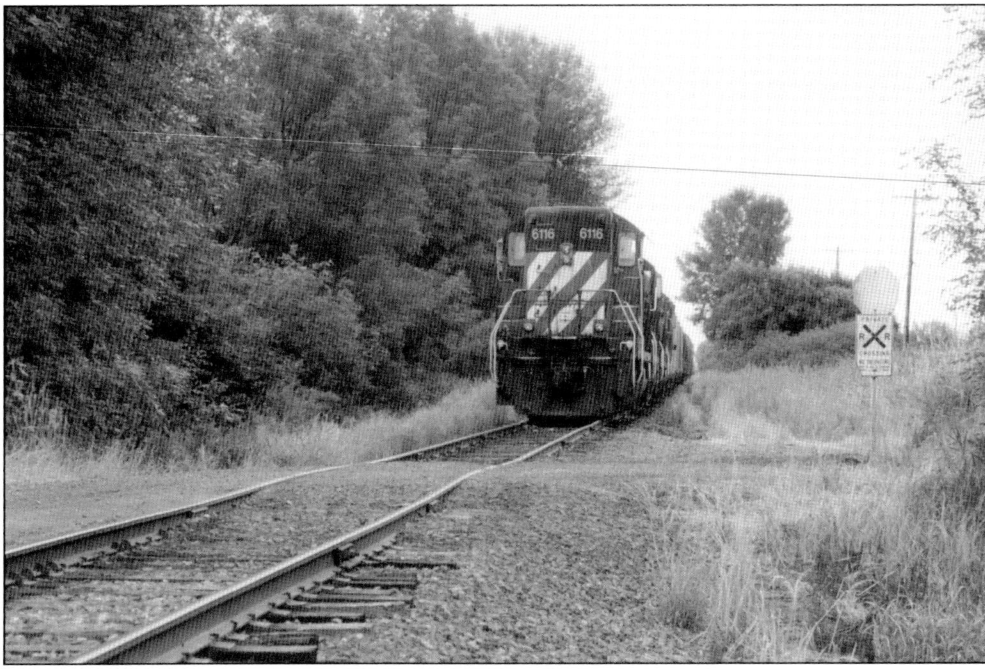

Staging at Banks. Until a December 2007 storm knocked out the Port of Tillamook Bay's tracks, trains operating between Hillsboro and Tillamook were routinely staged on the mainline directly west of Banks. After Tillamook-bound trains were assembled, the locomotives were shut down until a rested crew arrived to haul the freight cars to shippers along the line, primarily at Garibaldi and Tillamook. In the photograph above, in July 2005, a long line of mixed hoppers, lumber flatcars, and boxcars is headed by four SD9s, with the POTB's ex-BN SD9 No. 6116—still in its BN paint scheme—in the lead. Below, on September 3, 2007, the lead locomotive on a westbound is POTB No. 101, an ex-SP GP9 painted to resemble one of the dairy cows so familiar to the Tillamook area. Tillamook is home to the Tillamook Cheese Factory, and carloads of feed for the area's herds of cows were once a key commodity moving over the line. (Photographs by D.C. Jesse Burkhardt.)

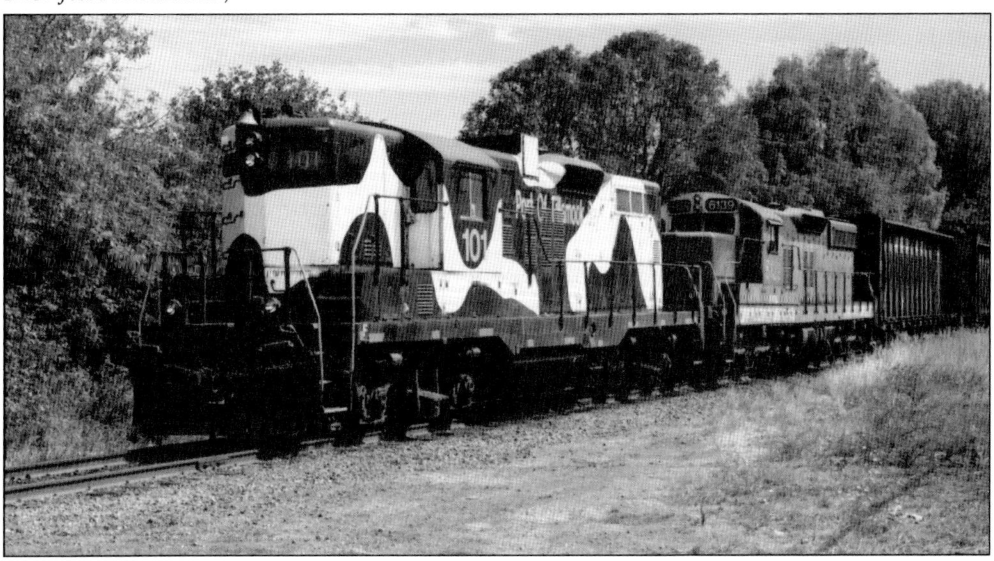

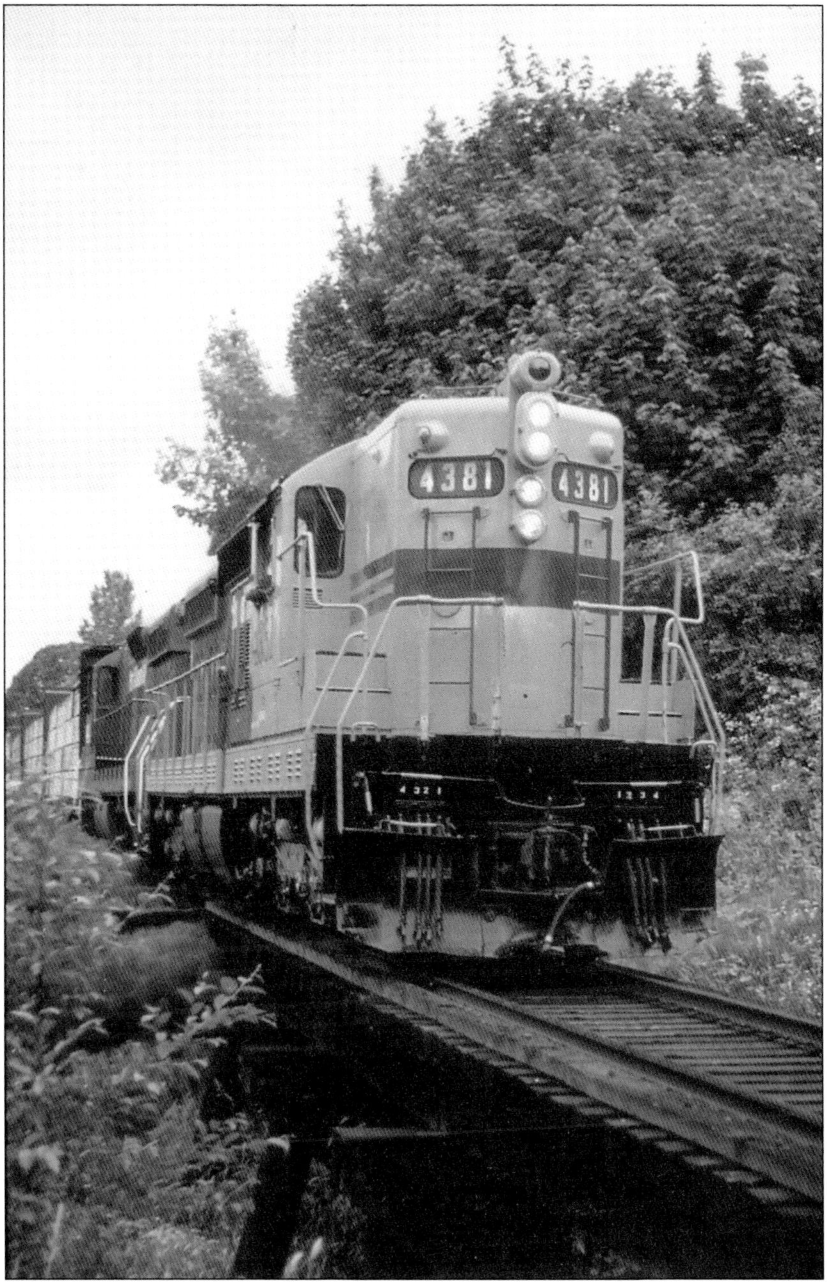

LUMBER FROM THE COAST. An eastbound Port of Tillamook Bay Railroad freight out of Tillamook, headed by ex–Southern Pacific SD9 No. 4381, arrives in Banks in June 1989 with a cut of lumber cars. The freight cars will be interchanged with Southern Pacific Railroad at Mahan, a siding just a mile west of the SP depot in Hillsboro. SP had operated trains on this line since 1915, but in May 1986, the POTB reached a trackage rights agreement with SP that allowed the POTB to operate over SP's Tillamook Branch from Tillamook to Mahan. On February 1, 1990, less than a year after this photograph was taken, the POTB paid SP $2.9 million to purchase outright 85 miles of the line from Tillamook to Schefflin, an agricultural center about halfway between Banks and Hillsboro. (Photograph by D.C. Jesse Burkhardt.)

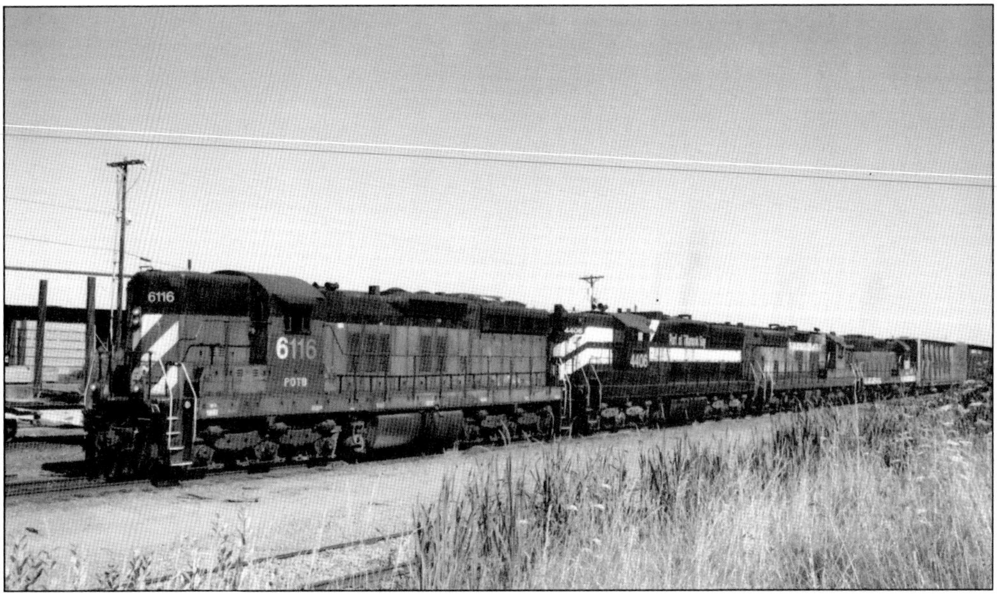

SD9s on Parade. A freight train rumbles through the rail yard at Banks in the photograph above, led by four of the Port of Tillamook Bay's 1950s-era SD9s (ex-BN No. 6116, ex-SP No. 4406, ex-SP No. 4414, and ex-BN No. 6139) in August 2005. Below, a short westbound train moves empties through the rolling landscape at Banks on the ex-SP&S Vernonia Branch on December 16, 1988, after interchanging cars with BN in North Plains. Engineers were not allowed to exceed 10 miles per hour on the Vernonia Branch, a neglected feeder line built mostly with 75-pound rail. Although this segment of track is still in active use, the portion of the branchline that once extended beyond Banks to Vernonia and Keasey was removed decades ago. The train, headed by POTB No. 4381, is running parallel to SP's Tillamook Branch. (Photographs by D.C. Jesse Burkhardt.)

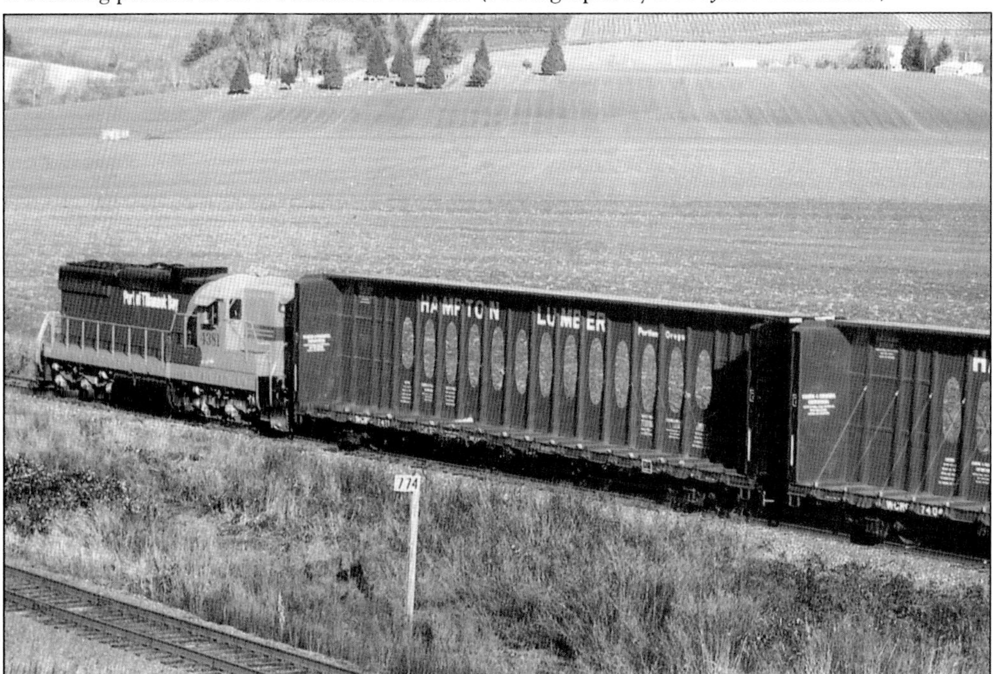

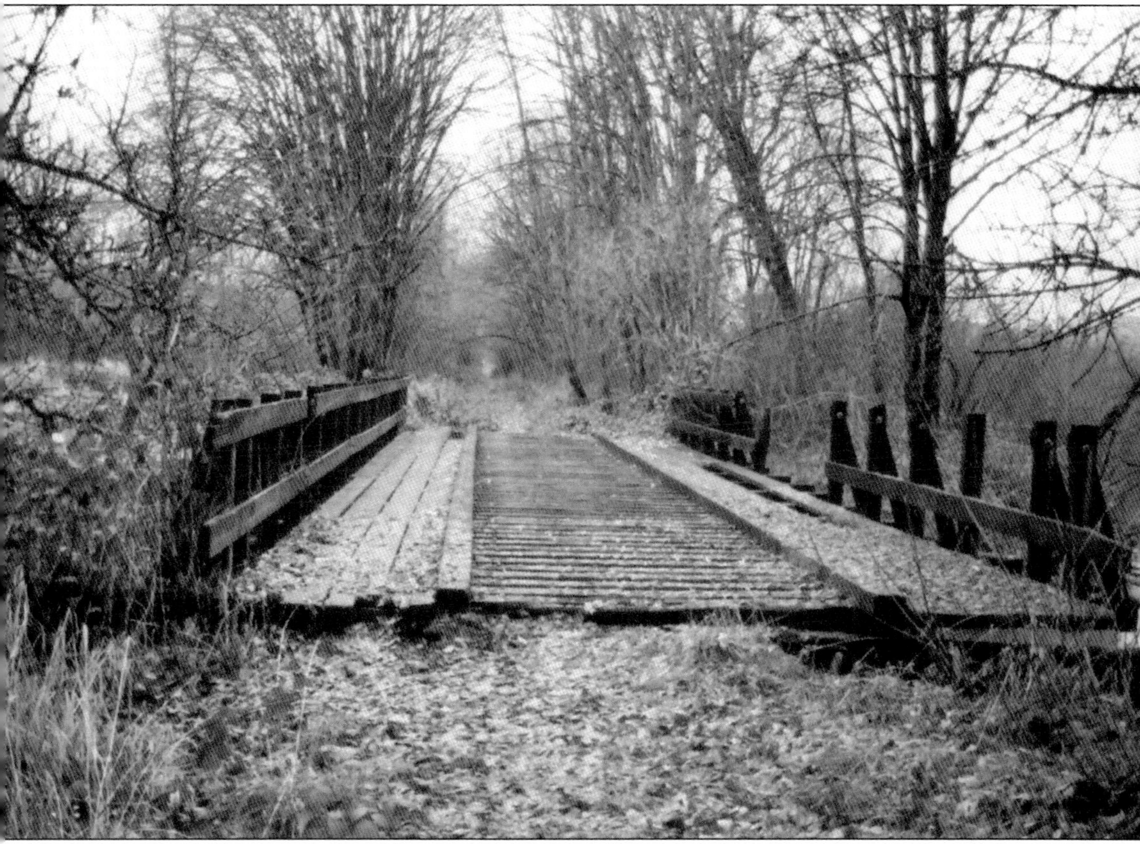

No Trains Today. A decaying, moss-covered bridge is all that remains of this portion of the former Spokane, Portland & Seattle Railway's Vernonia Branch just outside of Banks in this view from December 2009. Most of the Vernonia Branch, which once stretched as far north as Keasey, 31 miles from Banks, was abandoned in the 1970s. Oregon State Parks subsequently opened a trail along 21 miles of the old railroad right of way between Banks and Vernonia; the popular trail is formally known as the Banks-Vernonia State Trail. The ex–Southern Pacific Tillamook Branch, which ran directly parallel to the SP&S line for the five miles between Banks and Manning, is faintly visible to the left of the bridge. (Photograph by D.C. Jesse Burkhardt.)

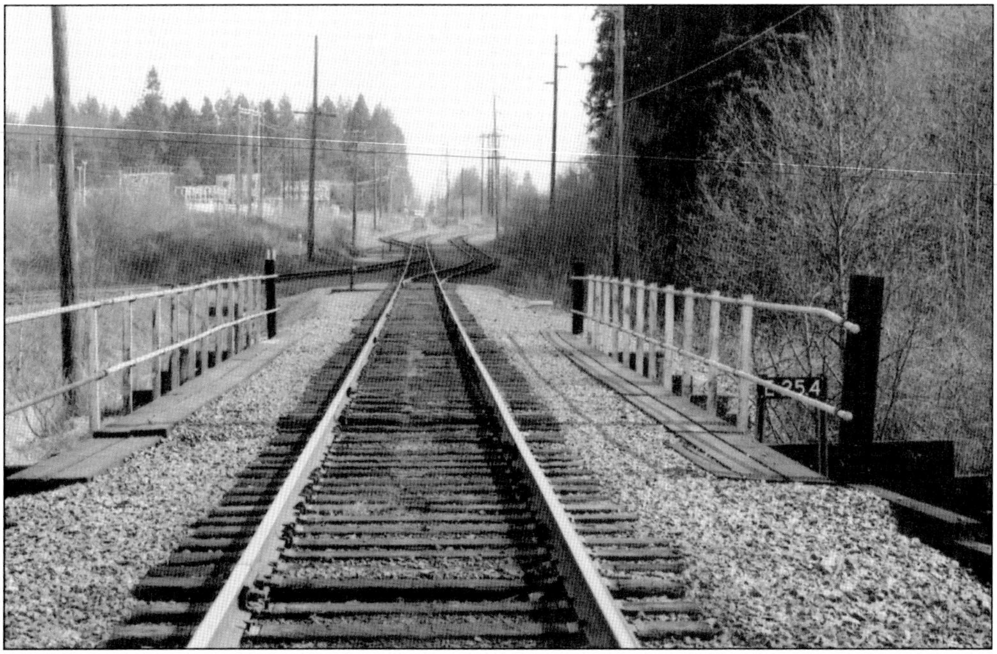

You Would Not Recognize It. The photograph above captures the scene looking east from MP 25.4 on Burlington Northern's Oregon Electric Branch at St. Marys Junction in 1995. Although tracks still exist at this location, the orientation is completely different in 2014; the tracks switching off to the right have been taken out of service and severed, while the track where the photographer was standing in 1995 is now abandoned and overgrown with weeds, as seen in the photograph below, taken on January 19, 2014. Straight ahead, a two-track light rail network, complete with overhead catenary, has replaced what was once a cargo route, and freight trains no longer move through this area. (Above, courtesy of the Library of Congress; below, photograph by D.C. Jesse Burkhardt.)

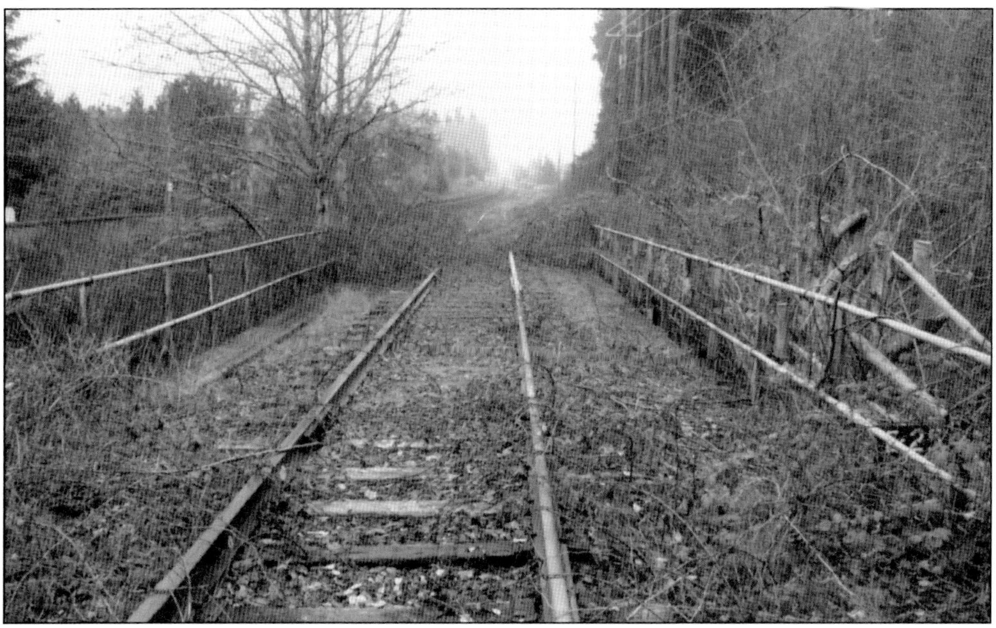

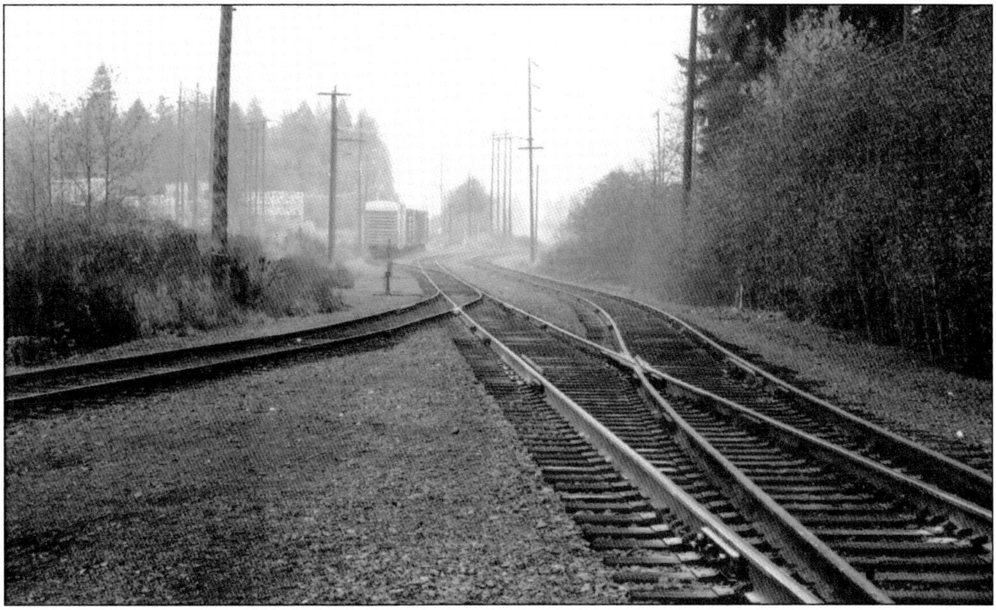

Changes at St. Marys Junction. These two photographs show another view of BN's St. Marys Junction, just a mile north of Beaverton, where the BN line connected with SP's Tillamook Branch. In the photograph above, taken in 1995, BN's Oregon Electric mainline cuts south from the junction toward Beaverton, while a string of boxcars rests on the track to the left. The boxcars were probably headed to the nearby General Motors auto parts warehouse. In the photograph below, taken nearly 20 years later in January 2014, and BN's once-busy junction has been abandoned. The freight corridor that continued east from here is now used solely for light rail transit operations, while the track to Beaverton has been removed. (Above, courtesy of the Library of Congress; below, photograph by D.C. Jesse Burkhardt.)

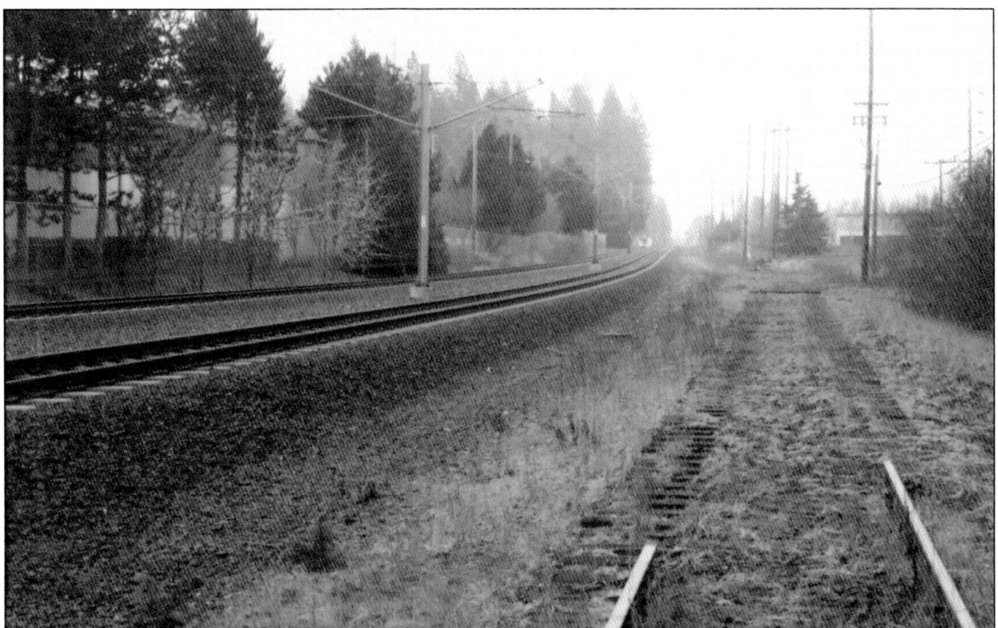

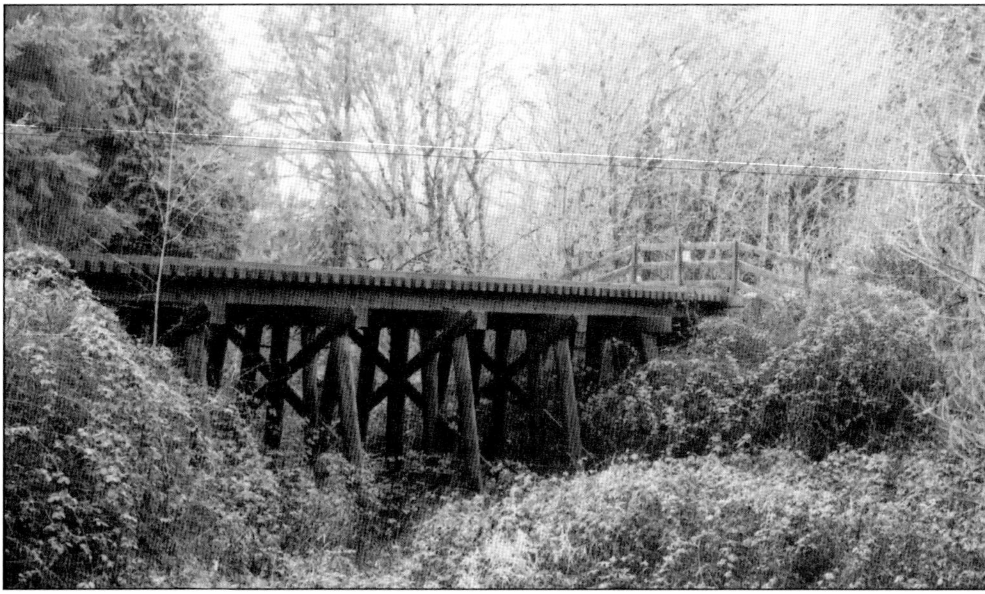

Fenced Off. This 1995 scene looks southwest at a trestle over Orenco Creek on Burlington Northern's mainline a few miles east of Hillsboro. The tracks have been blocked off by a wooden fence, as this segment of freight trackage was being readied for transformation into a light rail system. The last freight train ran on this stretch of track on December 31, 1994. (Courtesy of the Library of Congress.)

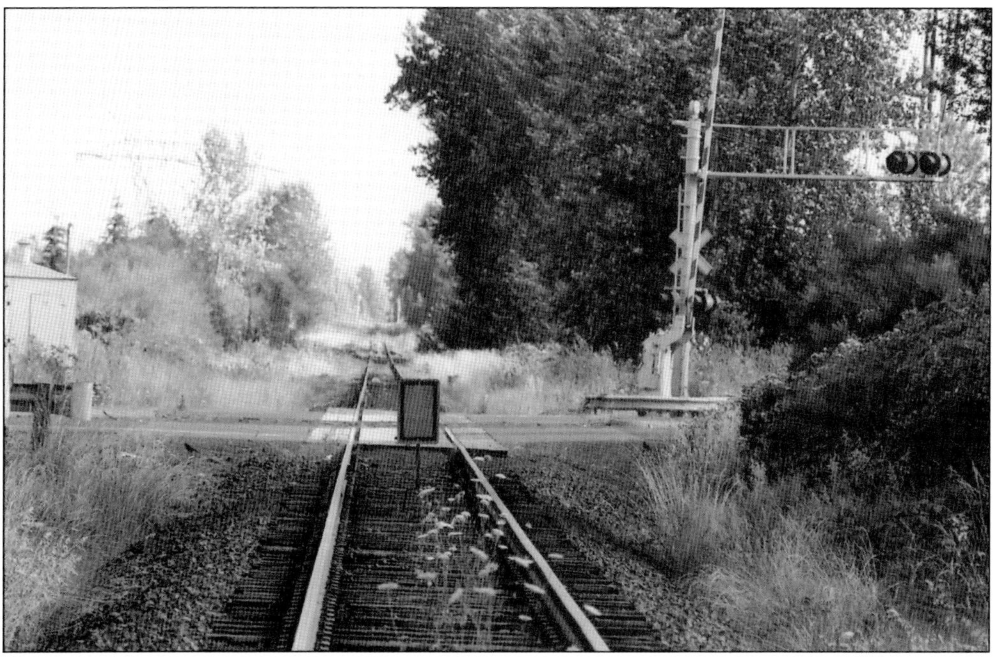

End of the Line. In September 1995, a railroad stop sign just west of Cornelius Pass Road in the Orenco area of Hillsboro indicates that the tracks beyond this point are out of service. This part of the former Oregon Electric mainline was lost when portions of Burlington Northern's right of way were taken to make way for light rail in the Portland metro area. (Photograph by D.C. Jesse Burkhardt.)

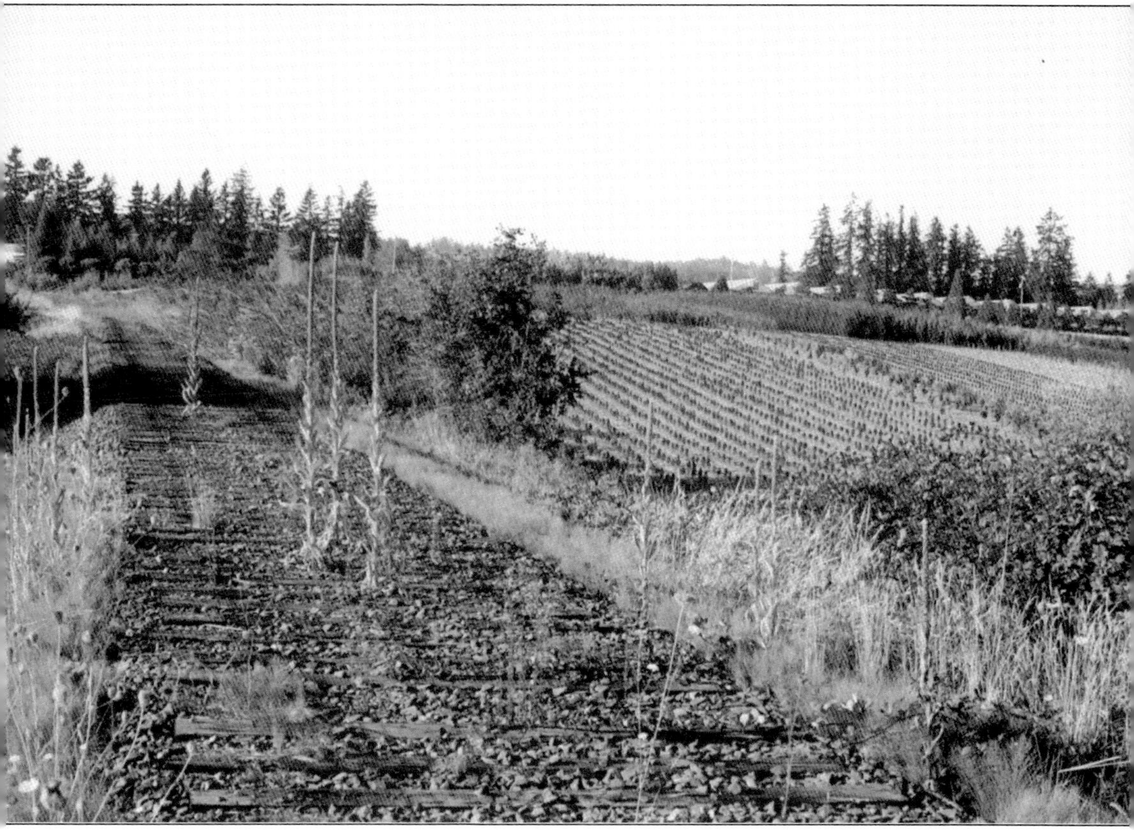

Ties and Weeds. It is the summer of 2008, and trains no longer pass through the rural community known as Bendemeer, just north of Hillsboro, on this stretch of what was once Burlington Northern's mainline between Eugene and Portland. Now only weeds remain where long freight trains once rolled on a daily basis. (Photograph by D.C. Jesse Burkhardt.)

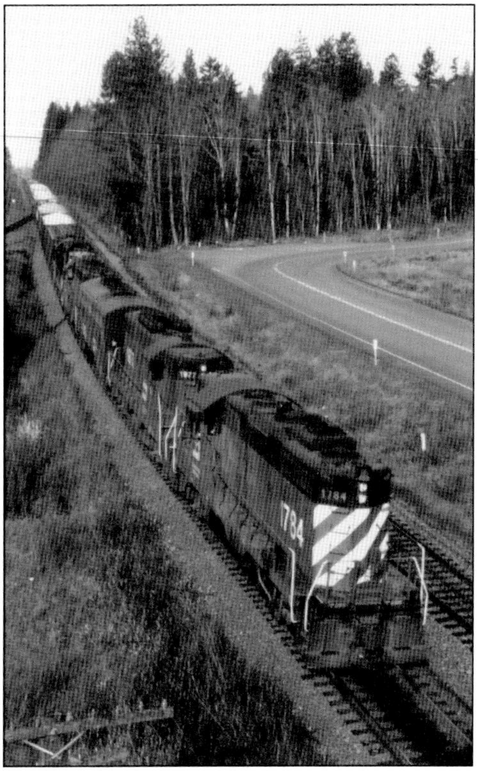

Differences of the Decades. In the photograph at left, a long, Vancouver-bound freight train is about to pass under the Murray Road overpass at the west end of the Burlington Northern siding at Beaverton in a glimpse back at February 1976. In the photograph below, at the same location 26 years later, the freight trains headed by multiple diesel locomotives are long gone as a light rail transit train powered by electricity glides along in October 2002 with two carloads of passengers. To mitigate the loss of its freight corridor, BN and Southern Pacific inked a trackage rights agreement in 1994 that allowed BN to route its Willamette Valley traffic onto a portion of SP's heavy-duty Valley Line—from East Portland (MP 770.3) to Labish (MP 721.3), just north of Salem. (Photographs by Randy Nelson.)

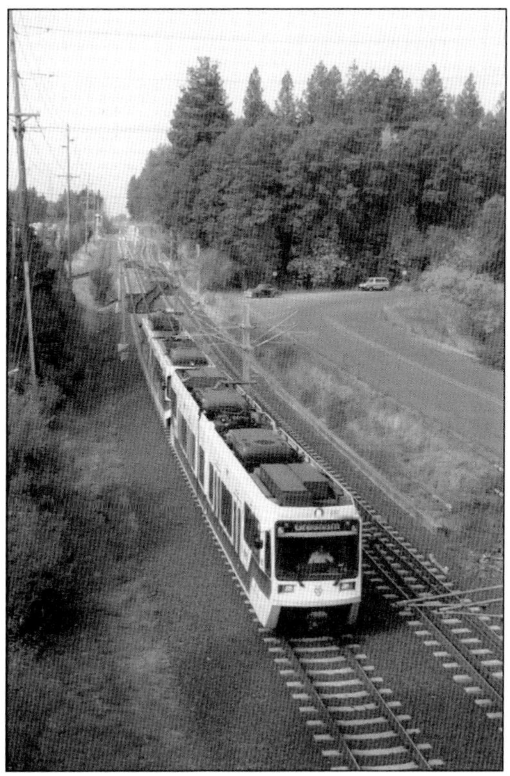

Four

CONNECTED COMMUNITIES

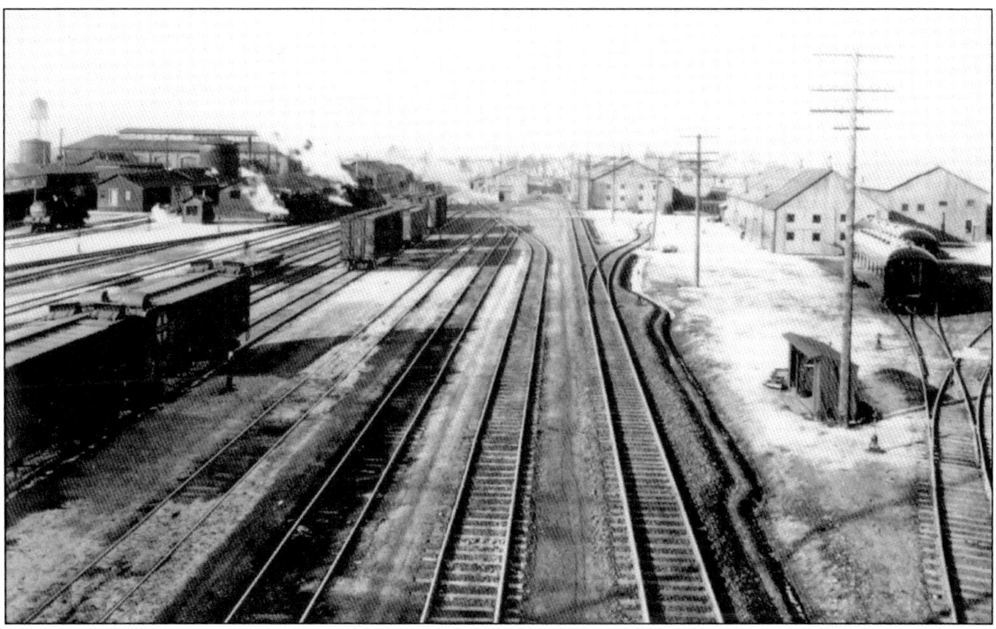

CRITICAL CONNECTION. No nearby community was more important to Hillsboro's growth than Portland, and in this 1924 look at Southern Pacific's Brooklyn Yard in Portland, a variety of activity is visible. On the left, locomotives steam away on a service track, while Santa Fe reefers and general service boxcars rest on another track. To the right, two passenger coaches await servicing or repairs. Most of the buildings in this photograph are long gone. (Collection of Curtis Culp.)

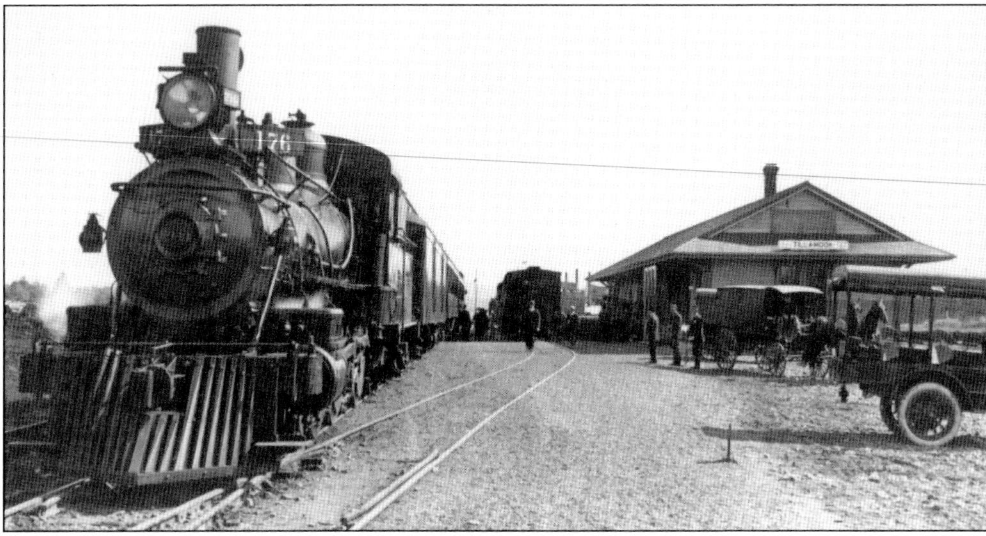

Outpost at the Coast. Tillamook and Hillsboro will always have a historic link, as the Pacific Railway & Navigation line that finally connected Tillamook, seen above, with the rest of the state's railroad network originated in Hillsboro. The route linking the two towns opened on November 10, 1911. Before reaching Tillamook (MP 855.8), westbound trains out of Hillsboro (MP 764.9) first arrived at Wheeler (below), at MP 833.6, twenty-two miles north of Tillamook. (The mileposts signified the distance from PR&N-successor Southern Pacific's headquarters in San Francisco, California.) In the scene below from 1915, Wheeler awaits the next train with one of the latest automobile models parked outside the station. The Wheeler Lumber Company mill in the background—note the locomotive switching the plant—is now gone, as is the depot. (Both, collection of Curtis Culp.)

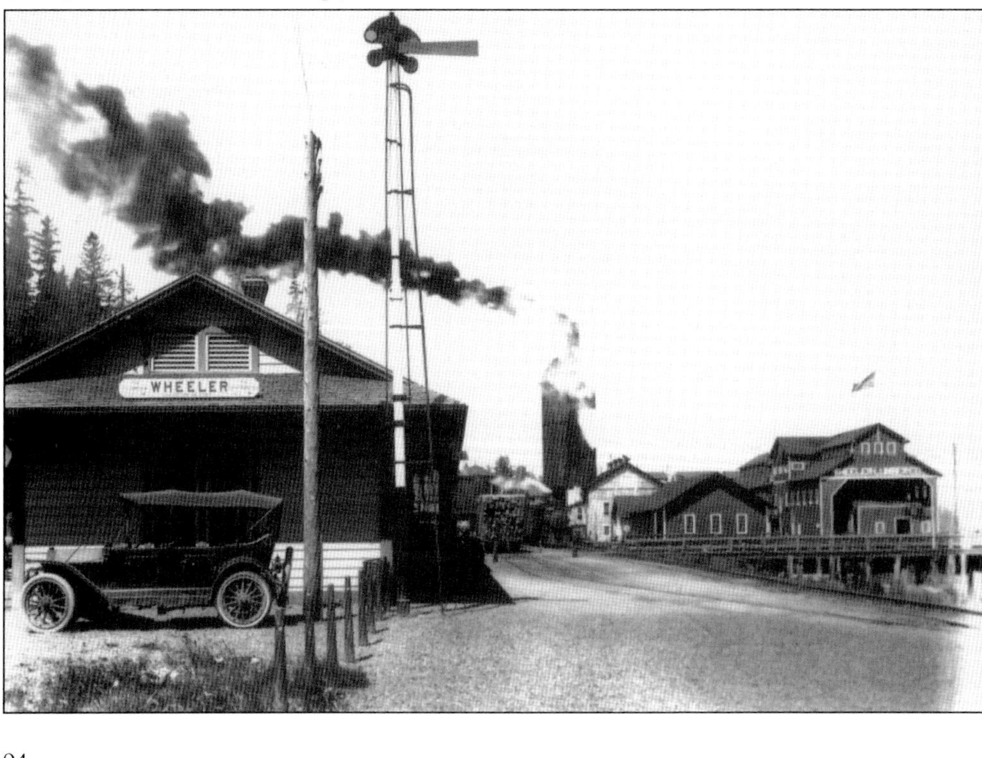

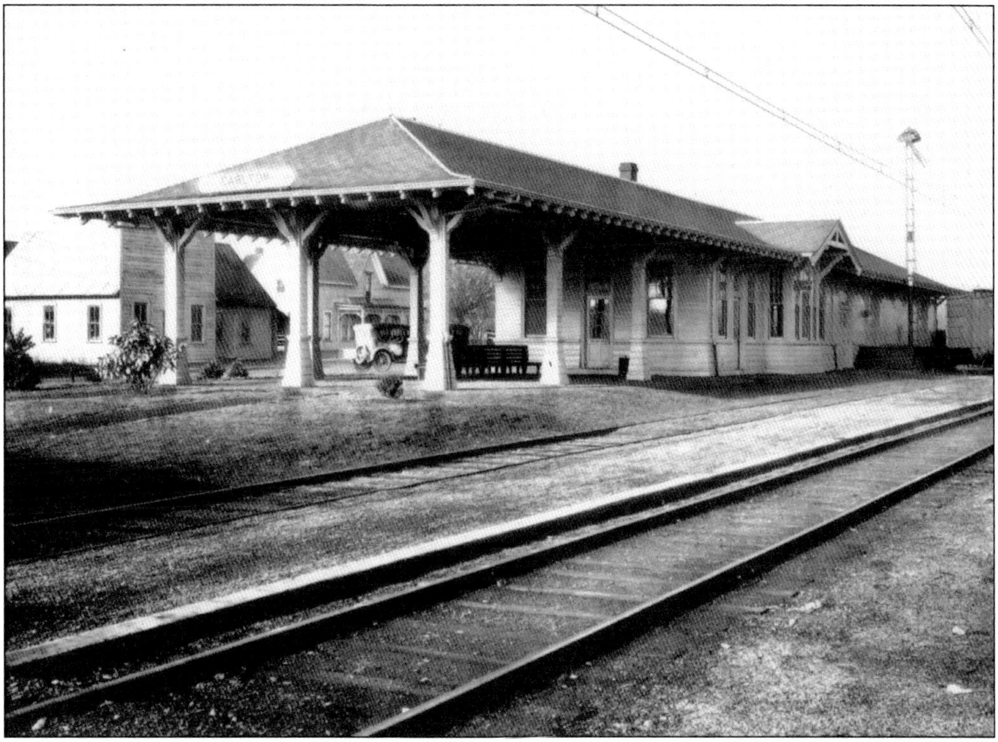

SOUTHBOUND STATIONS. Southern Pacific's depot at Carlton is seen above in 1920. Carlton (MP 742.2) is a small agricultural community located just 22 miles south of Hillsboro. Note the electrical wires above the tracks; in this era, the station was a stop on SP's "Red Electric" interurban passenger route. In the photograph below, a train has stopped to collect passengers at the McMinnville depot (MP 734.9) about 30 miles south of Hillsboro. Tracks reached Hillsboro in 1871, but soon after that, financial difficulties forced the railroad to put construction on hiatus for several years, and steel rails did not arrive in McMinnville until 1879. In 1985, Hillsboro lost its direct rail connection with Carlton, McMinnville, and points south when SP abandoned a 12-mile-long segment of the West Side Branch from Carlton to just north of Gaston. (Both, collection of Curtis Culp.)

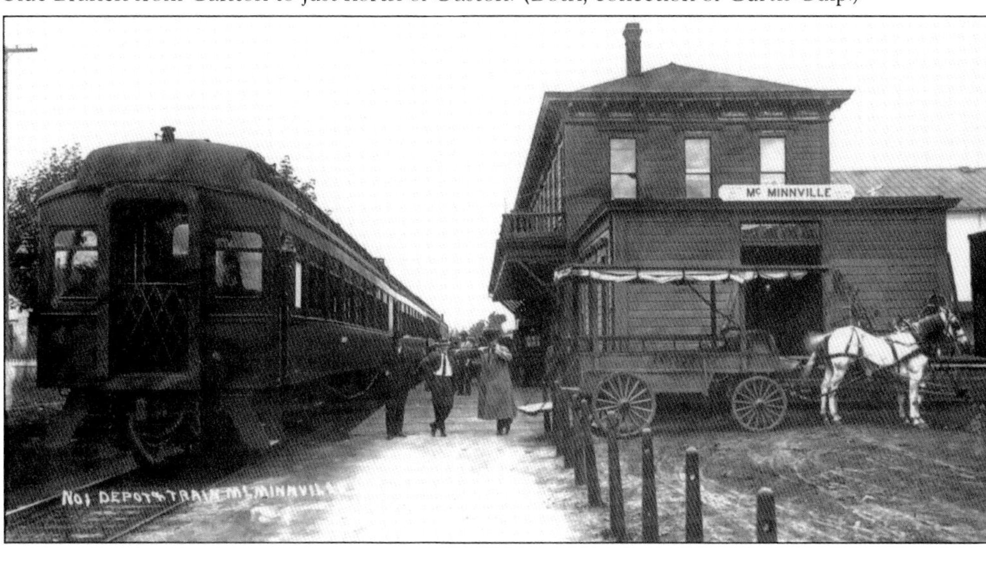

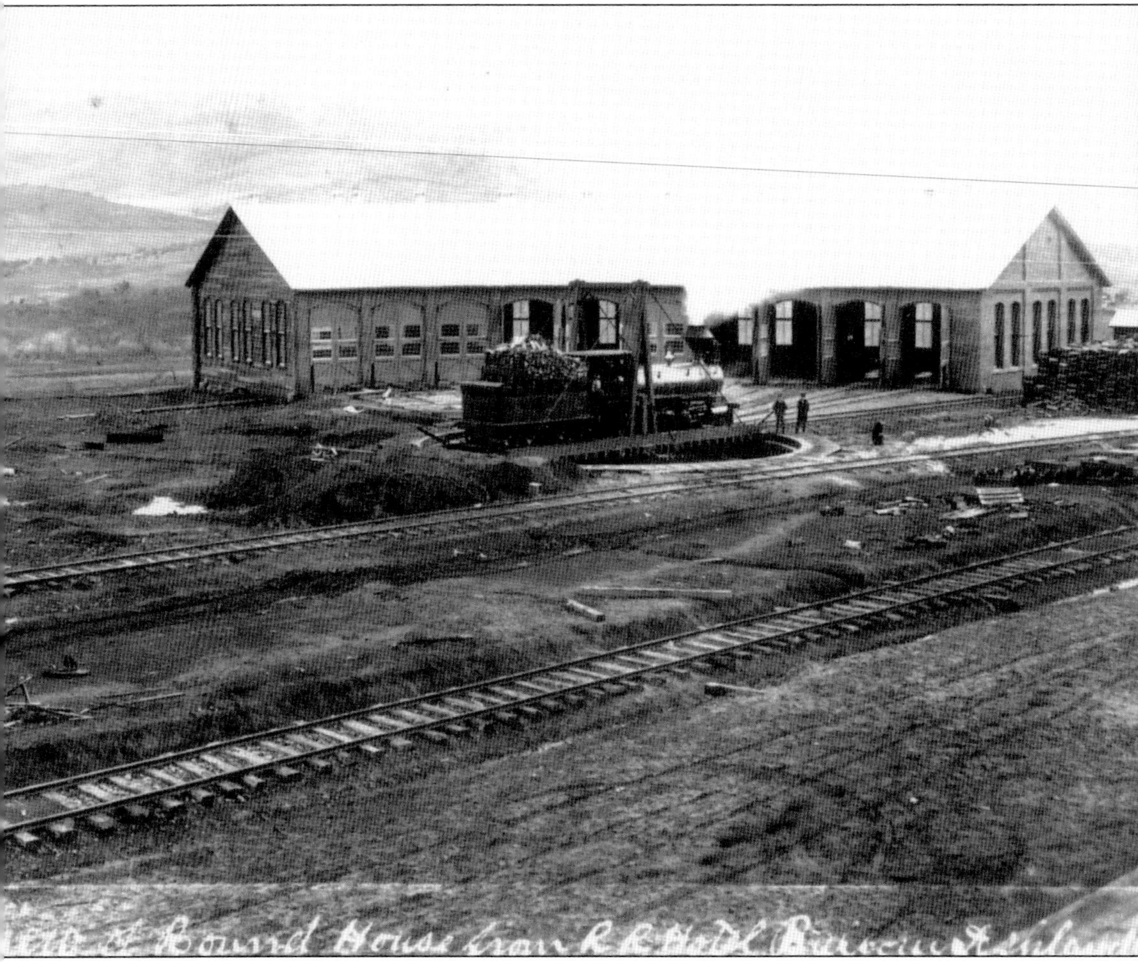

O&C Reaches Ashland. On May 4, 1884, thirteen years after the Oregon & California Railroad laid tracks through Hillsboro, the railroad essentially finished its southward extension when it reached Ashland (MP 429.1), about 20 miles north of the California border. This photograph shows the O&C roundhouse and turntable—with a wood-burning locomotive getting a ride—soon after the O&C completed its tracks into town. At this time, the railroad yard had not yet been completely built, as more yard tracks and structures were yet to come. On December 17, 1887, three years after this photograph was taken, the O&C line that came south from Portland via Eugene, Roseburg, and Medford was connected with a Southern Pacific mainline coming north from San Francisco. Thus, Portland—and by extension, Hillsboro—opened a direct rail link with one of California's biggest cities. (Collection of Curtis Culp.)

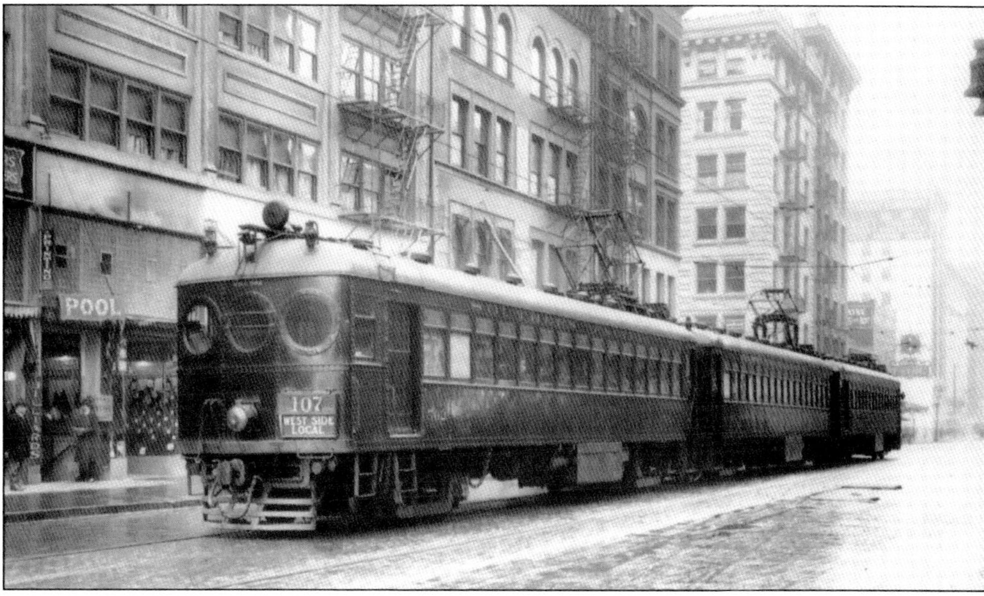

"Red Electric" Local. SP's *West Side Local* rolls through downtown Portland on its way south along the railroad's west side route through Beaverton, Reedville, Hillsboro, Forest Grove, Gaston, and Carlton. The train is lettered for Southern Pacific, but note the road number in small lettering on the top front of the lead car: O&C (Oregon & California) No. 502. (Collection of Curtis Culp.)

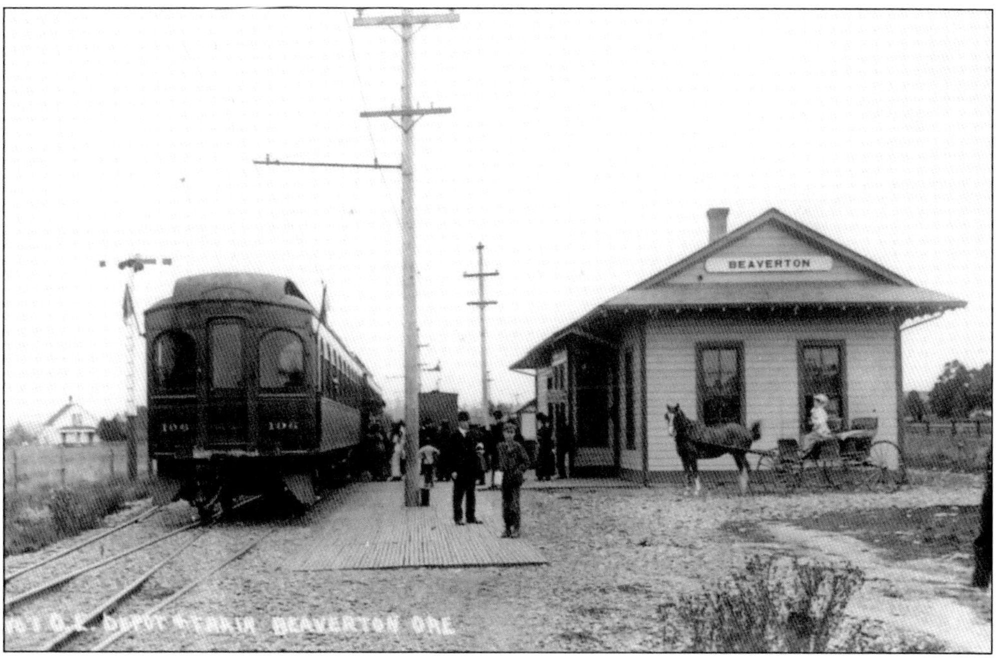

Meet the Competition. Like SP, the Oregon Electric Railway also served Beaverton, which was just nine miles east of Hillsboro. In fact, the OE brought its electrified interurbans to Beaverton in 1908, several years before SP arrived. In this 1912 view, a train has stopped at the depot, located at MP 10.2 on the OE's Forest Grove Branch. In a hallmark scene from the era, someone is waiting at the station with a horse-drawn carriage. (Collection of Curtis Culp.)

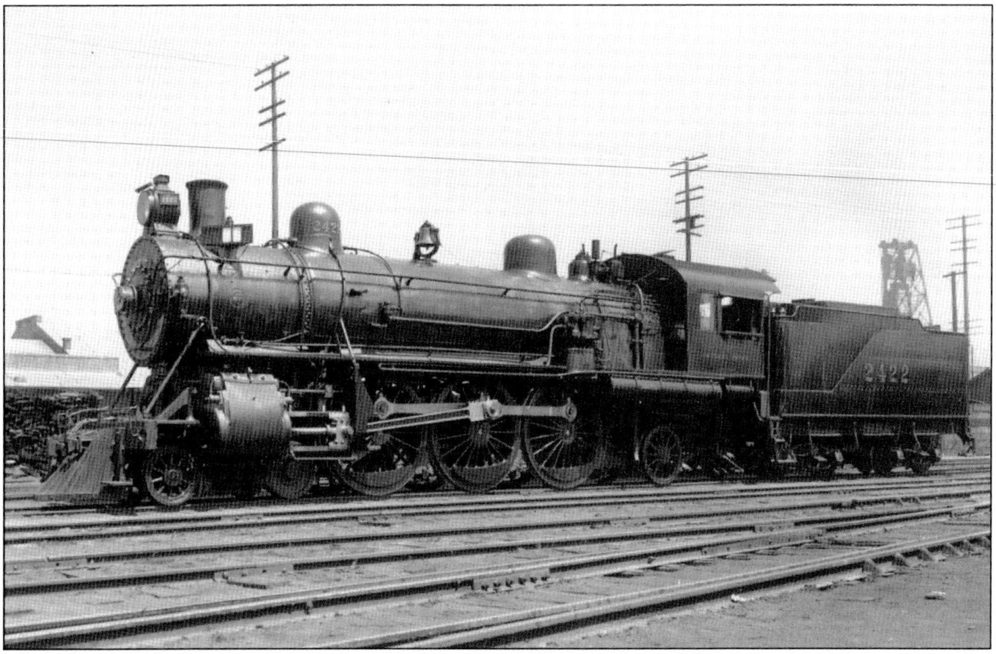

Once a Common Scene. Pictured above is an SP Pacific-class 4-6-2 steam locomotive—built by the Baldwin Locomotive Works—at rest in Portland's Brooklyn Yard around 1930. Dozens of similar locomotives once roamed the rails in the big freight yard here at the northern terminus of Southern Pacific's "Golden Empire," switching strings of freight cars, pulling long-haul freight trains or next-town locals, hooking on to crack passenger trains, or just running to the shop for servicing. In the photograph below, three locomotives stand on one of the 100-acre yard's service tracks in the late 1920s, ready to answer the next call to start moving passengers or freight. (Both, collection of D.C. Jesse Burkhardt.)

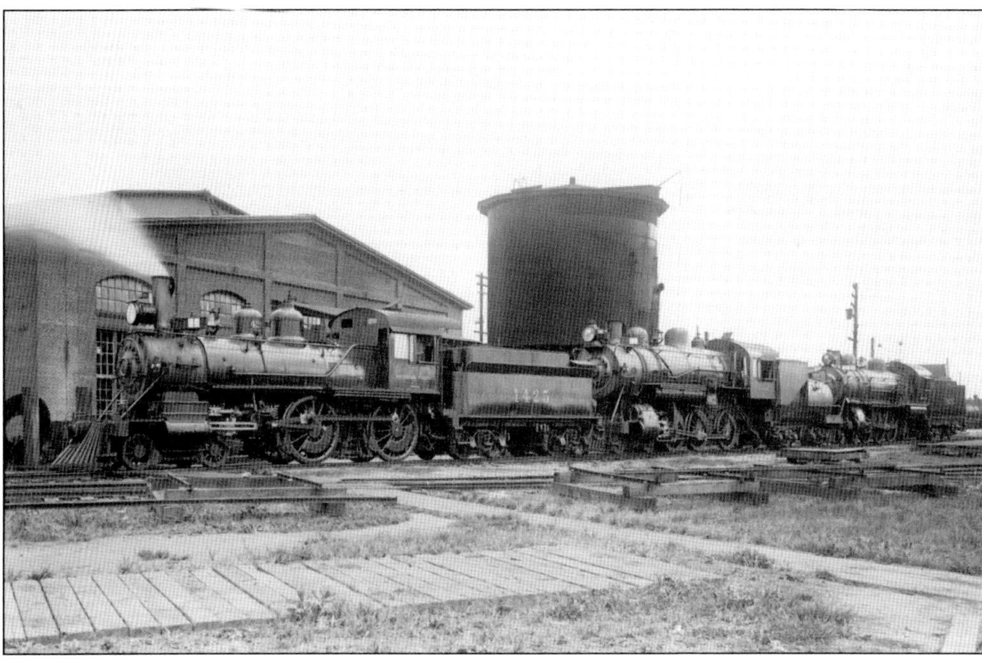

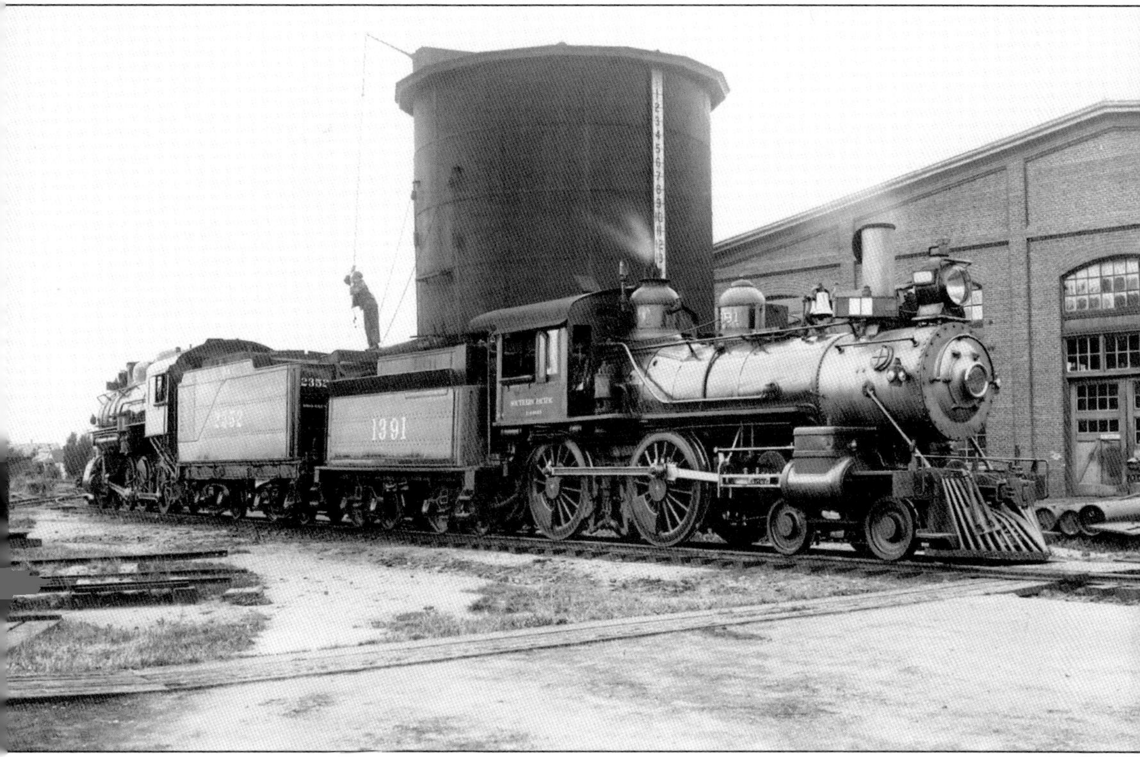

Lining Up for a Drink. Brooklyn Yard was a hub of activity for trains in Oregon's Willamette Valley region, providing servicing facilities for a large fleet of locomotives in mainline operations and in branchline duty. In this photograph from the 1920s, two Southern Pacific locomotives have been brought to a service track next to the water tower behind the roundhouse. One by one, a hostler fills the locomotives with water. To this day, Brooklyn Yard remains an important nerve center for Oregon operations, although the yard is now owned by Union Pacific Railroad, which took control of SP in 1996. (Collection of D.C. Jesse Burkhardt.)

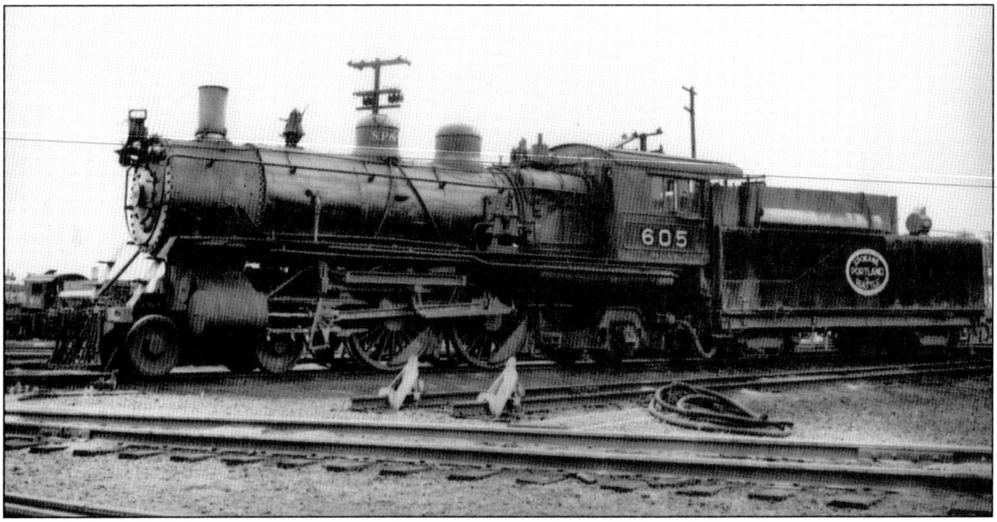

The Northwest's Own. Along with Southern Pacific, the Spokane, Portland & Seattle Railway had a big presence in Portland for many decades. In the photograph above, SP&S locomotive No. 605 rests in the SP&S yard in Portland between assignments on June 5, 1947. The image below has a different tale to tell. It shows an immaculate SP&S No. 2507 sitting in the freight yard next to the turntable. This 4-8-2 locomotive—built for Great Northern at the Baldwin Locomotive Works in Philadelphia, Pennsylvania, in 1923—was designed to power fast passenger trains. However, it had already been retired when this photograph was taken in 1965. In 2003, No. 2507 was put on display in Wishram, Washington. The SP&S, with its famous slogan, "The Northwest's Own Railway," faded into history when it was merged into Burlington Northern in 1970. (Both, collection of D.C. Jesse Burkhardt.)

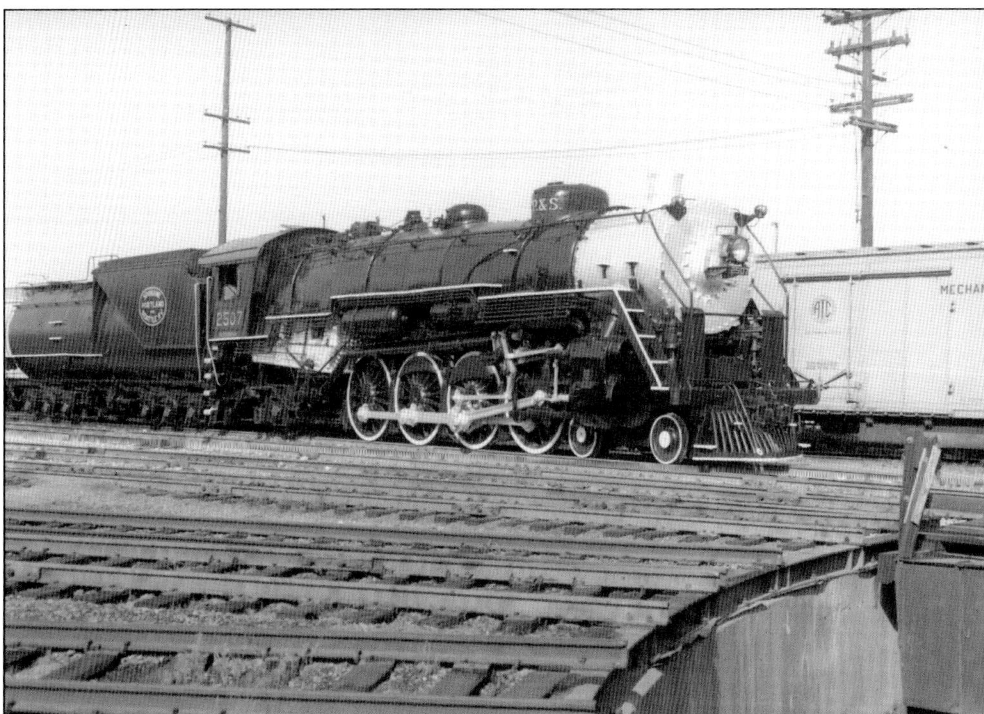

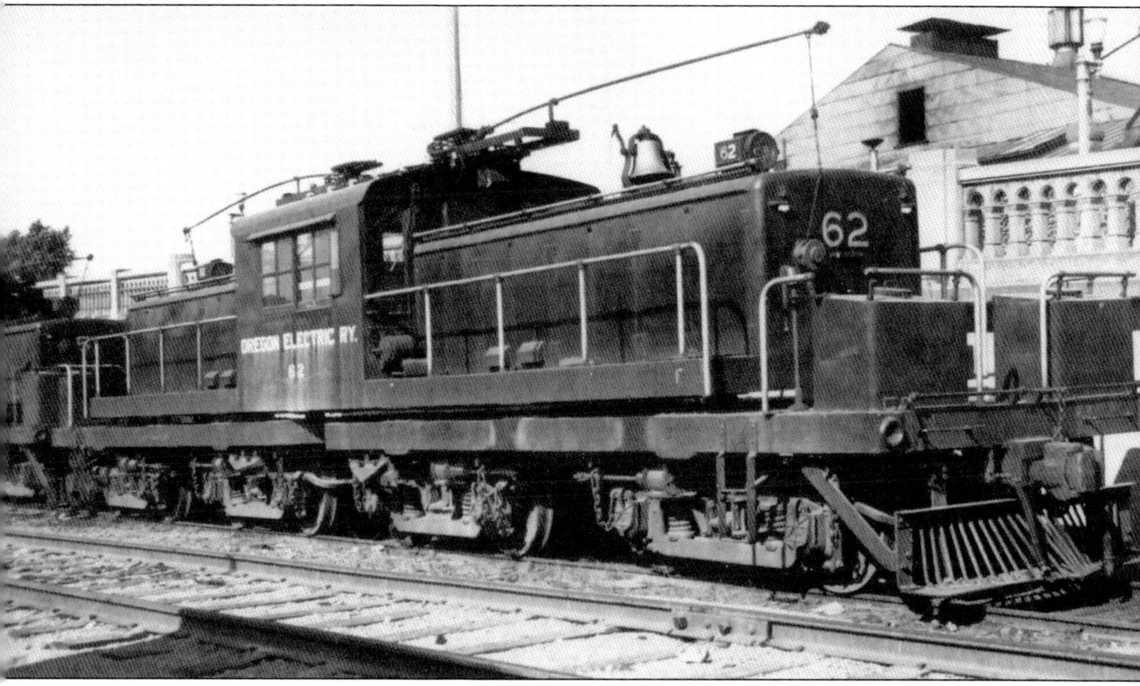

OBSOLETE FLEET. Although the Oregon Electric halted the last of its electrified passenger train operations in the Willamette Valley on May 13, 1933, the company continued to use electricity to run its freight trains until July 1945. At that point, virtually overnight, the railroad's fleet of electric freight motors was rendered obsolete. In this scene from Portland in 1946, several of the OE's electric locomotives have been stored on a siding to await their fate—most likely a date with a scrapper's cutting torch. (Collection of D.C. Jesse Burkhardt.)

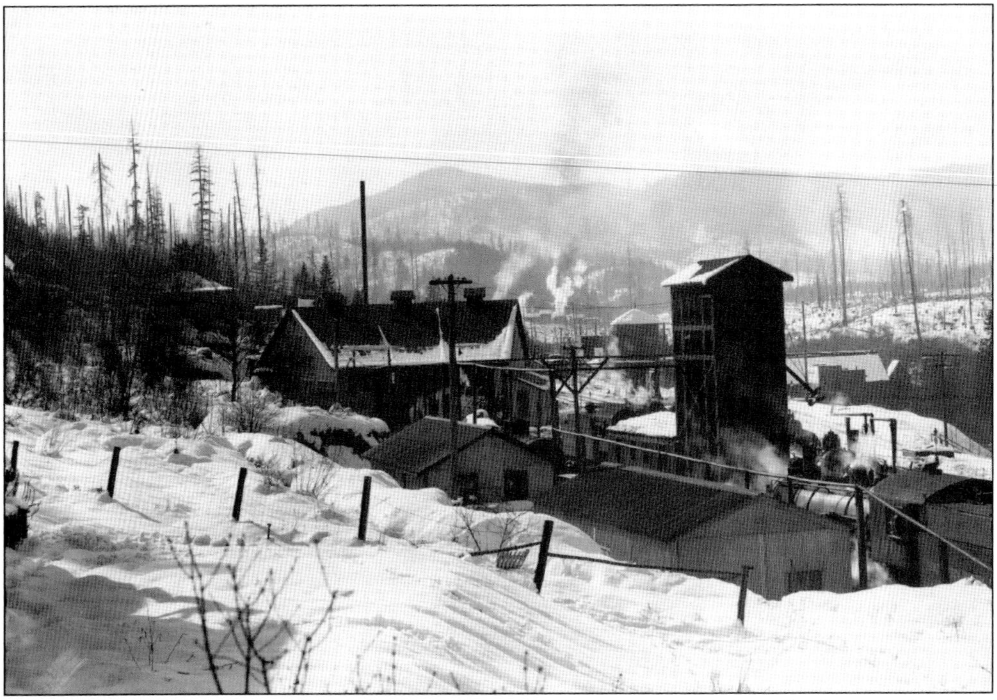

Backyard View. For several decades, Southern Pacific maintained shop facilities and a busy roundhouse in Timber (MP 793.1), 28 miles west of Hillsboro on the Tillamook Branch. In this 1920s view from a snowy yard overlooking the tracks, at least three locomotives can be seen steaming away, with two cabooses resting in the distance to the right of the roundhouse. (Photograph by H.L. Arey, collection of D.C. Jesse Burkhardt.)

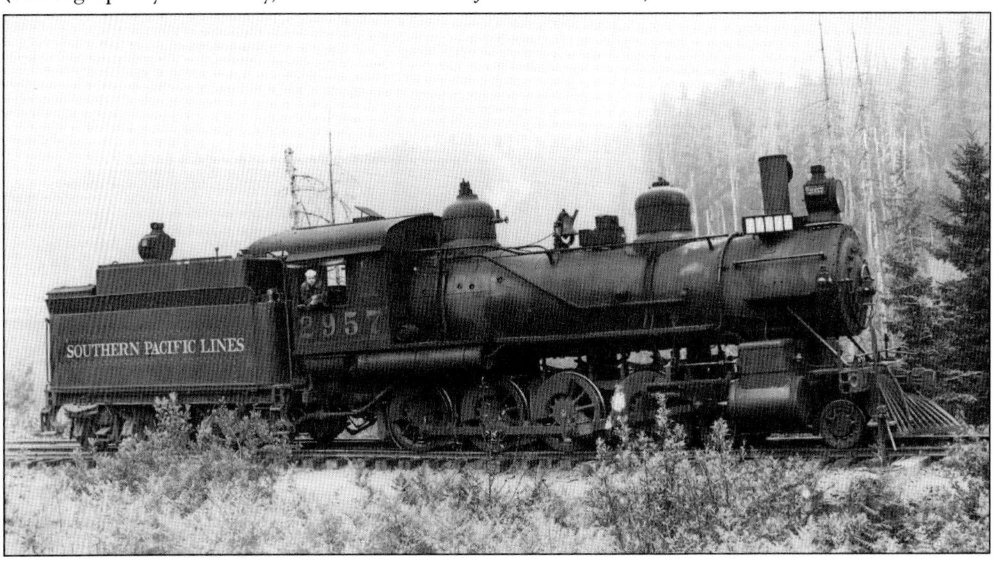

Helper Duty. SP No. 2957, with the iconic "Southern Pacific Lines" moniker in large lettering on its tender, pauses at the end of a siding not far from Timber, probably while waiting to hook onto the end of another freight train moving on the steep Coast Range grades between Hillsboro and Tillamook. Helpers were often needed to provide an extra power boost over the line's mountainous terrain. (Collection of D.C. Jesse Burkhardt.)

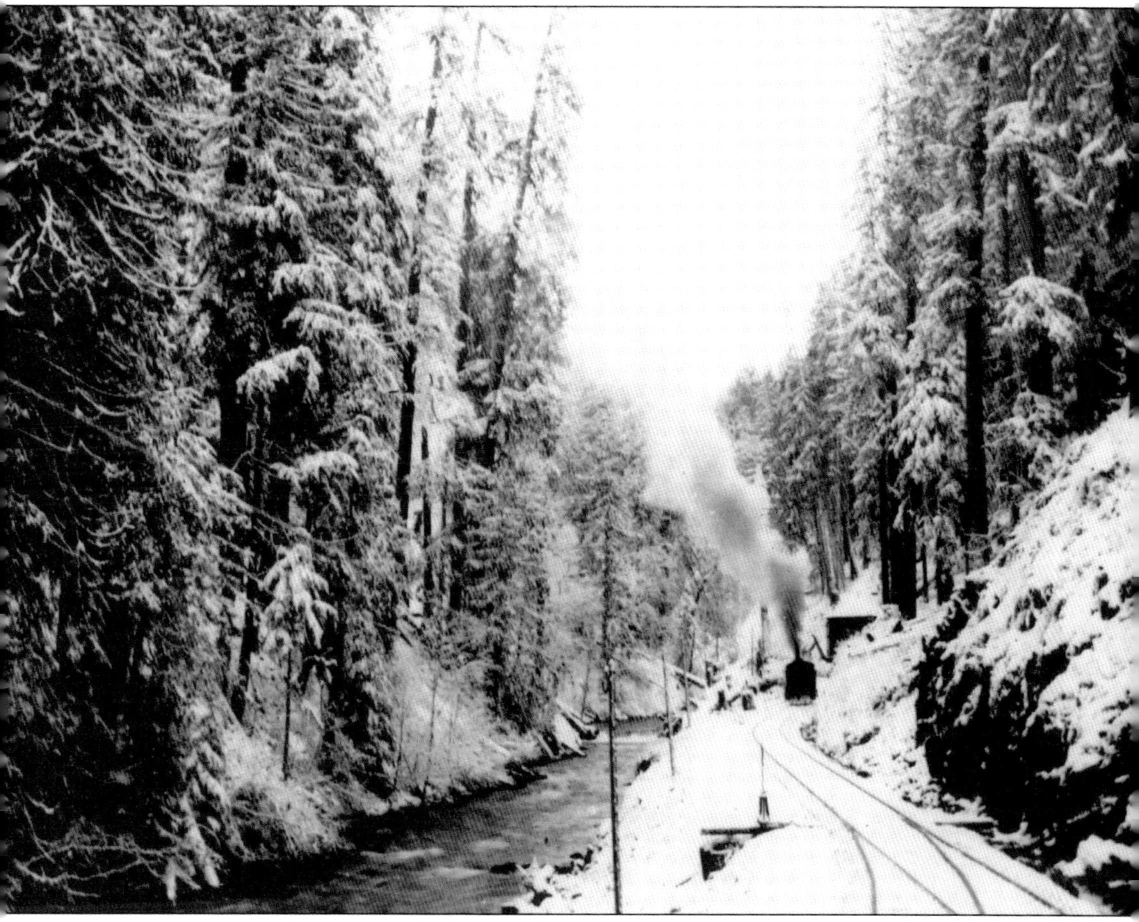

SMOKE AGAINST THE SNOW. A Pacific Railway & Navigation Company locomotive pours out smoke as it pulls up to a water tank somewhere on the Tillamook Branch around 1912. The Coast Range typically sees heavy snowfall in the winter months, and fighting snow on the line was an expected part of the railroad's operations to keep trains moving on the line that connected Hillsboro with several communities along the Oregon coast. Southern Pacific took over operations on this line on July 1, 1915. (Collection of Curtis Culp.)

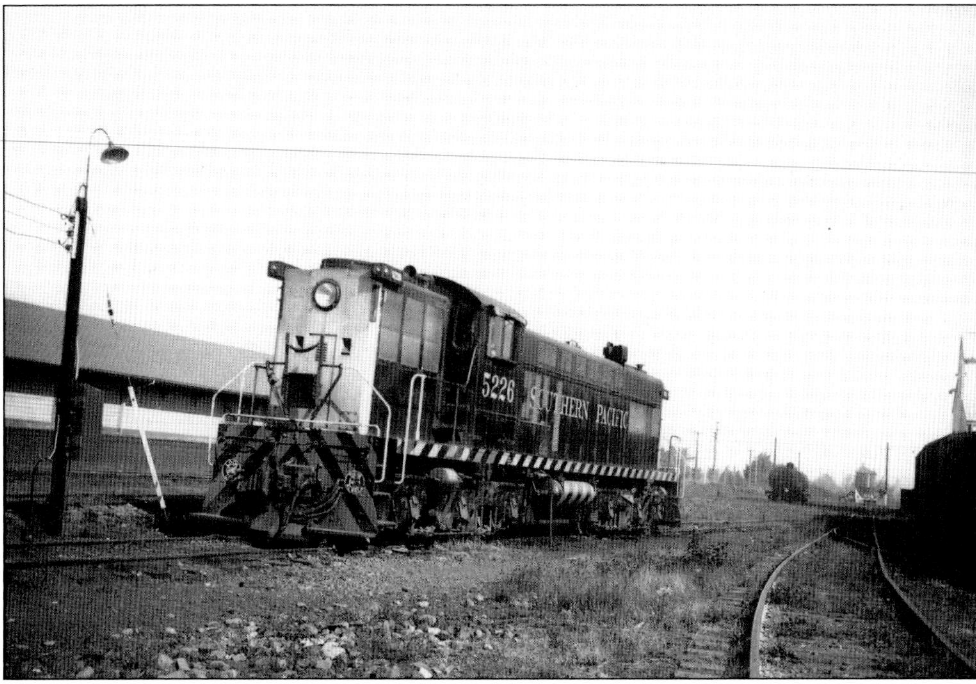

Taking a Break. In 1955, Southern Pacific locomotive No. 5226, a six-axle Baldwin, waits for its next switching assignment in the freight yard at Tillamook, at the western terminus of SP's Tillamook Branch. SP operated long trains out of Tillamook that came through Hillsboro every day on their way to or from Brooklyn Yard in Portland. (Collection of Curtis Culp.)

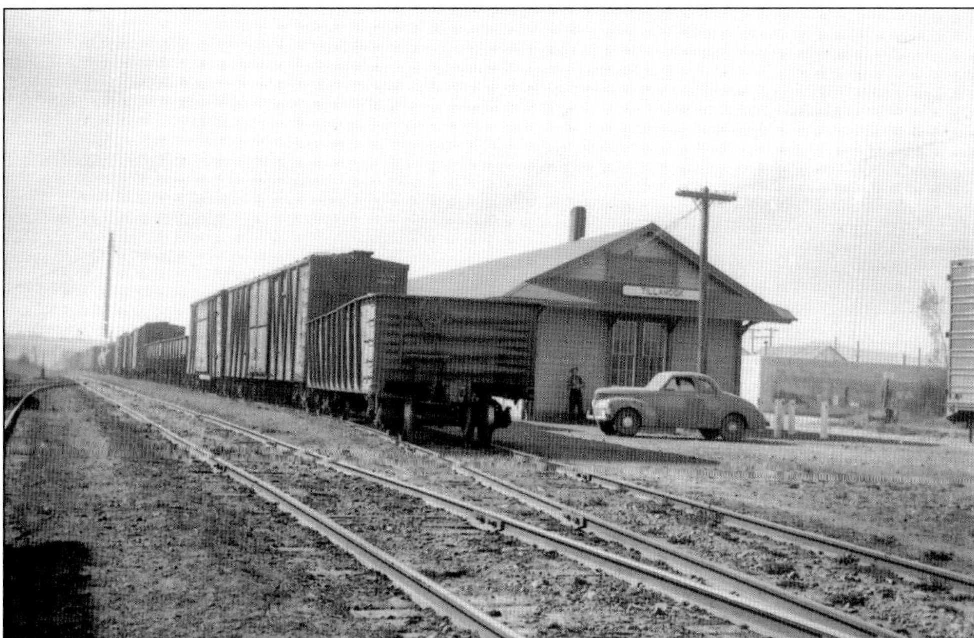

Waiting. In this 1955 scene of SP's freight yard in Tillamook, a freight train is made up and ready to be hauled east on the run over the Coast Range to Hillsboro and Portland. Note the classic SP depot behind the cut of freight cars. (Collection of Curtis Culp.)

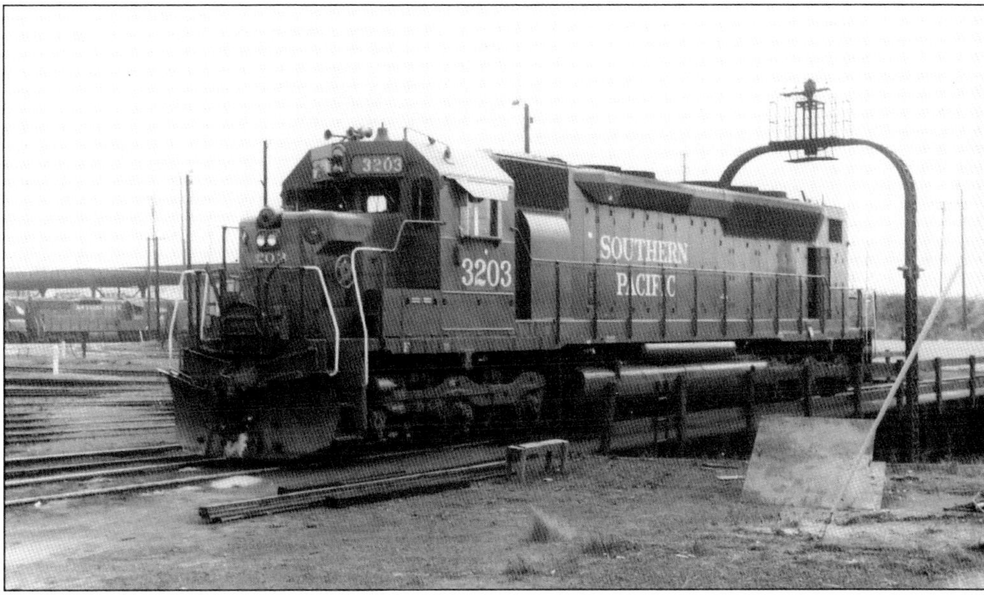

The Latest Technology. SP No. 3202, an SD45 from General Motors' Electro-Motive Division—one of the newest locomotive models in the 1960s—rests on the turntable at Southern Pacific's Brooklyn Yard in September 1969. The first SD45s came off the assembly line in 1965. (Photograph by Jack Holst, collection of D.C. Jesse Burkhardt.)

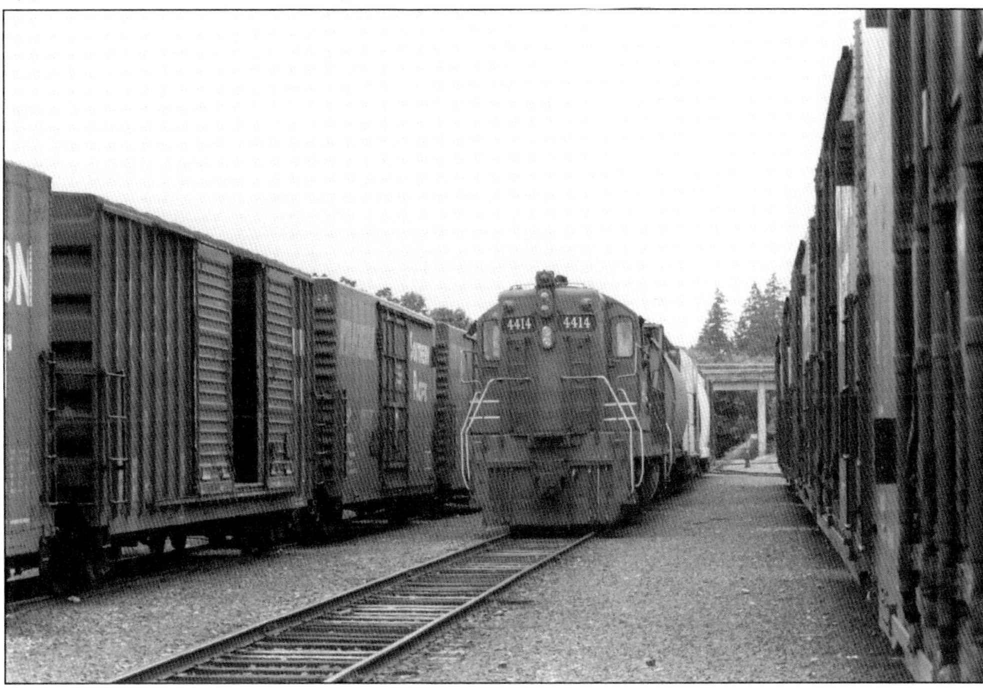

Corvallis Yard. Southern Pacific's small freight yard in Corvallis (MP 688.9) is quiet late on June 26, 1991. The yard was often busy in this era, as a local crew operated north to Dallas (MP 733.8) on Mondays, Wednesdays, and Fridays and south to the Hull-Oakes sawmill at Dawson (MP 679.9) on Tuesdays and Thursdays. In the 1920s, Corvallis, located 75 miles south of Hillsboro, was the southern terminus for SP's "Red Electric" operations. (Photograph by D.C. Jesse Burkhardt.)

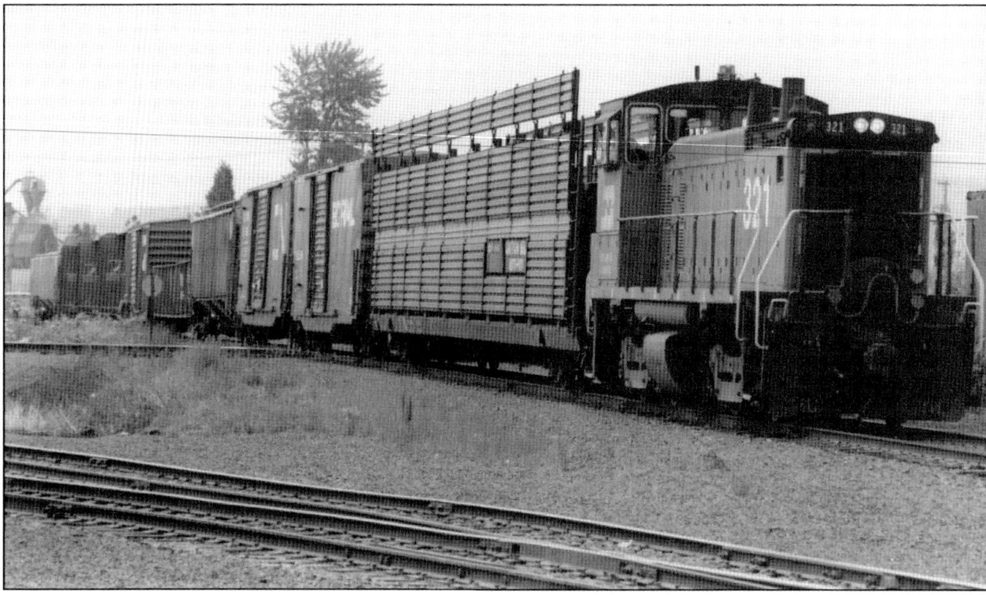

Diesels on the Oregon Electric. In 1912, the Oregon Electric Railway completed an electrified mainline between Portland and Eugene, and as it turned out, Eugene was the end point of the OE's southward expansion. Although proceeding into California was a key goal of OE owner James Hill, his competitors had other ideas. Southern Pacific owner Edward Harriman shrewdly purchased large strips of land south of Eugene to block the OE. In 1991, with the intrigue of that time long past, a Burlington Northern switcher moves cars on BN's Oregon Electric Branch in Eugene (MP 141.8) in the image above. Below, a long northbound train rolls through Salem (MP 69.0), Oregon's capital city, on January 13, 1996. When BN took over the trackage in 1970, the new company retained a bit of the OE's identity by naming the line to honor its history. (Photographs by D.C. Jesse Burkhardt.)

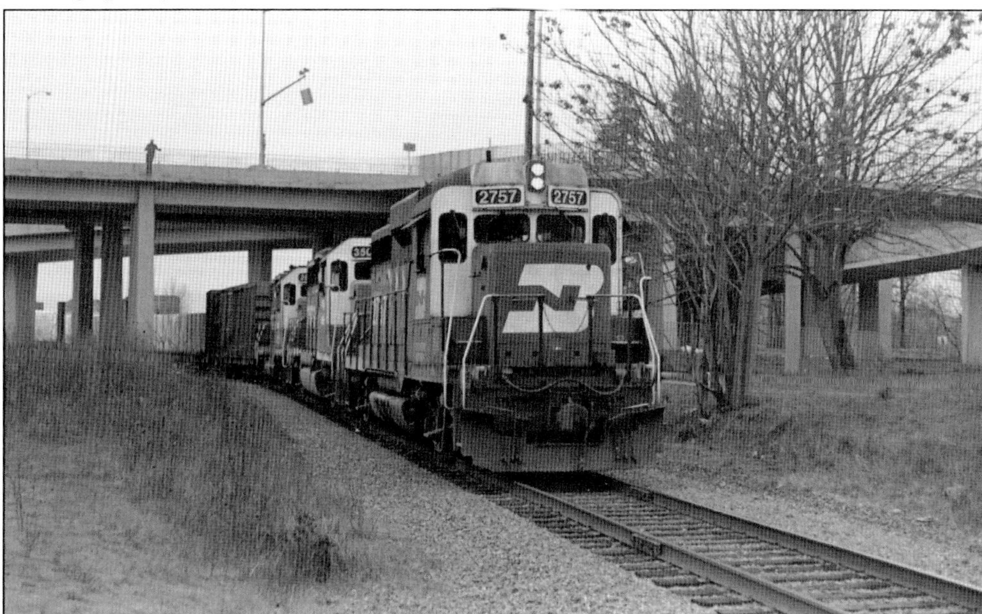

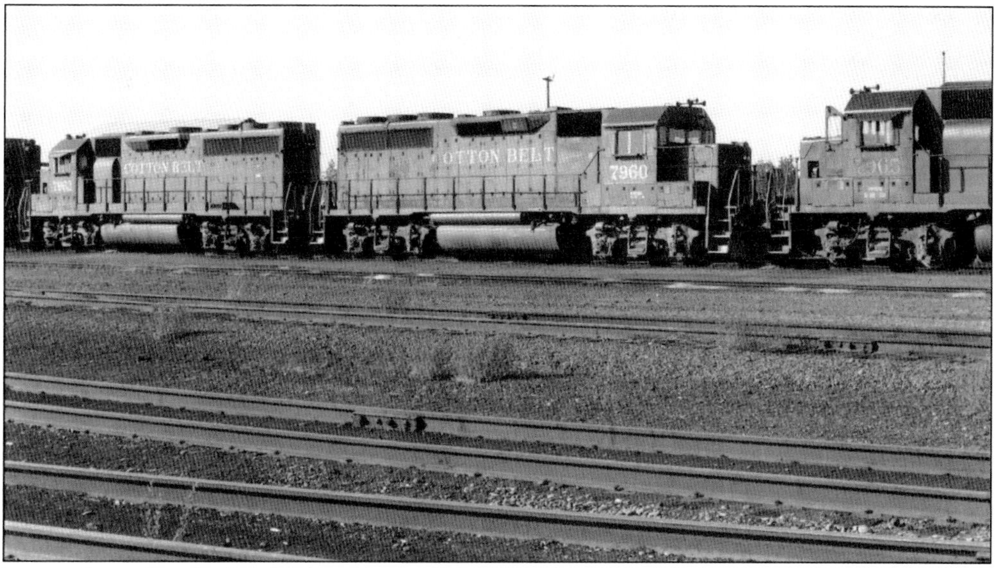

Power Line. Besides Portland, no Oregon station was more important to Southern Pacific than Eugene. Eugene (MP 647.3) was SP's largest classification yard in the state and a base for its Willamette Valley operations. In May 1988, several GP40-2s—lettered for sister carrier Cotton Belt—idle in the yard. GP40-2s were often used to power the *Toledo Haulers*, which served a huge Georgia-Pacific paper mill in Toledo, a coastal town south of Tillamook. (Photograph by D.C. Jesse Burkhardt.)

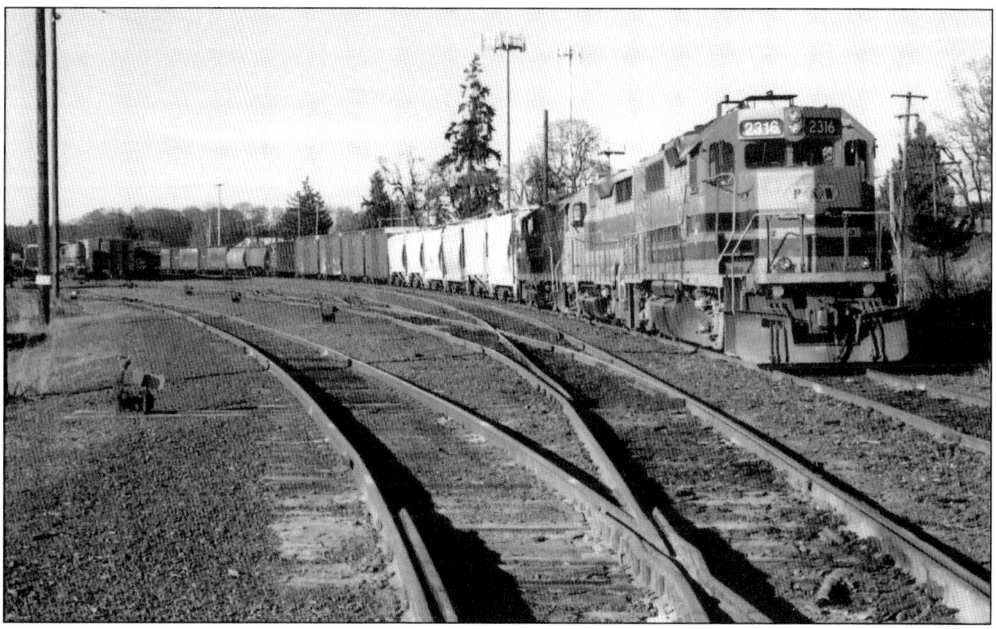

Central Hub. The former Oregon Electric yard in Albany (MP 96.5)—now operated by Portland & Western Railroad, as seen here on April 19, 2009—was the nerve center of the OE's freight operations in the Willamette Valley and now is key to the P&W. In the Burlington Northern era, long-haul mixed-merchandise trains bound for Vancouver and Pasco in Washington originated here, and locals made the 45-mile run to Eugene every weekday. (Photograph by D.C. Jesse Burkhardt.)

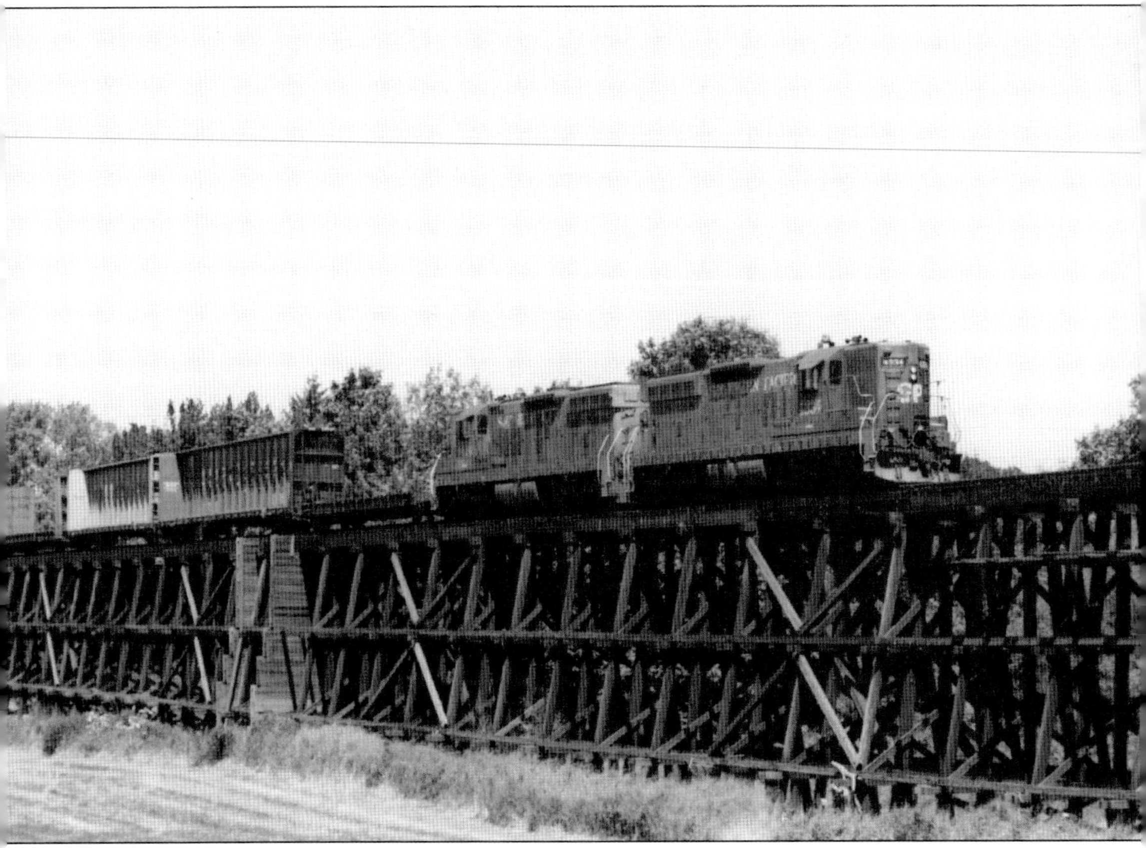

ON A TIGHTROPE. SP's *Willamina Local* crosses a long trestle with 20 cars as it heads south on the West Side Branch in June 1991. Before a 12-mile-long segment of this branch—from Carlton to just north of Gaston—was abandoned in 1985, the line extended south from Hillsboro (MP 764.9) to Monroe (MP 671.7), a distance of 93 miles. This train, headed by SD9s No. 4334 and No. 4424, is about to enter the yard at Whiteson (MP 730.6), where it will cut west to serve shippers on SP's 19-mile-long Willamina Branch between Whiteson and Willamina. (Photograph by D.C. Jesse Burkhardt.)

Five

Contemporary Operations

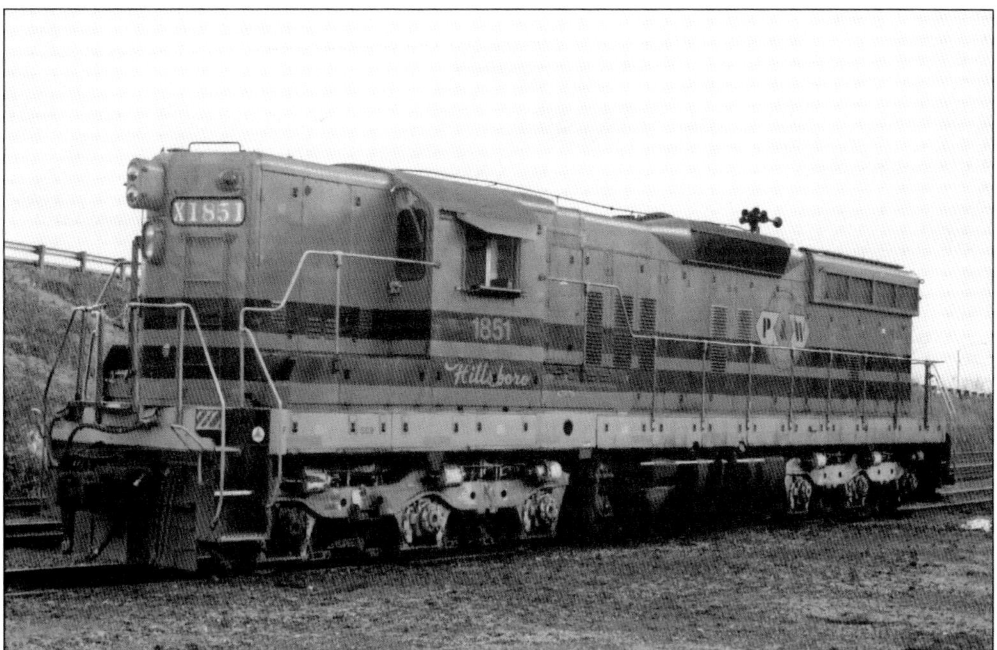

Hillsboro Tribute. The Portland & Western Railroad honors communities along its routes by naming locomotives after key cities. At St. Marys, just east of Hillsboro, P&W SD9 No. 1851—*Hillsboro*—waits for its next assignment. St. Marys was a relatively busy junction when Burlington Northern's Oregon Electric Branch and Southern Pacific's Tillamook Branch intersected here, but the BN trackage north of St. Marys was abandoned in 1995. (Photograph by D.C. Jesse Burkhardt.)

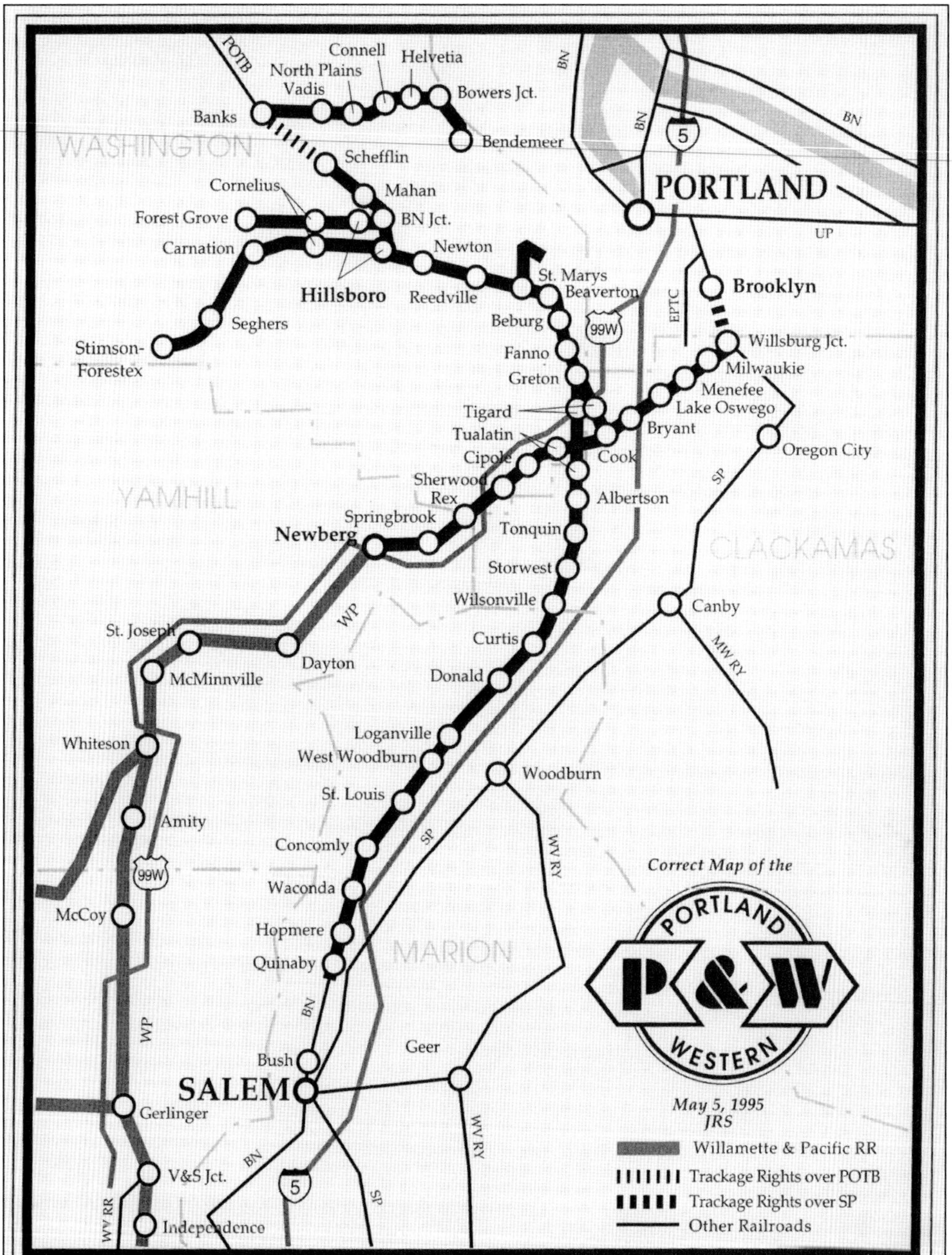

Portland & Western Takes Over. The official map of the combined lines of the Portland & Western Railroad and the Willamette & Pacific Railroad as displayed in the P&W timetable dated May 5, 1995. The heavy black lines show the route of the P&W, while the thick gray lines represent the tracks of the Willamette & Pacific. The P&W/W&P alliance combined much of the former Southern Pacific and Burlington Northern routes in the Portland metropolitan area and the Willamette Valley. As the map shows, Hillsboro is positioned as a key station for operations on the railroad's Tillamook, Seghers, and Forest Grove Districts. (Courtesy of Portland & Western Railroad.)

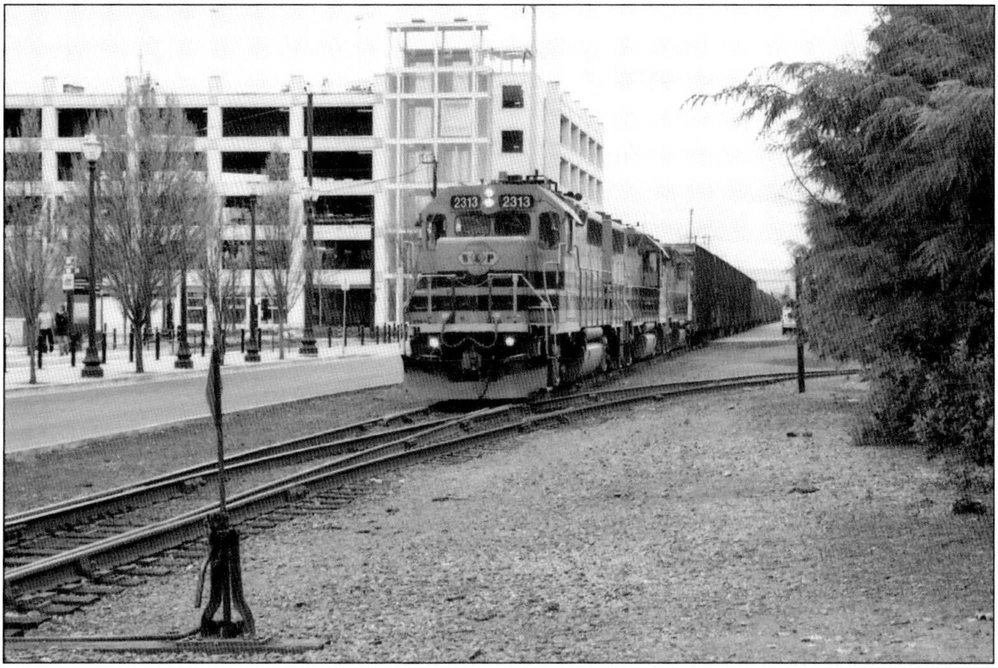

Five Days a Week. Portland & Western's *Harbor Turn* rolls west through downtown Hillsboro on April 11, 2009, with three locomotives leading the way. This train, which operates daily Tuesday through Saturday, moves freight between Albany and Linnton—a station about three miles west of BNSF Railway's Willbridge Yard in Portland—and switches Banks Lumber Company's woodchip and lumber tracks along the train's 89-mile-long route. (Photograph by D.C. Jesse Burkhardt.)

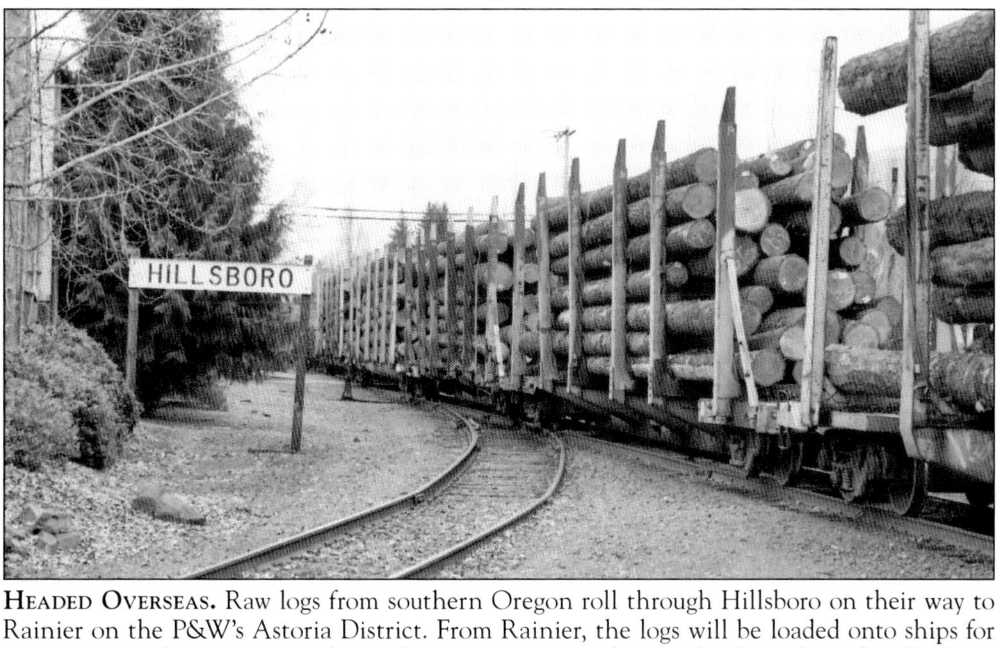

Headed Overseas. Raw logs from southern Oregon roll through Hillsboro on their way to Rainier on the P&W's Astoria District. From Rainier, the logs will be loaded onto ships for export, primarily to Asian markets. The train is passing the switch where the railroad's Forest Grove District begins; the track that cuts to the left in this photograph leads to Forest Grove. (Photograph by D.C. Jesse Burkhardt.)

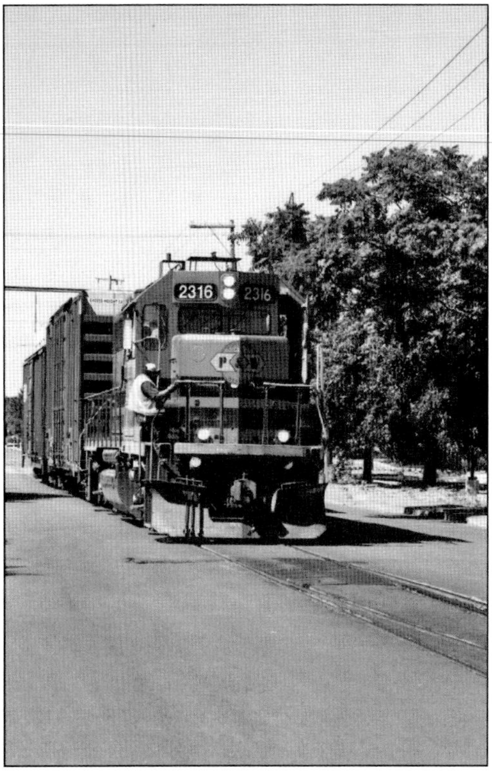

Running in the Street. The *Hillsboro Switcher* rolls down the middle of Adams Street in Hillsboro in July 2009. This trackage is part of the P&W's route between Tigard and Linnton, and it sees two trains each way most days of the week. The track diverges directly in front of the locomotive, with one set of rails veering east to Tigard and the other cutting south to Seghers. (Photograph by D.C. Jesse Burkhardt.)

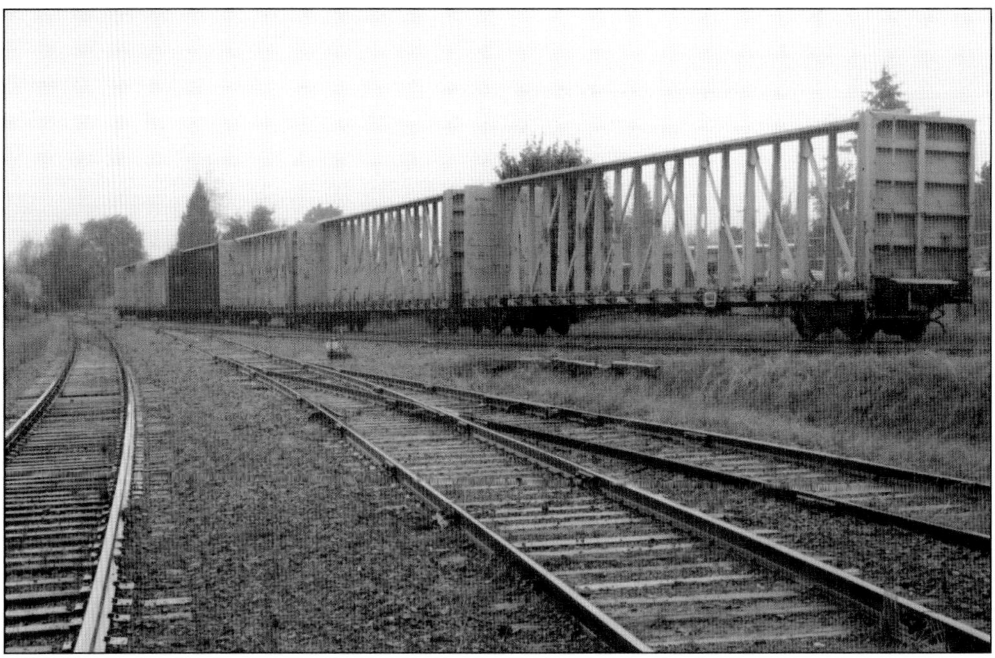

Empties for Stimson. A cut of empty centerbeam flatcars rests on a spur track in Hillsboro just west of the freight depot awaiting delivery to the Stimson-Forestex mill at the end of the line near Seghers. The mill is the main shipper on the Portland & Western's 12-mile-long Seghers District, which runs between Hillsboro and Seghers. (Photograph by D.C. Jesse Burkhardt.)

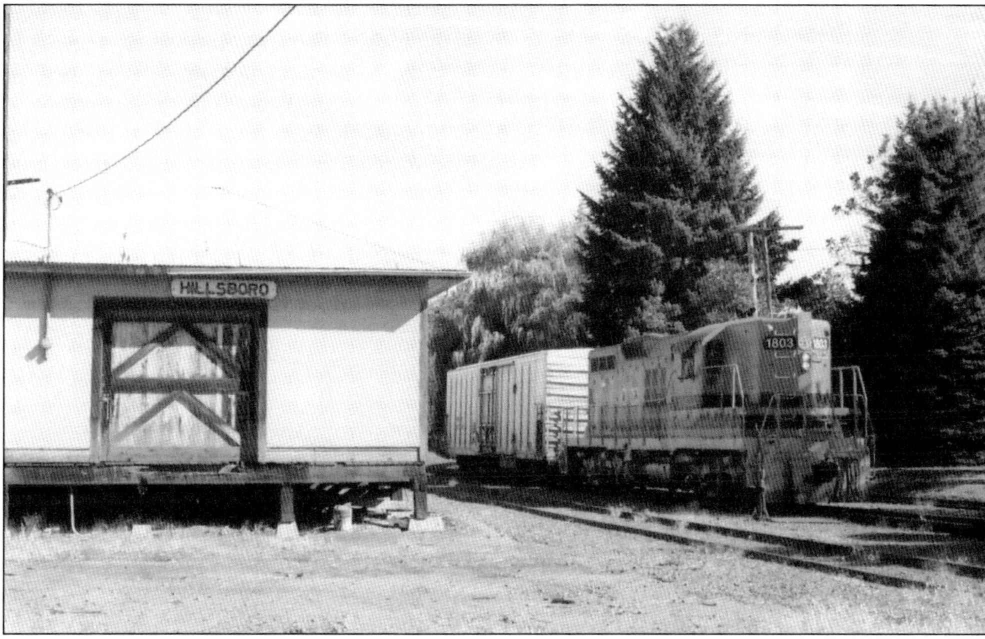

IDLING AT THE STATION. The *Hillsboro Switcher* rests next to the Hillsboro freight station in October 1995 with one reefer for delivery to a customer on the Forest Grove District. Until it was abolished in 2010, the *Hillsboro Switcher* worked out of Hillsboro Monday through Friday. Now, a local out of Tigard, which is about 14 miles southeast of this station, serves the territory. (Photograph by D.C. Jesse Burkhardt.)

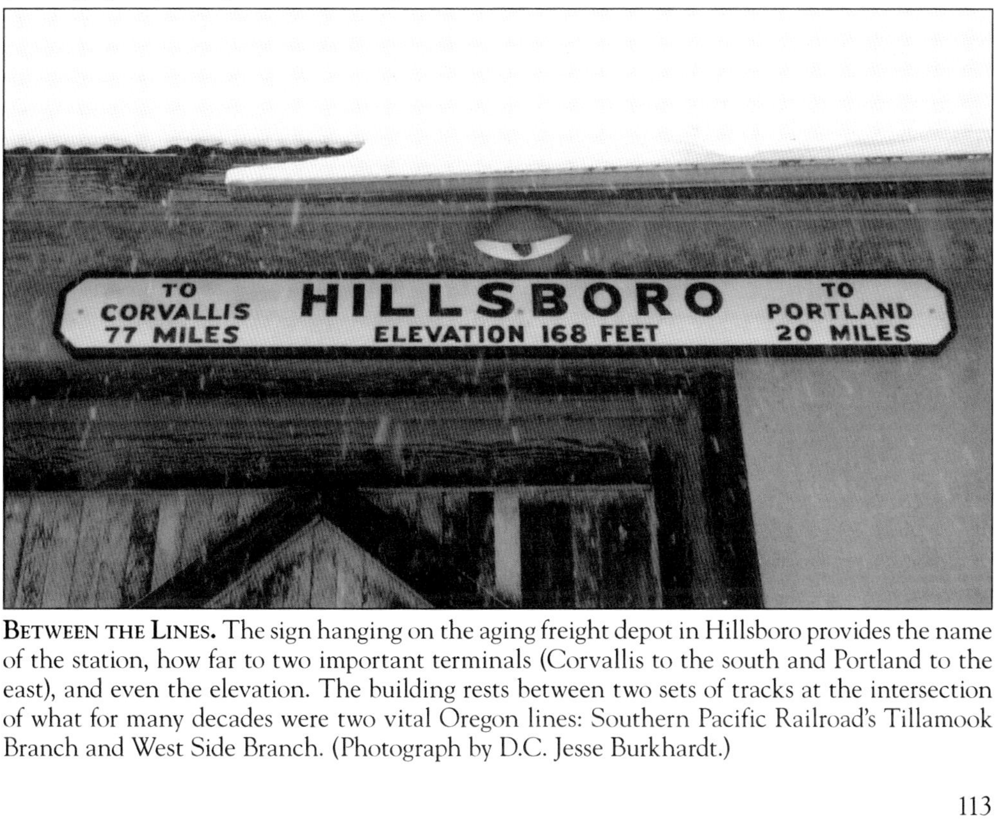

BETWEEN THE LINES. The sign hanging on the aging freight depot in Hillsboro provides the name of the station, how far to two important terminals (Corvallis to the south and Portland to the east), and even the elevation. The building rests between two sets of tracks at the intersection of what for many decades were two vital Oregon lines: Southern Pacific Railroad's Tillamook Branch and West Side Branch. (Photograph by D.C. Jesse Burkhardt.)

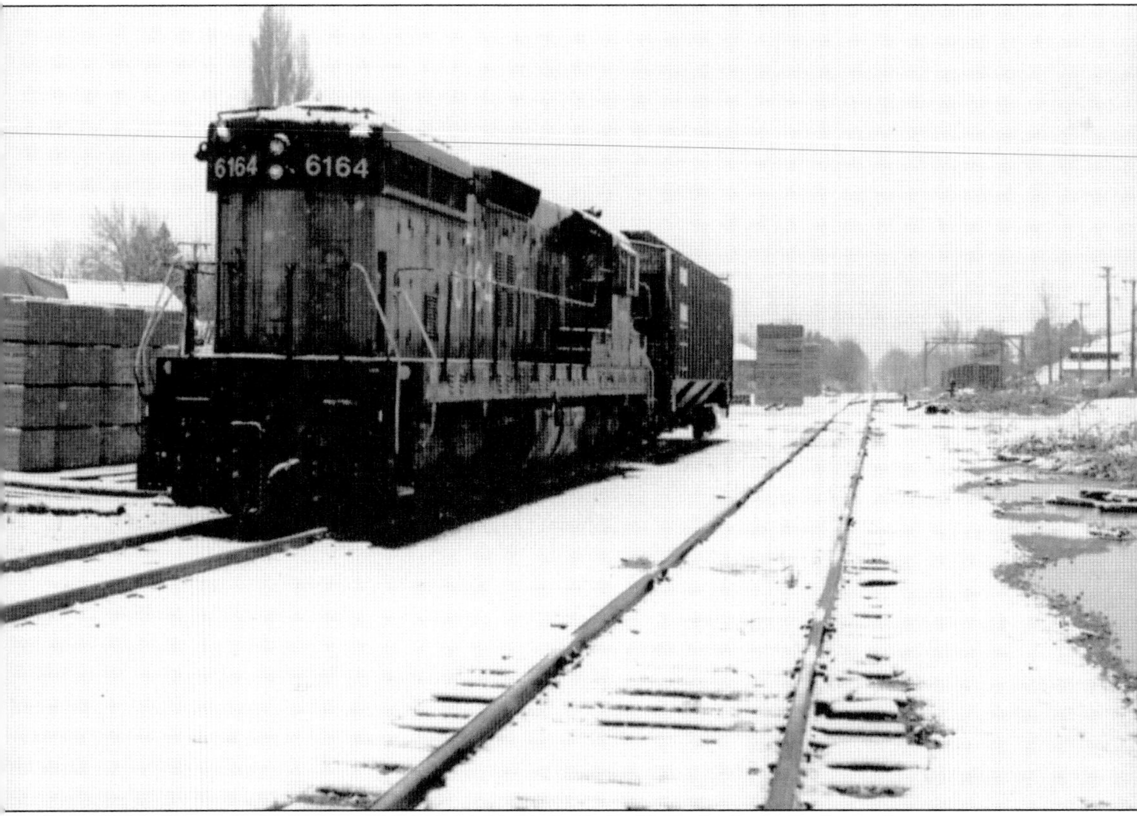

WAITING OUT THE SNOW. In this westward-looking view in Banks, one of the Port of Tillamook Bay Railroad's ex–Burlington Northern locomotives—SD9 No. 6164—is getting covered by snow as it rests on a spur track with a grain hopper in February 2008. Although a storm knocked the line going west from Banks to Tillamook out of service in late 2007, the POTB continued its switching services in Banks for several months before eventually turning the job over to the Portland & Western. (Photograph by D.C. Jesse Burkhardt.)

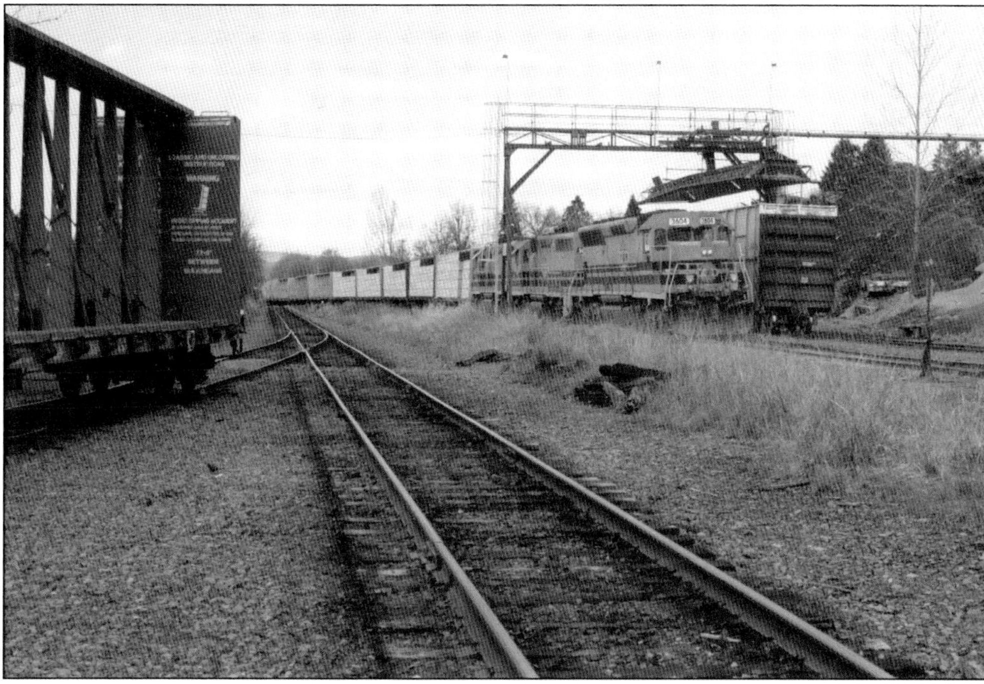

Harbor Turn. Switching the Banks Lumber Company mill is one of the duties of Portland & Western's *Harbor Turn*, the five-days-per-week train that operates between Linnton and Albany, via Hillsboro. In the scene above from March 5, 2006, the *Harbor Turn* passes the woodchip loading facility adjacent to the mill, pulling five loaded lumber cars and a cut of empty centerbeam flatcars. In the photograph below, after switching at Banks on January 17, 2009, the *Harbor Turn* prepares to head east on the railroad's United Railways District. From here, the train will roll through North Plains and Bowers Junction before finally reaching its northern terminus in Linnton. The track in the foreground is part of Portland & Western's ex-SP Tillamook District, which runs between Banks and Brooklyn Yard in Portland. (Photographs by D.C. Jesse Burkhardt.)

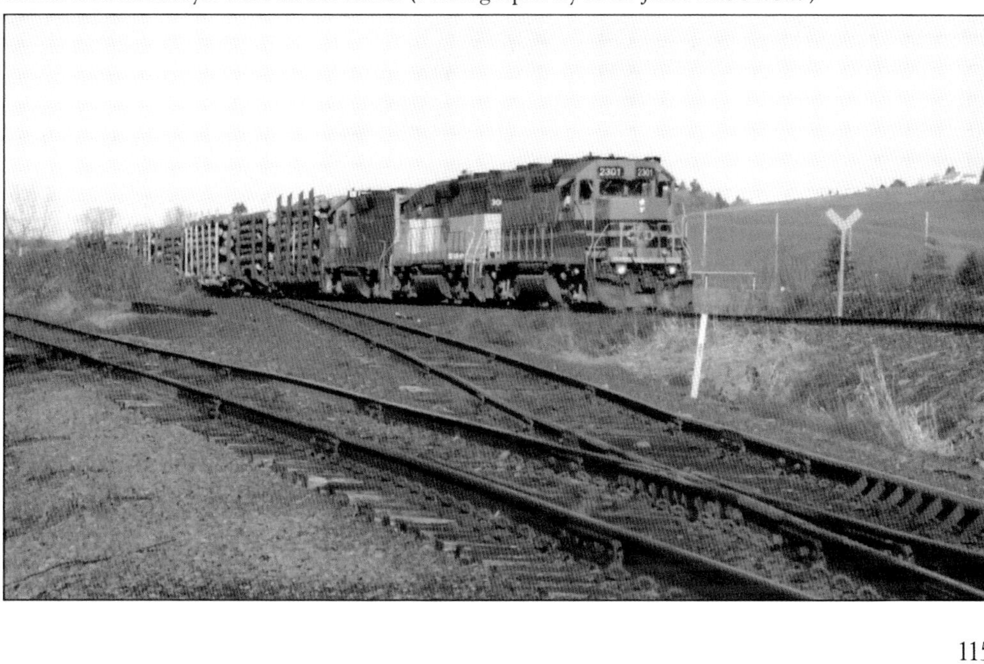

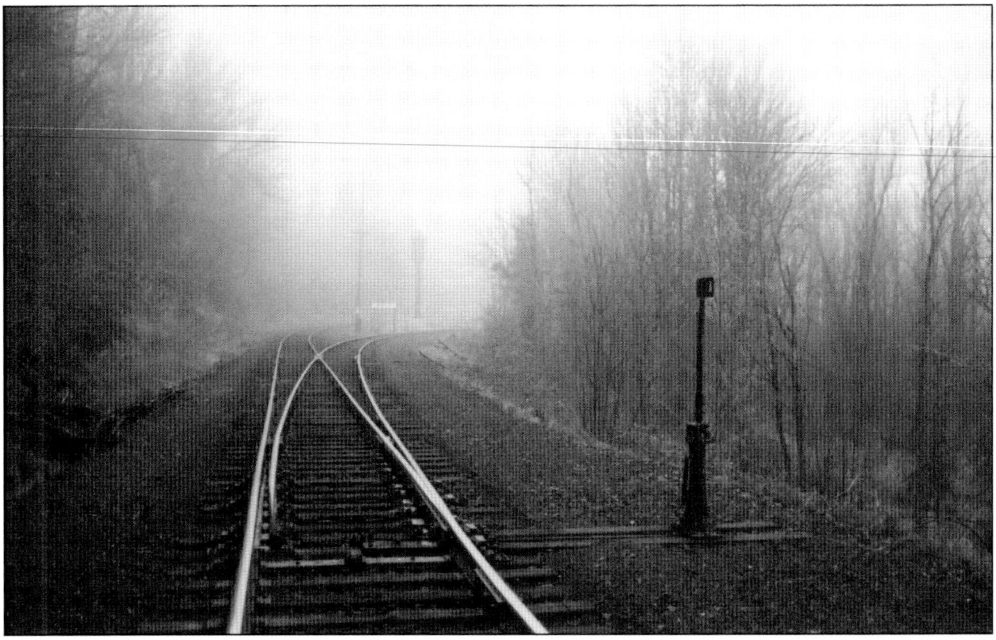

WINTER FOG. The P&W's tracks diverge at United Junction in this view looking west on February 17, 2007. From here, one line (left) cuts west to go toward Hillsboro and Tigard, while the other heads north toward St. Helens and Rainier. Note the sanding tower in the distance. Locomotives sometimes take on sand here to ensure trains climbing the grade out of United Junction have plenty for added traction. (Photograph by D.C. Jesse Burkhardt.)

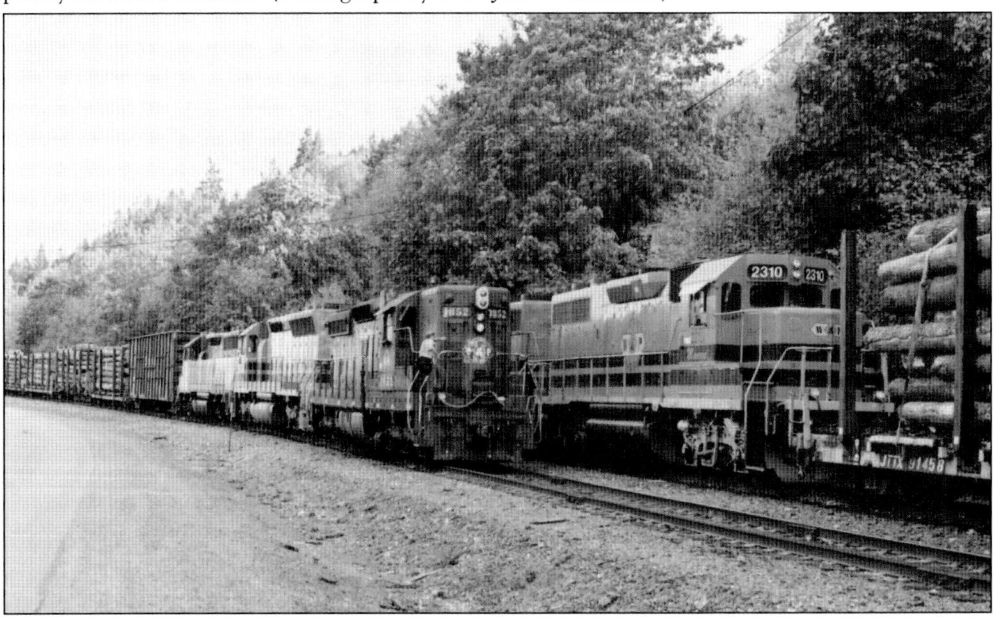

SIDE BY SIDE AT LINNTON. Two long freight trains meet at Linnton, a key terminal for the P&W's Oregon operations, on September 22, 2007. The train on the left is about to pull out of the two-track yard here and proceed to Tigard, located 44 miles away, while another train has just arrived. As is typical, both trains carry primarily logs and wood products. (Photograph by D.C. Jesse Burkhardt.)

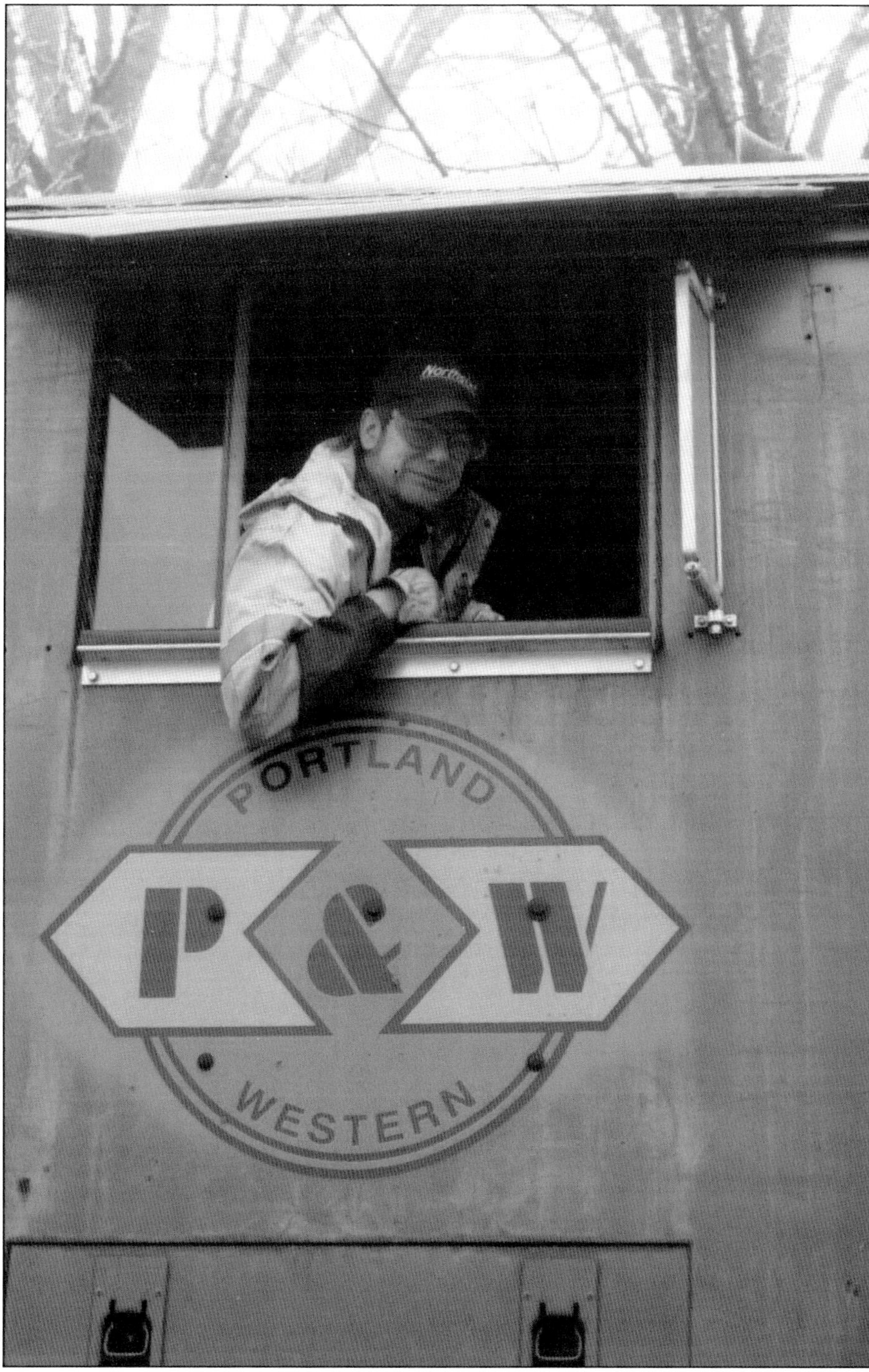

At the Controls. Portland & Western engineer Jan Zweerts offers a friendly smile from the cab of his locomotive, P&W SW9 No. 1201, as he waits to resume switching duties in the Hillsboro area on a foggy day in December 2011. Zweerts, who hired on with the P&W in June 1996, began his railroad career as a track laborer with Burlington Northern in Illinois in 1978. (Photograph by D.C. Jesse Burkhardt.)

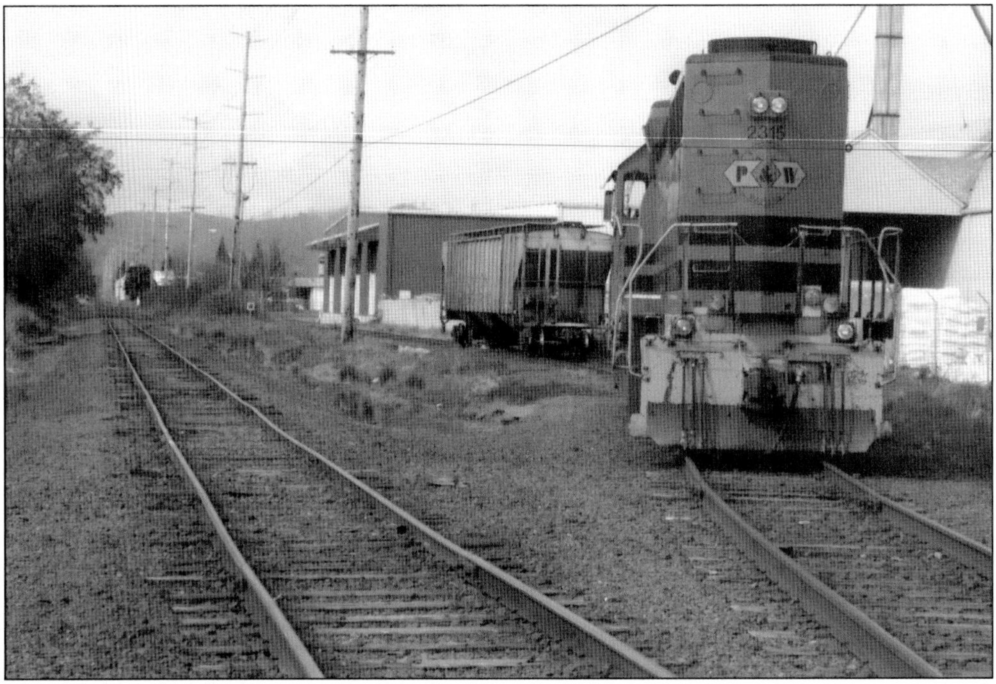

Cornelius Customer. P&W GP39-2 No. 2315, seen above, idles on the spur track at Crop Production Services—a Cornelius agricultural business and one of the Forest Grove District's most active customers—in this scene from April 2013. Once or twice a week, the company takes deliveries of hoppers loaded with fertilizers or tank cars filled with various chemicals. Cornelius is three miles west of Hillsboro on the Portland & Western Railroad's Forest Grove District, which is ex-BN trackage. In the photograph below, four hoppers are on the spur in February 2014 as an unusually heavy snowstorm blasts the region. (Photographs by D.C. Jesse Burkhardt.)

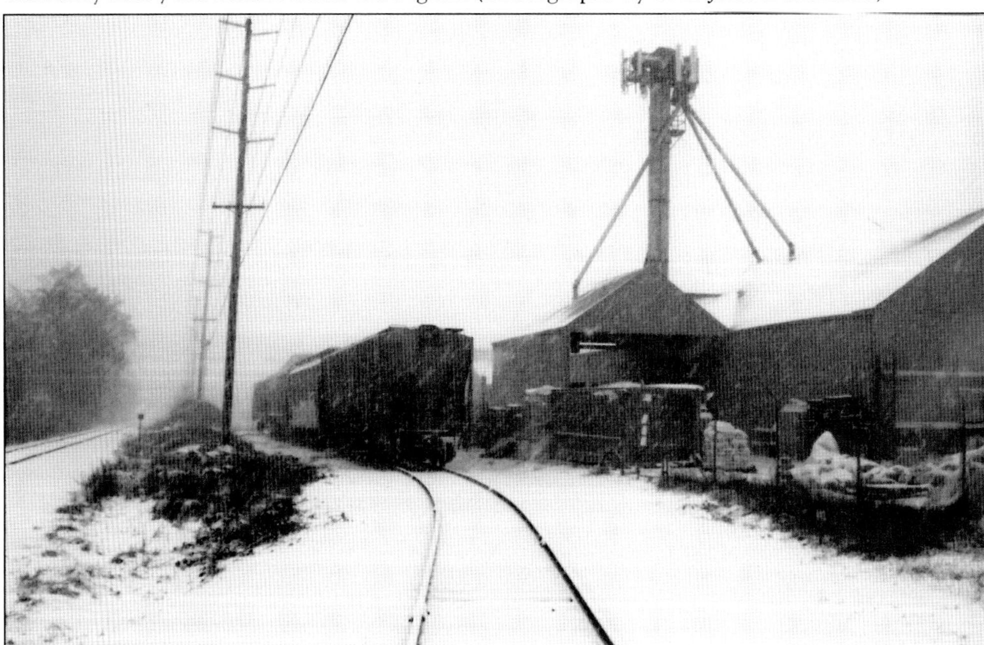

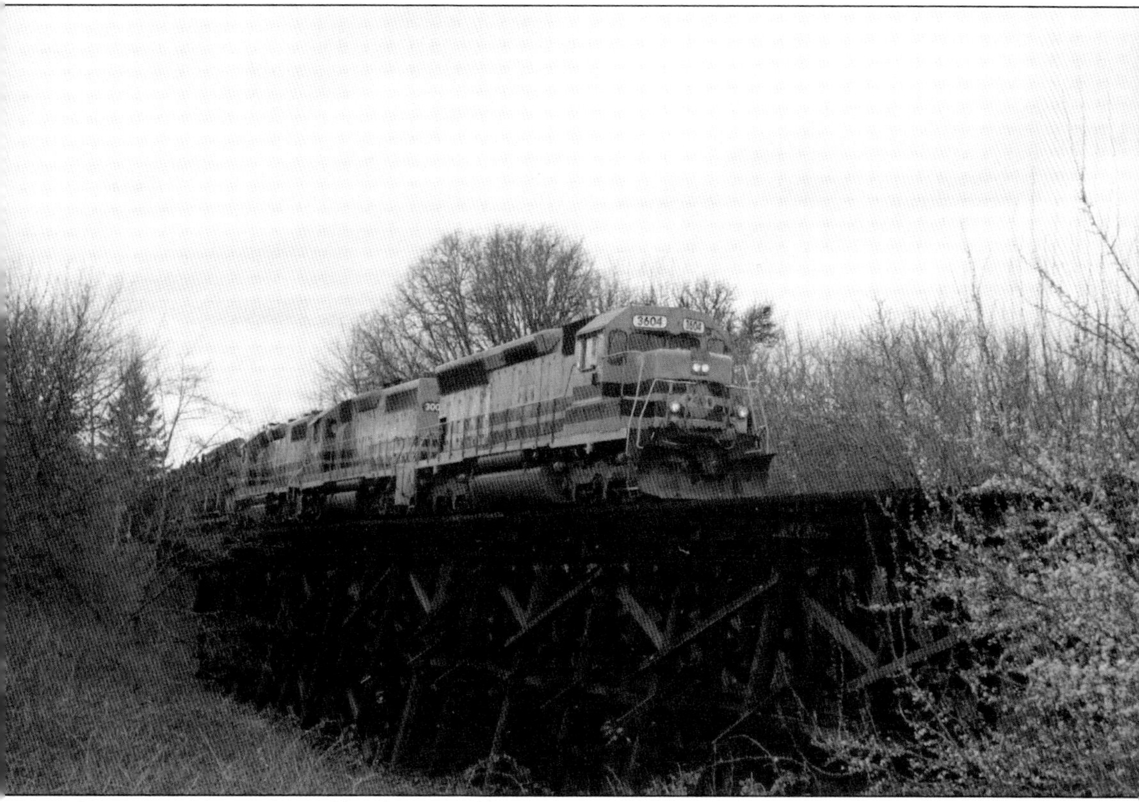

Spring Action. Powered by three road locomotives, the eastbound *Harbor Turn* pulls a long cut of log-laden flatcars across a bridge just outside of North Plains in March 2006. This stretch of track, once part of the Spokane, Portland & Seattle Railway's Vernonia Branch, is now known as the United Railways District of the Portland & Western, which reaches from Banks to United Junction, a distance of about 18 miles. United Railways was the name of the original company that built the route through North Plains as an electrified interurban railway. (Photograph by D.C. Jesse Burkhardt.)

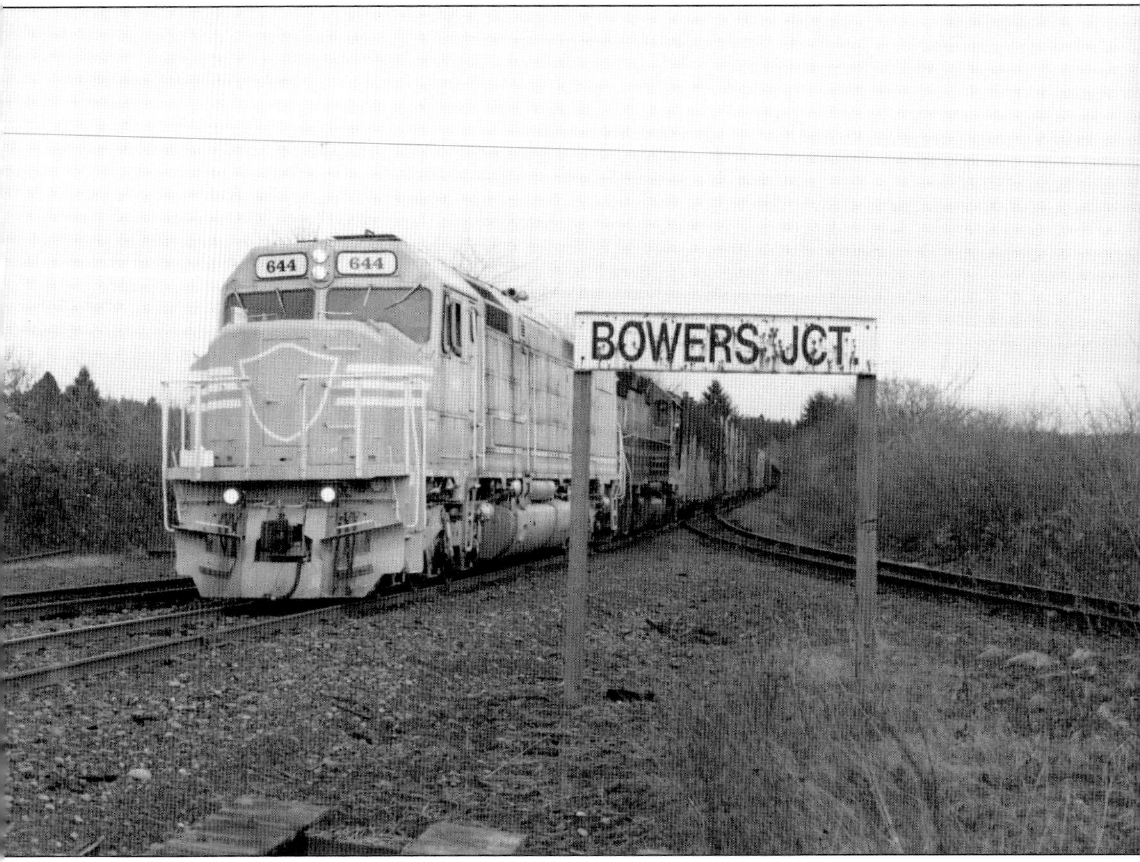

A Junction No Longer. The P&W *Harbor Turn* rolls past Bowers Junction with a leased 1974-era SDF40-2 No. 644 (in a Maersk paint scheme) in the lead. The date is December 16, 2006, and the long train is on its way from Linnton to Albany. Although the tracks curving south to the right of the train were still in place at this time, Bowers Junction was already a junction in name only, because the southbound tracks—which previously carried freight trains to Hillsboro, Salem, Albany, and Eugene—went less than half a mile beyond the switch here before coming to a dead end. The Oregon Electric route south of Bowers Junction, where Burlington Northern Railroad's Oregon Electric Branch and Vernonia Branch once connected, was abandoned in 1995. (Photograph by D.C. Jesse Burkhardt.)

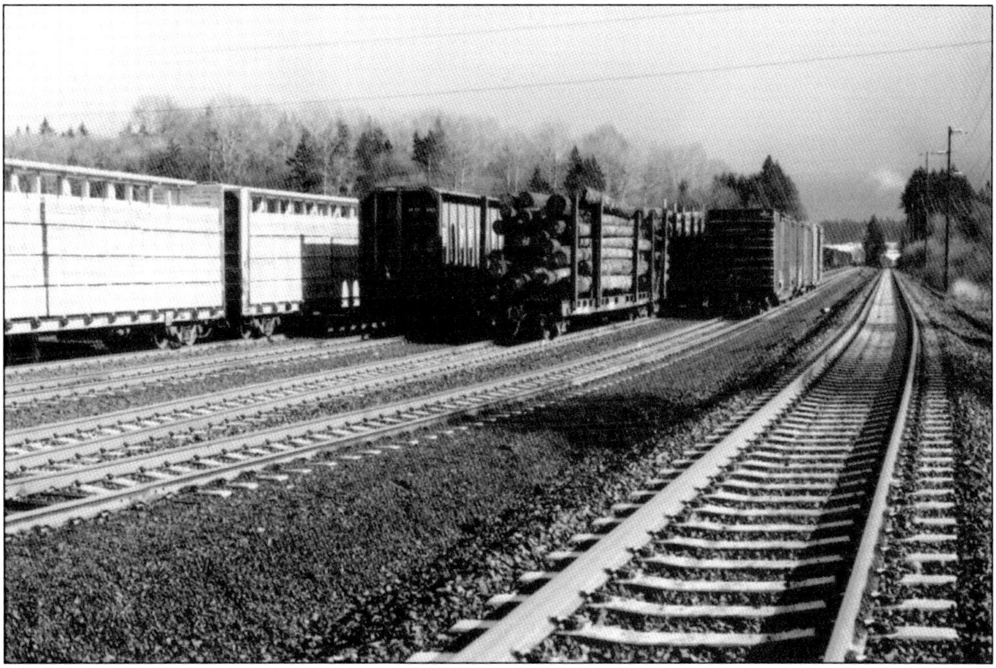

A Busy Place. To increase the efficiency of its operations, the P&W built a $3.7-million, four-track freight yard in Tigard between the mainlines of the railroad's Oregon Electric District and Tillamook District. The new facility, complete with concrete ties and heavy rail, opened in December 2007. Trains operating to Hillsboro, Seghers, and Forest Grove originate from this yard, which is often packed with a variety of freight cars, and Tigard is a crew change station as well. The mainline of the P&W's Oregon Electric District is in the foreground of the above photograph, taken on March 15, 2008, while the Tillamook District mainline is up front in the view shown in the photograph below, also taken in 2008. (Photographs by D.C. Jesse Burkhardt.)

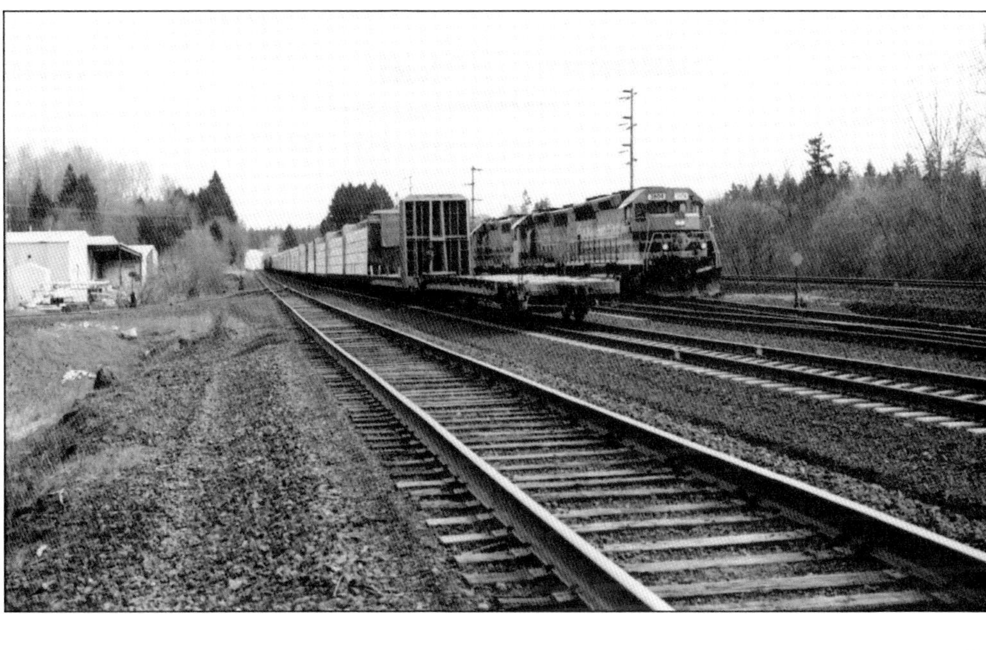

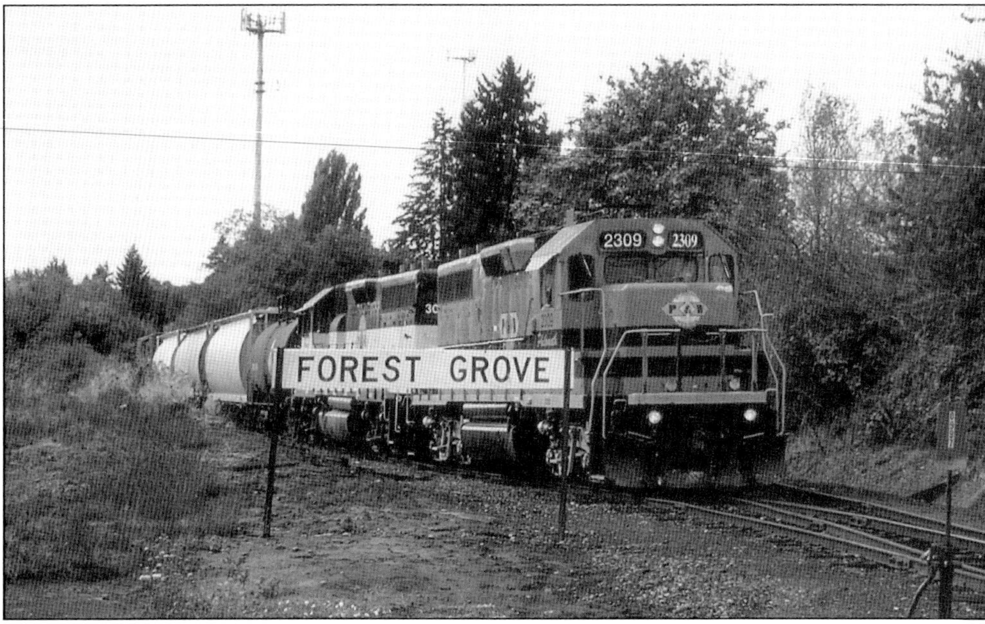

Five Cars East. Two locomotives are idling at the western end of the P&W's line between Hillsboro and Forest Grove in October 2005. With the crew's switching chores nearly done for the day, the train is preparing to head to Hillsboro with three covered hoppers, a boxcar, and a tank car. The entire 5.4-mile-long Forest Grove District—which P&W took over from Burlington Northern in 1995—is restricted to 10 miles per hour. (Photograph by D.C. Jesse Burkhardt.)

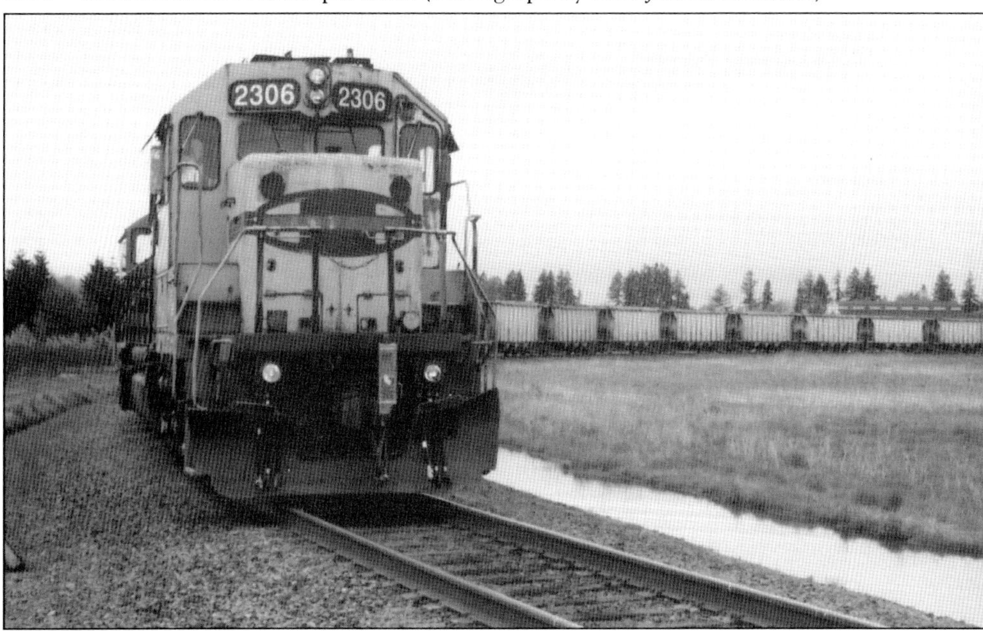

Rock Train. The P&W regularly moves unit trains of paving rock between Hillsboro and a gravel pit at Hopmere (on the railroad's Oregon Electric District about 45 miles south of Hillsboro) for the Knife River Company. These trains—like this one backing toward the Hopmere gravel pit in April 2012—operate with locomotives at both ends to make the shuttling back and forth more efficient. (Photograph by D.C. Jesse Burkhardt.)

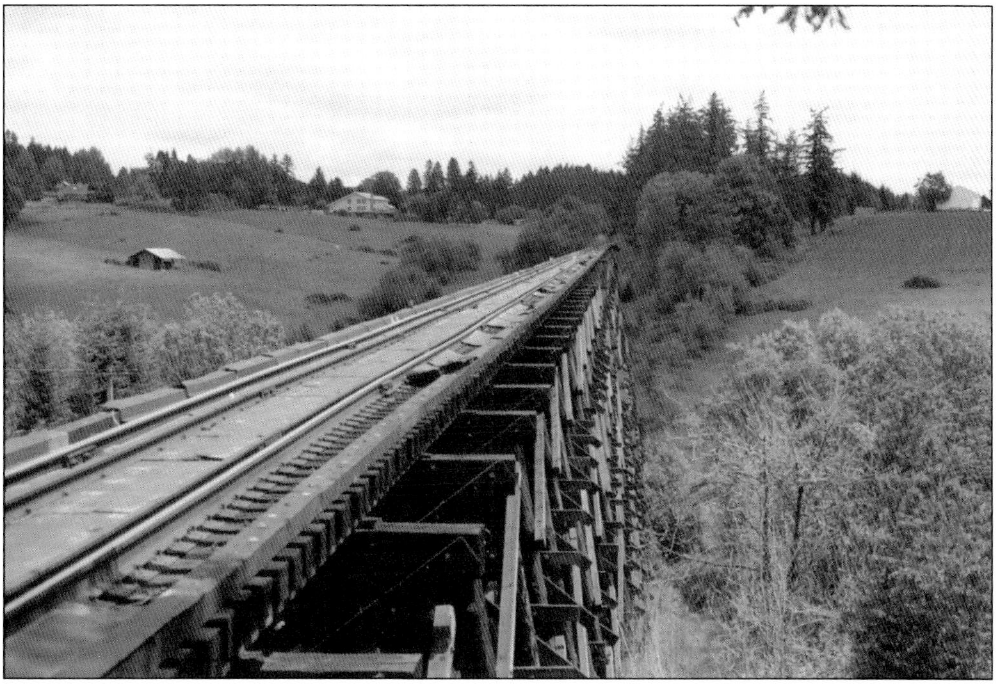

LONG AND TALL. The Cornelius Pass bridge over Holcomb Creek near Bowers Junction displays impressive engineering, especially considering it was built in 1905. It is a timber stringer trestle about 90 feet tall and 1,168 feet long and is reported to be the largest wooden bridge still in use in the United States. This view looks east from the top in June 2006. (Photograph by D.C. Jesse Burkhardt.)

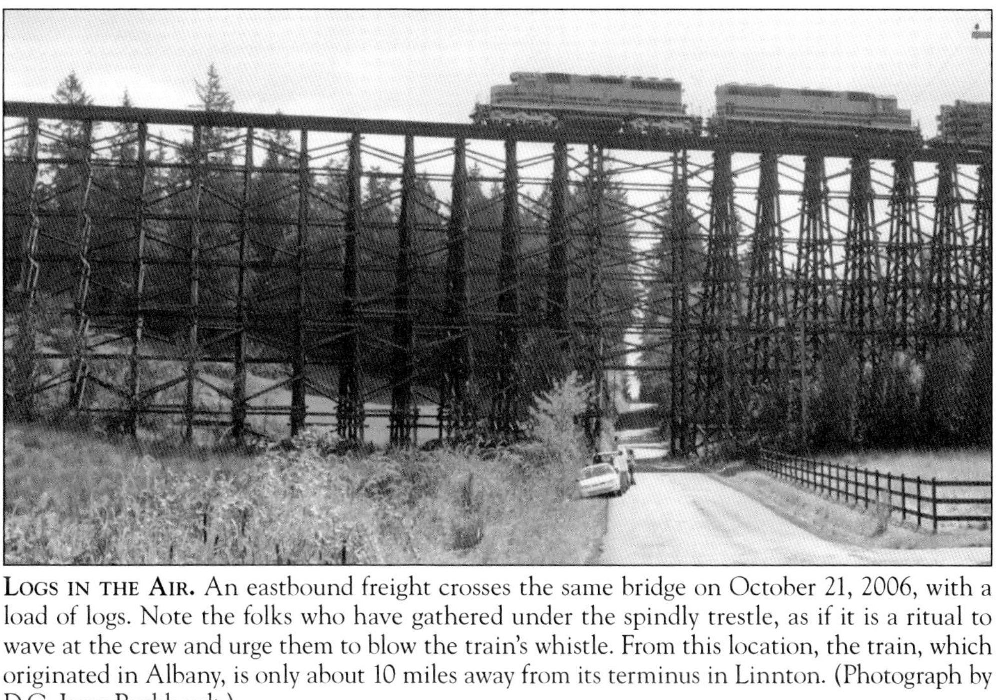

LOGS IN THE AIR. An eastbound freight crosses the same bridge on October 21, 2006, with a load of logs. Note the folks who have gathered under the spindly trestle, as if it is a ritual to wave at the crew and urge them to blow the train's whistle. From this location, the train, which originated in Albany, is only about 10 miles away from its terminus in Linnton. (Photograph by D.C. Jesse Burkhardt.)

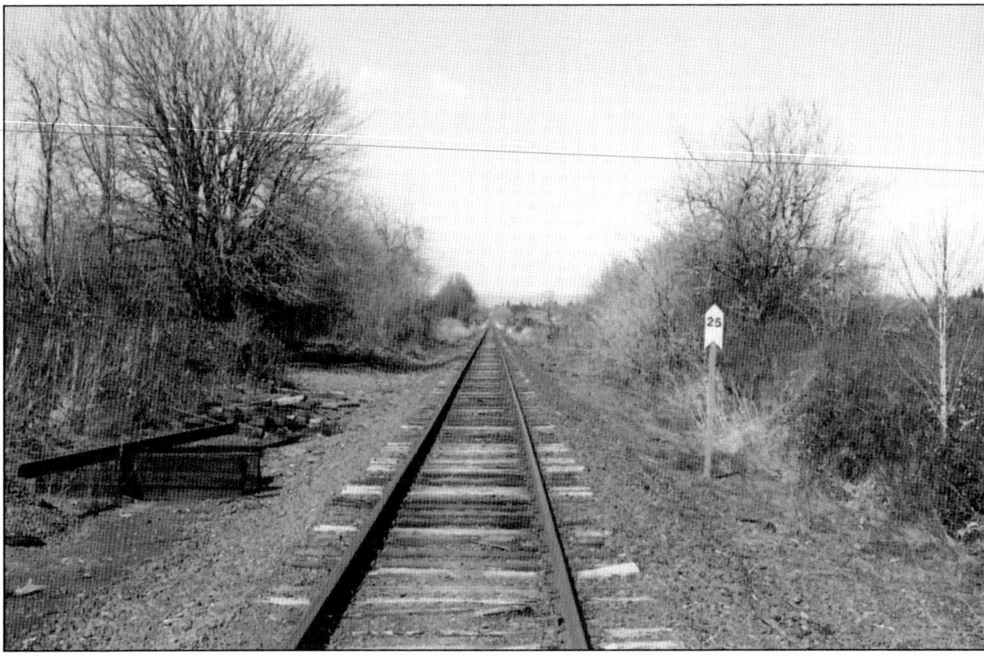

West Side Roots. The top photograph shows the view looking north along what was once Southern Pacific's West Side Branch, which ran along the west side of the Willamette Valley (hence the name of the line) between Hillsboro and Corvallis until a 12-mile-long segment just south of this point was abandoned by SP in 1985. This stretch of track, pictured here on March 15, 2009, is now operated by the Portland & Western and is officially known as the Seghers District. The signpost on the right tells engineers 25 miles per hour is the maximum speed on this portion of the railroad. Below, P&W GP40 No. 3004 rolls out of Seghers on March 17, 2007, hauling three loads of lumber from the Stimson-Forestex mill at the end of the line. (Photographs by D.C. Jesse Burkhardt.)

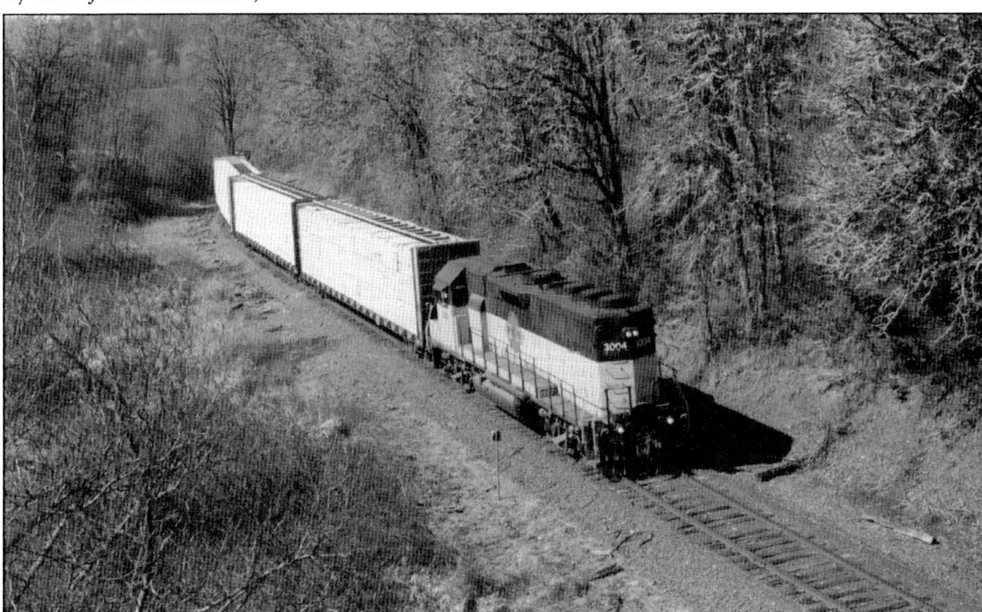

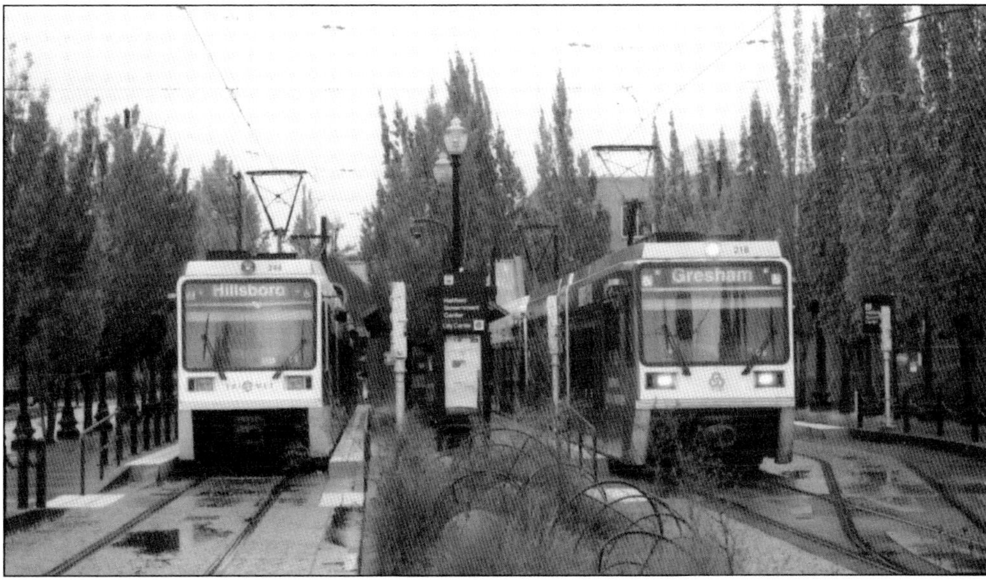

Return of the Electric Trains. In September 2013, two MAX (Metropolitan Area Express) trains are at the Hatfield Transit Center in downtown Hillsboro on transit agency TriMet's efficient light rail network, which serves 85 metropolitan-area stations. Using electricity to power these trains reveals a bit of "back to the future" thinking, as Hillsboro was once ably served by electric trains—including SP's famed "Red Electrics." (Photograph by D.C. Jesse Burkhardt.)

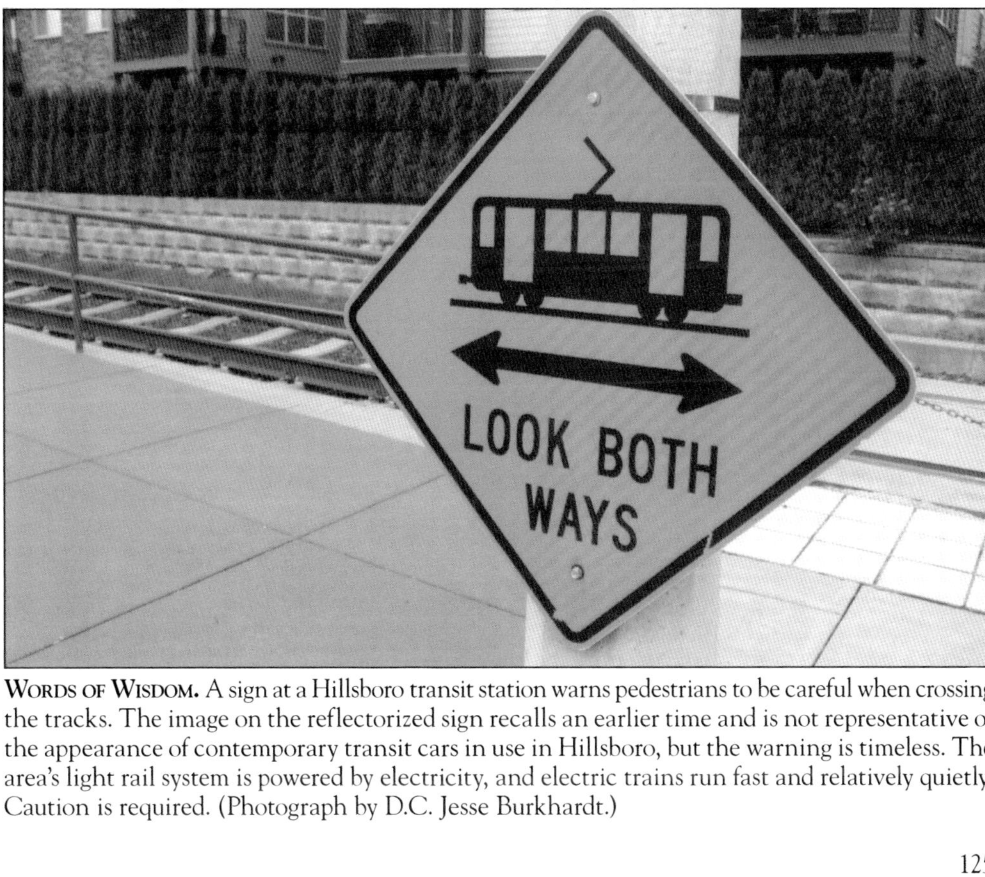

Words of Wisdom. A sign at a Hillsboro transit station warns pedestrians to be careful when crossing the tracks. The image on the reflectorized sign recalls an earlier time and is not representative of the appearance of contemporary transit cars in use in Hillsboro, but the warning is timeless. The area's light rail system is powered by electricity, and electric trains run fast and relatively quietly. Caution is required. (Photograph by D.C. Jesse Burkhardt.)

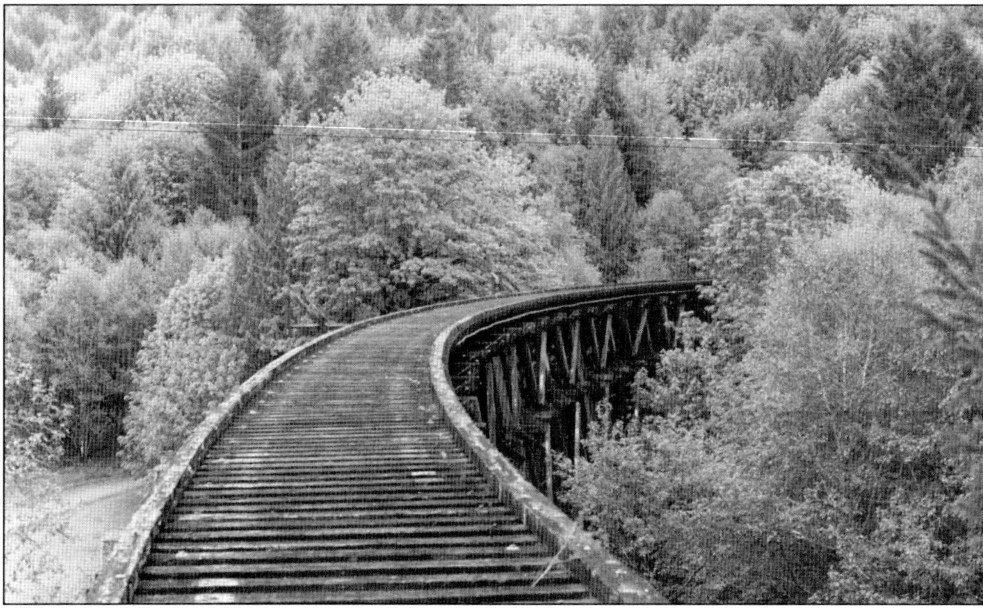

A New Assignment. Much of the former SP&S Vernonia Branch trackage—abandoned in the early 1970s—has been converted into a 21-mile-long hiking, biking and horseback riding trail that stretches from Banks to Vernonia along the former railroad right of way. In the photograph above, an abandoned trestle on the line near Buxton—the rails long since removed—stretches into the trees in May 2007. Compare this view with the photograph below, taken at the same location just a few months later, in September 2007, after Oregon State Parks converted the bridge into a highlight of the scenic trail. Until the bridge was decked, trail users had been forced to detour onto a steep service road to get around the structure, which had been fenced off and closed for obvious safety considerations. (Photographs by D.C. Jesse Burkhardt.)

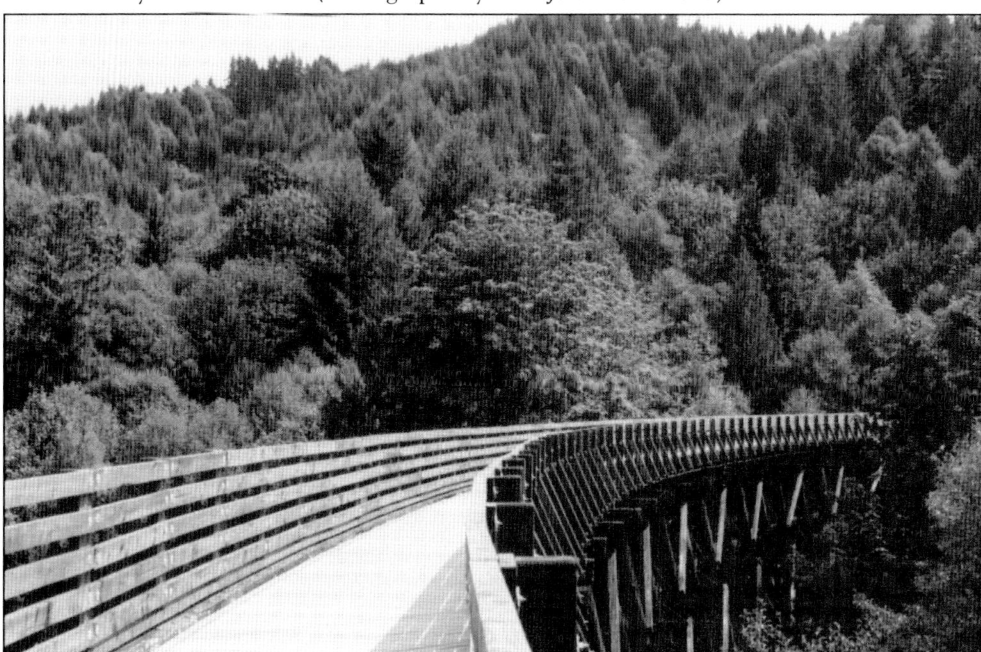

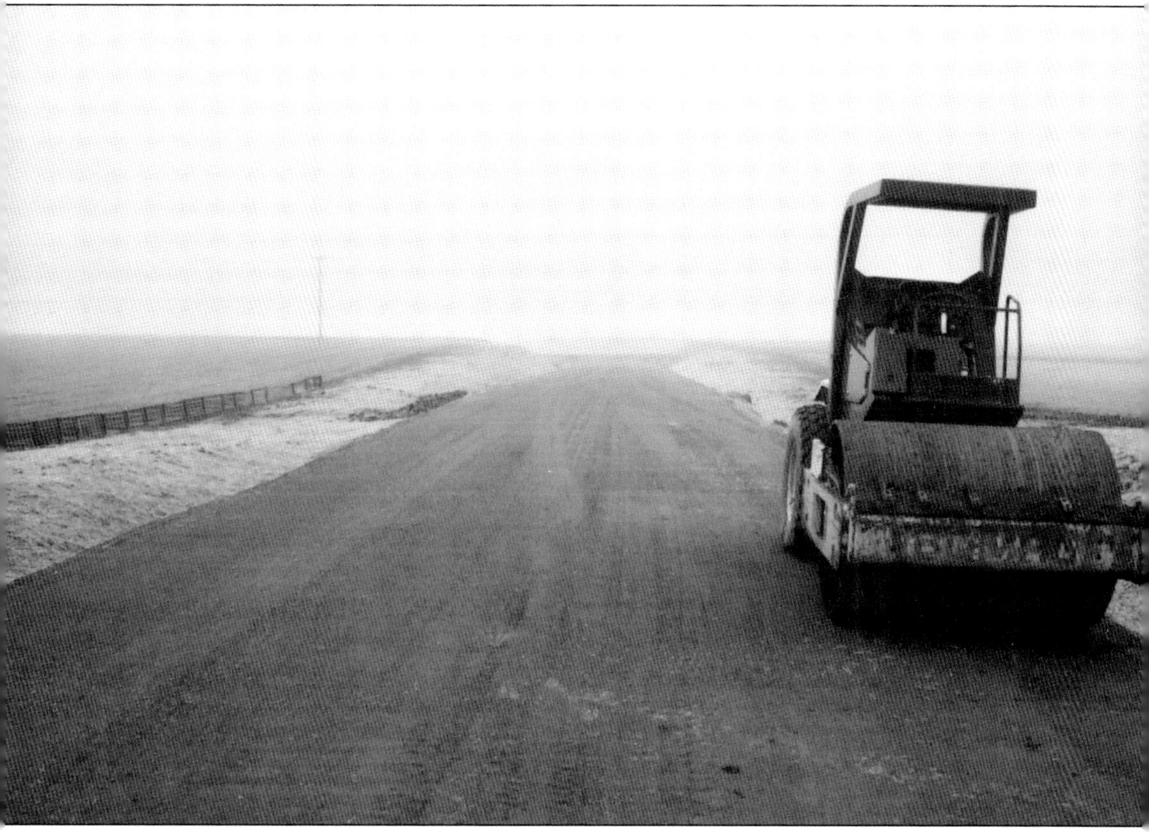

Making a Connection. The Portland & Western Railroad is building a new connecting rail line across a farmer's field at this site off Wilkesboro Road, located between Banks and Hillsboro. In November 2013, roadbed construction started on roughly two-thirds of a mile of track that more efficiently links the P&W's Tillamook District with its United Railways District. The new trackage, called the Banks Rail Connection, was expected to reduce the transit times of freight trains operating between Portland and Albany by at least an hour. The total cost of the infrastructure project was pegged at $3.1 million, with a transportation grant from the State of Oregon contributing about $2.4 million of it. The line was scheduled to be completed and in service by the summer of 2014. (Photograph by D.C. Jesse Burkhardt.)